The WorldWide Fundraiser's Handbook

A Guide to Fundraising for Southern NGOs and Voluntary Organisations

Michael Norton

A DIRECTORY OF SOCIAL CHANGE PUBLICATION

in association with the
International Fund Raising Group

The WorldWide Fundraiser's Handbook
A Guide to Fundraising for Southern NGOs and Voluntary Organisations
Michael Norton

Published by the Directory of Social Change in association with the International Fund Raising Group

Adapted from *The Complete Fundraising Handbook* by Sam Clarke, first published by the Directory of Social Change in association with the Institute of Charity Fundraising Managers in January 1992 (fully revised second edition published in March 1993)

Copyright © 1996 International Fund Raising Group and Directory of Social Change
No part of this book may be reproduced in any form whatsoever without prior permission in writing from the publisher. Permission will normally be given free of charge to non-profit making and charitable organisations.
The Directory of Social Change is registered charity no. 800517

Further copies of this book and a full catalogue of other books available can be obtained from the Directory of Social Change, 24 Stephenson Way, London NW1 2DP, UK. Telephone +44-171 209 5151;
Fax +44-171 209 5049; e-mail info@d-s-c.demon.co.uk
For more information on the International Fund Raising Group, contact IFRG, 295 Kennington Road, London SE11 4QE, UK.
Telephone +44-171 587 0287; Fax +44-171 582 4335;
e-mail wwp.ifrg@dial.pipex.com

Designed and typeset by Linda Parker
Printed and bound by Page Bros., Norwich

British Library Cataloguing-in-Publication data
A catalogue record for this book is available from the British Library

ISBN 1 873860 75 7

Acknowledgements

To *Sam Clarke* for his permission to take the manuscript of *The Complete Fundraising Handbook* and use it as the basis for writing this book, which still retains about 40% of the original text.

To *Richard Holloway* for compiling the section on *Income Generation*, which is an issue of growing importance to NGOs wishing to extend their funding base and become less dependent on aid donors.

To *Murray Culshaw* for his help with the section on international funding sources and advice on how to deal with a donor agency, and for the list of useful contacts at the end of the book.

To the *International Fund Raising Group*, *Per Stenbeck* and *Richard Tallontire* in particular, and also to the *International Federation of Red Cross* and *Red Crescent Societies* for collecting many of the real-life case studies that are used in this book.

To those who responded by submitting examples of their fundraising so that others could learn from their experience.

To the *Institute of Charity Fundraising Managers* for their permission to use their Codes of Practice, five of which are reprinted in an edited format at the end of this book.

And also to *Michael Eastwood*, *Anne Mountfield*, *Ken Burnett* and *Giles Pegram* for their comments on the draft manuscript.

Contents

Foreword 5
Author's Preface 7

1. Introduction 11
1.1 Why fundraising is important 11
1.2 The challenge for fundraisers 13
1.3 Who should read this book 14
1.4 How this book is structured 14

2. Getting started 16
2.1 Some key principles of fundraising 16
2.2 The skills required in fundraising 19
2.3 Who should do the fundraising 24
2.4 Equipping a fundraising office 30
2.5 Engaging a fundraising consultant 32

3. Fundraising strategy 34
3.1 Developing a fundraising strategy 34
3.2 Testing, evaluation and control 46

4. The sources 50
4.1 Individual donors 50
4.2 Government grants 56
4.3 International grant aid and development funding 60
4.4 Foundations 74
4.5 Company giving 84
4.6 Business sponsorship 94
4.7 Other sources 102

5. Income generation 107
5.1 The opportunities 108
5.2 Problems and issues 116
5.3 Getting started 120

6. Techniques 123
6.1 Setting up a local fundraising group 123
6.2 Organising a fundraising event 128
6.3 Collections 141

6.4 Direct mail 146
6.5 Committed giving and membership 156
6.6 Personal solicitation 163
6.7 Legacies and memorials 167
6.8 Capital appeals and big gift campaigns 170
6.9 Raising money from young people and in schools 175
6.10 Gambling activities that generate money 177
6.11 Advertising for support 180
6.12 Trading 185

7. Working with people 188
7.1 Working with volunteers 188
7.2 Working with patrons and celebrities 193
7.3 Working with trustees 196
7.4 Getting the most from your donors and supporters 198

8. Communication skills 205
8.1 Writing a fundraising proposal 205
8.2 Producing effective printed materials 214
8.3 Appeal letters 219
8.4 Annual reports 222
8.5 Using the telephone 222
8.6 Market research 225
8.7 Marketing 228
8.8 Public relations 231

Afterword 237

Appendices
1. Testing 239
2. Tax-effective giving 242
3. Using computers 244
4. Codes of practice 248
    Fundraising in schools
    House-to-house collections
    Static collecting boxes
    Reciprocal mailings
    Guidance notes for taking on a fundraising consultant

Sources of information
Useful organisations 259
Useful publications 263

Index of organisations 265
Index of topics 267

Foreword

This is a 'no-nonsense' handbook for both new and experienced fundraisers. It is a practical book and 'a very good read'. I have no difficulty in recommending it to the reader.

If fundraisers want a patron saint, I can think of no better choice than the Good Samaritan who demonstrated all the qualities that are needed in their profession for success:

- **Compassion**, when he crossed the road to pick up a badly battered man lying in a pool of blood in a ditch;
- **Courage** in getting off his horse in a particularly dangerous part of the road where the thieves might still be hiding;
- **Action** and **skill** – in knowing how to bind up the wounds with the use of a soothing oil; and finally...
- **The funds** so that he paid the Inn Keeper to look after the wounded man and promised that, if it was not enough, he would provide.

This parable illustrates that fundraising is not primarily about money. Rather, it is about:

- **Need** – about those human needs that cry out for help or for something to be done. And...
- **The response** to that need, to make things easier, to put things right, to make the world a better place.

So whenever you write or talk about your cause, always:

- Start with the need and explain it clearly and simply in human terms
- Then describe how your organisation can do something to relieve that need.
- But never exaggerate what you are capable of doing or make false claims of success.
- And do not forget that when you accept money from a donor, at the same time you are accepting a responsibility to that donor to ensure that his or her generous gift is used wisely and effectively and with economy.

This means that you as a fundraiser must be constantly asking all your colleagues who are involved in the work of the organisation how the work is going, what successes you are achieving and how you can demonstrate that the organisation is being well run.

You will want to keep in touch with your donors reporting back to them what you have been able to achieve with their money. Play your part as a truthful friend to your donor, telling of your successes and also your disappointments, and sharing your hopes and ambitions for the future.

People understand how difficult it is to bring about any real, lasting change for the better in human affairs, so you will find that an informed donor will support you through thick and thin – the first Director of Oxfam used to refer to this as 'the educated pound'.

Effective fundraising demands long hours, hard work, good communication skills and a proper understanding of the techniques that you will use to bring in the money, all supported by effective and well-managed administration. But at the same time it offers you a 'hidden agenda':

- A chance to be the agent of change for the betterment of the human condition, and to persuade others to help you in this.
- A chance to stand up effectively for human rights which are the key to human happiness, to justice and to the welfare of the human race. And
- A unique chance to play a tiny part in a vision of a new society in which all of us may dwell in peace and harmony.

So take up this challenge, be successful and enjoy yourself!

Guy Stringer CBE FRSA
Former Director of Oxfam UK/I
Chairman Emeritus of the International Fund Raising Group

Author's Preface

This book was originally published in the UK to provide a comprehensive overview of fundraising practice and techniques for those whose job it is to raise money for a charity or a development organisation – whether as a volunteer or as a paid fundraiser or as an external fundraising consultant.

A note on terms used in this book

This book is intended for people fundraising for non-profit organisations, and this includes:
- **NGOs** or **Non-Governmental Organisations**. This term may have different meanings in different countries.
- **Charities** – which are organisations established for charitable purposes under charity law, which again will differ from country to country.
- **Development Organisations**, which seek to promote community development. These are not charities in the real sense of the word, as they seek to empower and enable people to do things for themselves, rather than provide services for those in need – although most will be constituted under charity law.
- **Community-Based Organisations** and **People's Organisations** operating at the grass roots level.
- **Campaigning** and **Advocacy Organisations**, which seek to promote change through research, information, campaigns and lobbying.
- **Voluntary Organisations**. Voluntary Organisations and the **Voluntary Sector** (sometimes also known as the **Third Sector**), are terms used interchangeably with **Non-profit Organisations** and the **Not-for-profit Sector**. The term 'voluntary' is used because these organisations share a common feature – that they are all managed by a voluntary management board.
- **Trusts** and **Foundations**, which are grant making bodies, usually established under charity law with the specific function of making grants for charitable purposes. Many are endowed, but some have to raise money if they are to make grants. The two terms 'trust' and 'foundation' are used interchangeably. 'Trust' is used because many foundations are constituted under trust law.

All share the need to obtain resources for their work, which they do from a variety of sources. This book is intended for all of these types of organisation, and is particularly aimed at the Southern fundraiser, and has been written from that perspective, and is illustrated with examples from many Southern countries. **North** refers to the developed world; **South** to the countries of Asia, Africa and Central and Southern America where most of the world's poor live.

The Complete Fundraising Handbook was conceived and published by the Directory of Social Change, the UK's leading provider of information and training on management, fundraising and communication skills for charities and voluntary organisations. It was published in association with the Institute of Charity

Fundraising Managers (ICFM), the professional association which represents the interests of fundraisers and which promotes good practice in fundraising.

In 1994, the publishers were approached by the International Fund Raising Group (IFRG) with the suggestion that the book be adapted for use by Southern NGOs, charities and voluntary organisations. The IFRG was expanding its fundraising training worldwide, and felt that an accompanying handbook would be useful.

The author of *The Complete Fundraising Handbook*, Sam Clarke, formerly fundraising director of Oxfam and currently director of World University Service, very generously agreed to assign his interest in the copyright of his book to the publishers so that it could be completely revised, updated and fully adapted to the needs and interests of a Southern readership. About 60% of the text of the book has been newly written. This work has been done by Michael Norton, the founding director of the Directory of Social Change, an experienced fundraising trainer and author of a wide range of books on fundraising. He has been assisted by Richard Tallontire of the IFRG who has collected a number of examples and case studies which are used to illustrate some of the points being made, and by Richard Holloway of PACT and Murray Culshaw former Director of Oxfam (India) who have contributed to the sections on income generation and international funding sources.

There is one major difference between NGOs and voluntary organisations operating in the South as compared with their Northern counterparts – the availability in the South of large amounts of aid and development money from foreign sources, including governments, NGOs and charitable foundations. This has helped a great many voluntary initiatives to get started, to develop their work and even to grow into substantial institutions. International donors have been willing to part with quite large sums of money (at least in terms of purchasing power) and often for relatively long periods of time (in the UK a three-year grant is considered long term!). NGOs have been able to expand their work, obtain grants to meet their capital needs and even create corpus funds (sometimes known as endowments) as a 'nest egg' for their future.

But international help is fickle. This year's concern may not be next year's. In India, the NGOs in some of the Southern States are fearful that donors are becoming more interested in putting their limited resources into the more 'backward' States of Bihar, Madhya Pradesh, Rajasthan and Uttar Pradesh. Donors may decide to transfer their affections completely to other countries, such as Rwanda or for the reconstruction of the constituent countries of the former Yugoslavia, where they feel that there are real and immediate challenges for them. They may decide that countries such as India, which are undergoing relatively rapid economic development and which have even faster growth rates than in the North, are now able to look after themselves. Or they may simply feel that after the end of the Cold War there is no real reason for giving away aid money at all.

Whatever the reasons, and there may be several, it is not a very satisfactory situation for any NGO or voluntary organisation to make itself the victim of the whims of foreign aid donors – who are sometimes in a position to determine whether an organisation continues and to exert control over the nature and style of its work. This is where domestic fundraising steps in.

Domestic fundraising can:
- Help an organisation develop its own sources of income, and therefore give it more control in deciding its own agenda and future.
- Develop links between the voluntary organisation and the local communities in which the work is being done, for example by developing relationships in the local community with individual and corporate donors.
- Encourage those who are doing the work to understand the urgency and importance of what they are doing – which they will need to do if they are to successfully communicate their need for support to those with the power and the resources to help them.

Southern NGOs and voluntary organisations can succeed in fundraising, just as their Northern counterparts are doing. Two examples from India spring to mind:
- Lok Kalyan Samiti is an eye hospital in New Delhi. It now raises all the money it requires from a direct mail fundraising programme involving more than 30,000 active supporters. The director of LKS is now coordinating a network of over 30 eye hospitals in South Asia which are seeking to adopt similar fundraising methods.
- CRY – Child Relief and You is an Indian donor agency which successfully raises money from India's middle class and corporate sector, and also runs a substantial greetings card operation that contributes half its annual budget. CRY believes that it is only scratching the surface, and that the alleged 200 million strong Indian middle class presents a real challenge for fundraisers.

In Africa, and indeed in Central/Eastern Europe and Latin America as well as in Asia, there are similar possibilities for developing indigenous fundraising. Techniques including direct mail, organising fundraising events and involving volunteers can all be used successfully. There are many local companies as well as local branches of multinational companies that are willing to give support in cash or in kind.

As well as raising funds, there is another possibility of gaining an income for NGOs and voluntary associations – making your own money (or generating your own income). Many NGOs have pioneered techniques by which they sell their services (in part or in whole), run an enterprise – either linked to their main activity or not, or in some way generate income that they can use for their main humanitarian activities.

The problem is not so much a lack of opportunity, but rather knowing where to start and finding ways of building your fundraising (or your income generation scheme) from a small or not-yet-existent base. We hope that this book will provide you with the ideas, the techniques and the necessary skills to be successful. We hope that it will not only encourage you to identify the opportunities, but that it will also give you the enthusiasm and the confidence to make a good job of your fundraising and your income generation.

Michael Norton
February 1996

To Asang Machwe

Co-founder with me of Books for Change,
a new publishing venture in India to support the
NGO sector and promote development, organiser
of the highly successful Village Libraries programme
with the Rajiv Gandhi Foundation, Chair of the
Afro-Asian Book Council and one of India's most
successful independent publishers, a very special
person and a friend whose untimely death in 1996
is a great loss to all of us.

1. Introduction

1.1 Why fundraising is important

Fundraising is an extremely important component of your organisation's success. Some of the reasons for this are described below.

Survival

Every organisation needs money to survive – to meet project costs and develop programmes for the future, to pay the wages and salaries of its staff and all the office and organisational overheads that are needed for this, to keep buildings and vehicles in a good state of repair and to pay for new equipment. The list of needs is endless. And the stark truth is that if the money is not raised, the organisation will not be able to do the work. And if the work is not done, then all those pressing needs will remain unmet.

The tool you will use to manage your fundraising is your annual budget. This will show the amount of money you plan to spend, and it will also indicate the amount of money that has already been raised or has been promised, and what extra support needs to be raised during the year so that you can meet your outgoings.

You will monitor your progress in fundraising through keeping records of money received or promised, and by preparing and discussing management accounts at regular Management Committee meetings (which may be held monthly, or perhaps quarterly for smaller organisations). If the income isn't coming in as planned, then you will need to take some sort of action – put more effort into your fundraising, cut costs, defer planned projects, or agree to subsidise the deficit out of your reserves.

Expansion and development

If the organisation is to meet the challenges of the future, it may need to expand and develop its work – to improve its services, to extend its work into other regions and areas, to undertake research, campaigning and advocacy alongside its basic service delivery work, to experiment and to innovate. This all requires more money – money that will need to be raised.

You may want to prepare a business plan, or at least to prepare a 'sketch budget' for the next few years so as to plan for any major developments or expansion that you wish to undertake. In this way you can set about raising the necessary resources for this. Remember, fundraising always takes longer than you think. The more you plan ahead, the more successful you will be in getting the resources when you need them.

Reducing dependency

Many organisations are funded with one or perhaps several major donors providing most of the funds that they need. This can put the organisation into a state of dependency. If one of the grants is withdrawn, this could create a financial crisis. And it may be difficult for the organisation to determine its own agenda when it is constantly having to adapt to the priorities of the donor organisation.

Broadening the fundraising base by bringing in other donors and by generating other sources of money can reduce this dependency. You have to decide whether your organisation is too dependent on any one source, and if this is the case, whether to negotiate some form of long-term funding partnership with your current donors or to develop alternative sources of income.

Building a constituency

Fundraising is not just about money, it is also about numbers of supporters. Each supporter is important to you. They can all be persuaded to give again and to give even more generously. They may be able to volunteer or to find friends who are willing to support you. They are an indication of the level of support that your organisation is attracting, and therefore can add strength to your lobbying and campaigning work.

You need to think about the sorts of constituencies that you would like to mobilise and who will be attracted to the sort of work you are doing. Is it businesses? Or middle class people? Or students and activists? Or women? Or retired people with time on their hands? Or doctors? Or lawyers? Or other special categories? And you will need to think about how best to reach them and the sort of message they will respond to.

Creating a viable and sustainable organisation

Fundraising is not simply about generating the resources you need to survive from this year to next year, and planning for any expansion and development. It is also about helping create a viable and strong organisation which is able to sustain itself into the future.

There are many ways of doing this. One way is to build a substantial and active donor base – getting people to support you who feel involved and important to the organisation, and who will continue to give their support over a long period of time. Other ways include: organising successful fundraising events (which can create a regular and continuing source of income); creating capital within your organisation, such as buildings and equipment (which reduce your need for running costs or can help you generate an income) or an endowment or corpus fund; and developing income generating schemes for the organisation itself.

Many organisations are addressing long-term needs – for example through community development which will not yield immediate results, or in looking after disabled or elderly people where there is a continuing commitment to provide care. It is important that you create an organisation that is financially strong and positive about its future, rather than one that is plagued by annual deficits, which is at or near bankruptcy, and where the financial concerns are beginning to affect the morale of the whole organisation. Most organisations should be able to find ways of strengthening their financial position and developing a sensible fundraising or income generation strategy for their future.

1.2 The challenges for fundraisers

Fundraising is never easy. And there are particular challenges for Southern fundraisers at the present time:

The development of fundraising

Fundraising in the South is not as well developed as it is in the North. This means that the Southern fundraiser has to become part of the process of developing the habit and practice of giving, developing the fundraising methods and techniques which work well within the local culture, and identifying and mobilising those constituencies of support you wish to tap. In the North, there is plenty of experience, good practice, published case studies, practical training and support services for the fundraiser to draw upon. The South is starting lower down on the learning curve. Which is perhaps where this book comes in!

Growing need

Many countries implementing structural adjustment policies are cutting back on their welfare and educational programmes, and this is creating greater burdens for the poor. In those countries where population growth outstrips economic advance, the poor are growing poorer year by year. And even where some countries are experiencing rapid economic growth, wealth is not trickling down to the marginalised and the dispossessed. Then there are always new needs and new concerns – from the growing impact of the AIDS epidemic to the consequences of rapid urbanisation.

The challenge for NGOs and voluntary organisations is to develop 'solutions' to people's needs rather than simply provide 'services' that improve the quality of life. They need to create more imaginative and effective approaches to the problems that exist in society, so that they can respond to the growing levels of need without necessarily creating a continuing demand for funding that is just not there.

Competition

The fundraising world is extremely competitive. More organisations are thinking about fundraising and beginning to develop independent sources of income for themselves. This means that many of the 'more obvious' sources, such as the larger local companies and rich individuals, are receiving increasing numbers of requests for support – and they can't support all of them, however worthwhile the requests are.

New organisations, full of energy and enthusiasm, are continually being formed to meet many of the needs that your organisation is addressing. And your existing 'competitors' are each struggling to show that they are 'the best'.

Your job is to try to show that your organisation is successful, effective, cost-effective, innovative, lively – in short that it is the best recipient of a donor's funds.

The difficulty of making money

It is not easy to start and sustain a money making enterprise in the South. If it was then there would be more successful business people. NGOs and voluntary organisations are also largely inexperienced in business methods. Many of them have doubts, moreover, about the validity of making money as a strategy for an NGO. Despite all this, there are a variety of rich opportunities, however, for

NGOs to manufacture and sell products, both linked to or separate from their main work, or to sell services that they are well positioned to offer on the market. A growing body of experience is building up. Hopefully this book will help to spread the word about the possibilities.

1.3 Who should read this book

The simple answer is that everyone who has any sort of fundraising responsibility needs to understand the fundraising process:

- **Board Members** will want to know what to expect of fundraisers, how to employ them, what qualities they should have and what support they will need to succeed. They will also want to know the options in income generating schemes.
- The organisation's **Director** and other **Senior Managers** will want to know when it's time to employ a specialist fundraiser or a fundraising consultant and how to manage them to achieve the best results. They will also want to know what is likely to be involved in starting an income generating scheme.
- **Fundraisers** will of course need to have a good background guide to the many techniques that are available, and an understanding of which are likely to be the most relevant to them.
- **Volunteers** who are raising money should have a copy to give them good ideas for improving their own contribution.
- **Consultants** and **Advisers**, who will often be charging for their services, to ensure that they give the best fundraising advice to help their clients raise real money.
- **Trainers**, who might wish to use some of the material as handouts or checklists for those attending their courses.

So the book has been written from as many points of view as possible, taking into account the interests of both large and small organisations, those with some experience of fundraising and those considering the possibility for the first time.

1.4 How this book is structured

The book is divided into eight sections:

- **Introduction**, which is this section, which sets out why fundraising is important and the challenge for fundraisers.
- **Getting started**, which describes some of the key principles of fundraising (to give a better understanding of the process) and some of the personal skills required in a fundraiser (so you will know your strengths and weaknesses for the job). It also explores who should do the fundraising, and what is needed to equip a fundraising office.
- **Developing a fundraising strategy**, which describes some of the factors to take into account and suggests ways of developing a strategy for your own organisation. This section also covers testing, evaluation and control, to enable you to be more cost-effective in your fundraising.

- **The sources**, which covers international aid and grants, grants from government sources and programmes, foundation support, company giving and business sponsorship, getting support from individuals, and a range of other possible sources for you to consider. This section will give you an understanding of how money is given away, and will help you identify opportunities for getting support for your own organisation.
- **Making your own money**, which covers the opportunities for developing income generation schemes to earn money for your organisation as part of a strategy for developing more financial independence and less reliance on grant aid.
- **Techniques for raising money**, which covers everything from house-to-house collections and direct mail to organising a fundraising event, getting a legacy, raising money from overseas non-resident communities and running a capital appeal. The full list of topics covered in this section is given on the contents page.
- **Working with people**, including volunteers, overseas volunteers, celebrities and patrons, board members and donors.
- **Communication skills** to help you state your fundraising need and communicate this to someone with the resources to help you. This section covers writing an effective fundraising proposal or appeal letter, producing effective literature for your organisation, using the telephone, marketing and market research, and effective public relations (which is an essential ingredient of successful fundraising).

The book ends with:

- **Appendices**, covering *testing, tax-effective giving* and *using computers*, which give more detailed information on subjects covered elsewhere in the book, and **five codes of practice** on: fundraising in schools (which means working with a vulnerable and impressionable group of people); reciprocal mailings (where you swap your list of supporters with another organisation); house-to-house collections and the use of static collecting boxes (where proper management and some assurance that the money collected is reaching the organisation is important); and guidance notes on taking on a fundraising consultant. These codes of practice have been adapted from those used by the Institute of Charity Fundraising Managers (ICFM) in the UK.
- **Sources of information and advice**, where we concentrate on a few organisations and publications which we think will be helpful. Mostly, you will have to find relevant sources in your own country.

2. Getting started

This section covers some of the key aspects of fundraising. It will help identify the people, the attitudes and the approaches that you will need to get a successful fundraising programme under way.

2.1 Some key principles of fundraising

"Fundraising is a science. But its rules are more like a rainbow than a formula. You need to paint with the most delicate shades of colours and moods. You will surely become a success if you paint with love and friendship."

Ekaterina Kim, Contacts-I, Moscow

You have to ask

A piece of research commissioned by a major charity asked non-supporters what was their main reason for not giving. The answer was simple – the main reason for not giving was that they had never been asked.

Some fundraisers do not exploit the opportunities that exist to raise money. Others ask, but do not do so effectively. The whole purpose of fundraising is to raise money, and it is often forgotten that the call to action, the punch-line asking people to give, is the essential piece of the message.

The good fundraiser must ask clearly for exactly what they want, having regard to the donor's ability and willingness to give when deciding what to ask for. They may also need to repeat the message to emphasise the point. And they must make it as easy as possible for the donor to respond.

The personal approach

The general rule is that the more personal you can make your approach, the more effective you will be. So:

Asking in person at a **face-to-face** meeting is better than...

Giving **a presentation** at a meeting to a group of people, which is better than...

Telephoning someone to ask for support, which is better than...

Writing a **personal letter** to someone, which is better than...

Sending a **circular letter** to lots of people.

Many fundraisers prefer to work by sending letters asking for support. This is not the most effective way of asking, and you may need to think carefully about how to make your approach. Two other factors are worth considering:

A meeting at your project where the prospective donor can see your work and meet some of the beneficiaries is often the most effective of all. If that can't be managed, you can try to illustrate your work with a short video, or with photographs, or by taking along some of the people you are working with to fundraising meetings.

A request from someone who has given or from someone important (such as a business leader or expert in the field) can often be more effective than a request from a fundraiser or from the project director. Part of the skill in fundraising is knowing the best person to do the asking.

Understanding the donor's viewpoint

In making a decision to give, a whole range of feelings and thoughts may be aroused in the donor. It is important for the fundraiser to understand this process.

The act of giving includes elements of faith, hope and charity. Faith that the fundraiser truly represents the cause and will act as an efficient conduit for the donor's money. Hope that the gift, however small, will make some difference. Charity as an act of altruism, a gift without the expectation of any material return. It is also important for the fundraiser to understand that the donor might have some personal reason for wanting to give, and to build on that interest. People may want to support a cancer charity, for example, through fear that they might get the disease, or because a family member or close friend has recently died of it. They may feel strongly about an issue – such as the environment – and want to do something about it. In supporting your cause, they are also supporting their cause, doing something that they feel needs doing and that they want to see done.

> **The return to the donor**
>
> People support charity without the expectation of any material return. But they do want something for their money, even if it is intangible. For example:
> - **A feeling of having done something worthwhile**, and perhaps that they have been able to make a difference to someone else's life.
> - **Recognition** from other people and from the public of their generosity – although some people prefer to give anonymously.

Fundraising is a people business

People do not give to organisations. They do not give to abstract concepts. They give to help people or to do something to create a better world. Your job as a fundraiser is to show how you are helping do this. One way of doing this is through case studies – illustrating your work with actual examples of the people you have been able to help, showing how you have been able to change their lives, showing what you have done to create a better environment, etc. In this way you can show donors how their money can make a difference.

Another is to focus your fundraising on particular aspects of your work: the income generation project you are planning to introduce in the village, that you hope will transform people's lives; the community publishing programme that is getting underway, where you are all full of enthusiasm and excitement about its potential. By focusing on specific projects rather than the overall work of the organisation, it is easier to excite and enthuse your donors.

Fundraising is selling

Fundraising is a two-stage process. The first stage is showing people that there is an important need which you can do something useful about. If they agree that the need is important, and that something should be done; and if they agree that your organisation is doing something significant to make a difference; and if you can show them how some extra support could be used to do even better – then asking for money becomes easy. Fundraising is more about selling an idea that the donor can make a difference than about asking for money. Once people have been sold the idea, then they will want to give. Fundraising is also more about 'selling' than 'telling'. It is about persuading people to give, and showing reasons why the work is important. Your success depends on your ability to get people to do something to help.

Credibility and PR

People prefer to give to organisations and causes that they have heard of. This means that the organisation's credibility and good public relations are extremely important. Press coverage of your work, trumpeting your successes in the newsletters you send to supporters, getting endorsements about the quality of your work from experts and prominent figures can all encourage people to realise the importance of what you are doing and have the confidence that you are doing a worthwhile and successful job – which makes it much easier for them to support you.

Ways of asking for a specific amount

- **Ask for a specific sum** for a item of expenditure (for example, £200 to sponsor an afternoon eye clinic at the hospital).
- **Give a shopping list** of different items at different prices (for example, if you are equipping a hospital, you can list all the items you will need to purchase and ask a donor to contribute to one or more; the Lok Kalyan Samiti eye hospital suggests donations of Rs100 (£2) per patient for eyecare and Rs200 per patient for cataract operations and asks donors to sponsor 1, 5 or 10 patients).
- **Give examples of gifts** already received. This will give people a good idea of how much to give, depending on their level of generosity and whether they see themselves making a largish or a smaller gift.
- **Break down the total** into numbers of gifts of different sizes that you will need to achieve if you are to reach your target.

Donors don't know how much to give

One problem is that donors don't know how much they are expected to give. They may not want to give an enormous amount. On the other hand, they may not want to give too little, and so seem mean.

Saying thank you

Saying thank you is extremely important. It recognises and values the donor's generosity. It can also be an act of enlightened self-interest in getting donors to feel more warmly about your organisation, and perhaps to consider giving again at some time in the future.

Many organisations follow the policy of saying thank you to supporters only when they have actually received something. Those who say thank you on every appropriate pretext will see this investment repay itself handsomely in donor loyalty and may well be surprised at the level of repeat giving that can be stimulated by this process. But many donors complain that many of the organisations they support never even bother to say thank you!

Saying thank you can pay

A former Director of a major aid charity made a point of telephoning donors who had given £500 or more at home in the evenings to thank them personally. *"We're thrilled with your support. We're going to put it to good use immediately by using it to help establish a new health clinic for the Turkana. And we'll keep you in touch with progress."* All this makes the donor feel that the charity is doing a good job and that their money is actually having some impact.

A fundraiser from an Asian NGO made a personal visit to thank a donor who had recently given 30,000 rupees (£600). At the end of the visit, the donor made another donation of more than twice as much again.

Long-term involvement and commitment

What you really want are people who will give to you regularly and substantially. All the effort to find a donor and persuade them to give will really only bear fruit if they continue to give over many years and maybe increase their level of giving. And if they are then prepared to ask their friends to help you or to put in long hours as a volunteer, then that's an added bonus.

To achieve this means getting them involved with the work of the organisation and committed to its success.

Accountability and reporting back

When you take money from somebody, you are responsible for seeing that:

Involvement and commitment

The difference between involvement and commitment is well illustrated by the Bacon and Eggs story. A chicken and a pig were discussing the upcoming breakfast in which they were both to play a part. The pig said crossly to the chicken, *"It's all very well you being so cheerful. You're just involved. I'm committed!"*

You want your donors to be committed. You can try to achieve this by:
- **Saying thank you** immediately and telling them what you plan to do with their money.
- **Regular reporting back** showing them what you have achieved with their money.
- **Sharing your ideas** and hopes for the future.
- **Encouraging them to visit you** to see your organisation at work and getting them to meet some of the people that they have been helping.
- Offering opportunities for them to **meet with the staff and volunteers** who are actually doing the work, and with prominent personalities associated with the cause.

- The money is spent on the purposes for which it was raised. Failure to do this is a breach of trust.
- The money is well spent and actually achieves something.

You may be obliged to report back to the donor as a condition of the grant. But you will want to do this anyway to show them that you have used their money effectively. This is not only polite, it is good fundraising practice – as an enthusiastic donor who has seen the money make a difference may consider becoming a more committed supporter.

2.2 The skills required in fundraising

There are a number of important skills that you will need if you are to be successful. If you understand what skills are required, you can:

- **Assess your strengths**, so that you concentrate on doing those things you are good at.
- **Learn what skills you need to acquire**, and set about obtaining the necessary training or experience.
- **Find ways of compensating for your weaknesses** by mobilising others to help you where appropriate.

Commitment to the cause

Commitment is one of the most important attributes that a fundraiser can bring to the job. If the cause does not seem important to you, then how can you convey to others the importance and urgency of doing something about it? You must really believe in the cause you are addressing and in the work that your organisation is doing. Your enthusiasm and commitment will encourage others to become equally committed through their giving.

The starving baby syndrome

You are watching TV. There is a programme about a refugee camp in Rwanda. People have arrived there with nothing, absolutely nothing. They have walked days to get there and are near starvation. A picture flashes up of a starving baby, who seems to be crying out to you *"Help me. Please help me. Please."* How can you resist giving your support to the aid charity running the feeding programme at the refugee centre? Then you think about the cause you are working for. "If only I were having to raise money for starving babies, it would be so much easier", you think.

But your cause is important too. You have to make it seem as important to yourself and to others as saving starving babies. And interestingly the fundraiser for the starving baby charity probably believes that it would be much easier to be raising money to save endangered animals from being poached. And the animal fundraiser would much prefer to be raising money for a cancer charity.

You have to believe wholeheartedly in what you are doing, and make your cause compelling to others. If you can do this, fundraising will become very much easier.

The ability to ask

Many people feel uncomfortable with the notion of actually asking for money. Anyone who has this difficulty will not be a natural fundraiser – whether the task in hand is to write a four-page appeal letter, make a speech at a meeting of the Rotary Club, telephone a business to ask for an in-kind donation, organise a committee to run a fundraising event, or pay a personal visit to seek the support of a major donor. All this requires an ability to ask effectively for what you need.

Persuasiveness

People have choices as to what to do with their money. They have competing demands on what to spend it on. Your job is to persuade them that supporting your organisation is a really worthwhile 'investment' of their hard-earned money. You need to make a really good case and to present it in a persuasive way. This requires good selling and communications skills. In particular you need to be able to marshal compelling arguments, to be able to write letters which excite interest, talk fluently and interestingly about the cause in public or in private, create a sense of excitement through your enthusiasm, and share your hopes and visions for the future.

Confidence and dealing with rejection

When you are asking for money, you need to radiate confidence. If you are apologetic or hesitant, people will not give to you.

One of the biggest problems is maintaining your confidence in the face of rejection. Since more people are likely to say "no" than say "yes" – that's a fact of fundraising life – it is very easy to get downhearted. Many approaches will be unsuccessful, simply because of the enormous competition for funds, or just through bad luck. After a couple of rejections, you really begin to believe that nobody wants to support you. You then start acting as if nobody wants to support you. You become apologetic and you talk as if you expect to be refused. And maybe you even avoid asking – so as not to be rejected.

A good fundraiser has to be able to cope with rejection, starting each fresh approach as if it were the first, and to be prepared to learn from experience.

Persistence pays

"Some years ago I produced an environmental colouring book for children for a schools education programme. I thought that this might be sold in bookshops, so I decided to see whether bookshops might be interested in taking copies. I went first to my local bookshop. *"Not our sort of book"*, they said. *"No thank you."* I had a similar experience at the next three bookshops I visited. I really was beginning to feel that nobody wanted the book. But I decided to go to one more bookshop before giving up. It was just as well that I did. *"That's just the book we've been looking for. We'll take 70 copies for our Christmas table... And what's the next title in the series, as we'd also be interested in that!"* I felt elated." It is exactly the same with fundraising. Your next approach might be your big success! So keep trying.
Michael Norton on his book 'Colour in Your Environment'

Persistence

Most fundraisers give up too soon. People often take "no" to mean "no" – rather than as a challenge to try to convert the "no" into a "yes". If you give up immediately, then there's no chance at all. If you feel that they really should be interested in supporting you, then you will try to find a way of getting them to change their mind, or find some other thing that they might like to support. You have approached them in the first place because you need support and you feel that they might potentially be interested in giving it. Don't just give up at the first setback. You will find that persistence really does pay.

What to do if you are turned down

- Telephone to try and find out why they decided not to support you this time.
- Ask about the possibility of submitting another application, and try to find out what aspect of your work they might be interested in supporting.
- Ask for a meeting, so that you can put your case in person.
- Suggest that they come and visit your project to see the excellent and exciting work you are doing.
- Tell them that you will keep in touch – sending them information on your work and news about progress.

Turning a NO into a YES

I asked a group of fundraisers who were approaching charitable foundations to telephone them when they had received a letter of rejection to find out why they had been turned down, whether there was any possibility of their application being reconsidered, or what else they might apply for. What was interesting was how many eventually succeeded in getting a grant. If you are a donor receiving hundreds of applications, there is a tendency to say "no" as an immediate response to any request. It is far harder to say "no" to someone who feels that they have a good project which you really should be interested in and who has the courage to come back and try to enter into a discussion with you.

Truthfulness

The fundraiser has to be truthful at all times. The need to persuade people creates a pressure to tell only partial truths and to claim more for your work than is the case. The very complex socio-economic factors that create poverty today are a good example. If we are to raise funds by writing a short letter to a potential supporter, how can you hope to describe what lies behind the poverty? And can you give a proper explanation without straying into the politics of the situation, however unattractive or contentious that may be to the donor?

There is also a tendency to present the beneficiary as a victim. It makes it easier to elicit sympathy and support. This is as true for people with physical disabilities as it is for refugee families. The beneficiary may see the fundraising material and even be represented on the boards of organisations, and be offended at how the cause is being presented. The need to present a sensitive but truthful case, whilst making it powerful enough to persuade donors to give, can cause conflicts within the organisation. To resolve this demands sensitivity and understanding from the fundraiser.

Social skills

A good fundraiser needs confidence, patience and tact. Confidence, because a confident appeal is harder to refuse. Patience, to deal with the particular concerns of donors (for example, when they ask to hear about the income ratios of the organisation for the third time). Tact and sincerity, to ask a supporter face to face for a legacy, or to suggest a variation in a Will. A good fundraiser should also like meeting and dealing with people.

Dealing with your donors

"A fundraiser should never give up. Much depends on his (or her) approach and personality. To ask for financial or other support for people who are in need does not mean that you should look unhappy. Your appearance, open smile, courage and challenge should light a beam in the heart of your donor. Your belief in the future for the people you are helping should convince the donor. It is useful to remember that the donor is also a human being who lives in the same world as you, and is anxious to do his bit to improve the community. My modest experience in fundraising says that it is very important to create feedback with your donor. Generous people do not necessarily need to be praised up to the sky, but they will be delighted to know that their support has helped improved something or made a better world for somebody. We have become close friends with many of our donors and try to build long-term relationships with them."

Contributed by Ekaterina Kim, Contacts-I, a group with disabilities working for people with disabilities in Moscow

Organisational skills

Fundraising often involves keeping in touch with thousands of supporters, all of whom imagine that they are special and that you have some personal relationship with them. Good organisation is essential. Fundraisers have to keep accurate records of correspondence and information on donation history for each donor. All this must be organised so that no past event or piece of generosity is forgotten. A good memory for faces helps too.

Imagination and creativity

Fundraisers who come afresh to an organisation will find that imagination is an invaluable asset. The task may be to dream up new activities that will inspire existing supporters and to create events that the public is going to be enthused by. Or to present your work in an exciting and imaginative way. Circumstances are continually changing and new opportunities emerging, so fundraisers need to identify new approaches and not simply rely on what has been done in the past.

Contacts and the ability to make contacts

The fundraiser who already has a number of existing contacts in an area or sector will be at an enormous advantage. But this is not a prerequisite. Having contacts does not necessarily mean that they will be the right people for the organisation. A good alternative is to have the confidence to ask anybody for what is needed, the ability to make new contacts and the good sense to ask others to do the asking for you.

Opportunism

You need to grasp every opportunity that presents itself. For example, when a well-known supporter is awarded libel damages, should your letter asking for support not be in their in-tray next morning? Or if a leading company has just announced a major hike in profits or has been awarded a major construction contract in your area, then a cleverly constructed appeal for funds might just succeed.

The clearest examples of opportunistic fundraising are to be found in newspaper coverage. If, for example, there is a feature in the paper focusing on your cause, then the results of any advertising placed in the paper on the same day may be substantial (provided of course that the editorial coverage is supportive of what you are doing). So if you know you are going to get coverage, then consider taking an advertisement to ask for support – or better still, get the journalist to add this request at the end of the article, with a reply address where donations can be sent.

The annual calendar provides opportunities at different times of the year. For example in Christian communities, Christmas and the New Year provide extremely good fundraising opportunity, and other faiths have similar points in the year. And then there are anniversaries or centenaries which can be used as a basis for major appeals.

Zubin Mehta and the Shalom India-Israel Centre in Bombay

How Zubin Mehta, the Indian-born international conductor and Music Director for Life, became involved with the Shalom India-Israel Centre in Bombay

"Having nurtured the dream of an India-Israel Centre, I visited Israel in 1991, tramping the offices of umpteen cultural institutions, following up on every tenuous connection, meeting with Israeli government officials. Finally on my way back to the airport, I felt the kind of empty fatigue that comes with carrying a load of promises but nothing tangible. I knew we needed a respected and powerful patron, and many names came up, including Zubin's. But it needed both familiarity and courage to access high places. That first time, in 1991, I'm not sure I had both. Suddenly, there was Zubin before me in the bustling airport. On impulse I went up and congratulated him, and said that he had done every Indian proud. He thanked me politely, then it was over. *'In that crowded place'*, I anguished with myself, *'I could have done more'*. Two hours later airborne, I noticed Zubin up front, reading glasses perched on his nose. I mustered the courage to send a polite note requesting to talk to him. From that and many subsequent meetings I realised that I was with a very special human being. Zubin's warmth and easy accessibility, his ability to get as excited as a child with an idea, astonished me. Here was something he had always wanted to do – to bring together the people of the two countries he loved together culturally."

Salome Parekh, Hon Director and Trustee, the Shalom India-Israel Centre, Bombay

2.3 Who should do the fundraising

Who then should be actually doing the fundraising work? There are several options to consider:

The Management Committee or Management Board or Trustees of the organisation

These are the people who are legally responsible for ensuring that the organisation has sufficient funds to carry out its work and ensure that it doesn't become insolvent. They have to ensure that the fundraising is done effectively and on time. But that does not mean that they have to do the fundraising work, although in many smaller organisations it is the committee members who will be doing most of the fundraising.

The Chairperson

The Chairperson of the organisation occupies a special position of leadership within the organisation. And part of the responsibility of heading up the organisation may be to deal with major donors, along with the Executive Director, and to attend various meetings with foundations and businesses where this will be helpful.

A Fundraising Committee

Where the fundraising is being done by Committee Members, it is important to remember that some people don't like doing fundraising or are no good at it. This leads some organisations to appoint Committee Members for their fundraising skills and personal contacts – if they know the 'captains of industry' and the 'good and the great', then they may be in a good position to bring in the money. This is not always a good strategy. Any Committee needs to include people with a range of skills, expertise and standpoints, as it has responsibility for the proper management and strategic direction of the organisation as well as to ensure that the organisation has sufficient funds. It might be better to form a Fundraising Committee or Development Committee with people who are interested in the organisation and are also keen to help raise money for it. This group can then be charged with overseeing the fundraising, and even undertaking much of the fundraising work.

The Executive Director

The Executive Director of the organisation is the senior staff member. As such he or she is in a good position to do the fundraising – with an expert knowledge of the work being done and sufficient seniority to be an effective persuader. Fundraising can also be an extremely creative process. For if you are dealing with donors, you will be testing out new ideas and getting feedback, negotiating different forms of support and having to think creatively about how to turn people's goodwill into support. All this is extremely useful for a successful Chief Executive.

One problem though is lack of time, which means that the fundraising will not be given sufficient priority. One solution is to give the Executive Director sufficient administrative assistance so that the fundraising part of the job can be done well.

A Professional Fundraiser

Organisations of sufficient size or where fundraising is to be given a high priority may decide to create a specific post of 'Fundraiser' within the organisation. This will ensure that a person with the required skills and with sufficient time to do the job properly is responsible for the fundraising.

However, it is easy to delegate a job that nobody really likes doing and then forget about it. There are many instances of organisations appointing a Fundraiser and telling them to get on with it, then finding a couple of years later that nothing has been achieved. So even if you decide to delegate the job of fundraising to a professional, both the Executive Director and the Management Committee need to keep management control of the process, setting goals and monitoring progress, providing active support where needed and giving encouragement.

A Volunteer

Yet another option is to find a part-time or even full-time volunteer who is prepared to do the fundraising. Some organisations have been able to do this successfully. A recently retired businessman might find this a challenge.

Volunteers are more often given a responsibility for a particular aspect of the fundraising, such as organising a fundraising reception or a charity gala film evening. This has the advantage that a slice of the fundraising work can be handed over to someone else who takes full responsibility for it; but the volunteer should be set targets and held accountable for performance, if the arrangement is to be a success.

A Fundraising Consultant

There is a new breed of person thriving in Northern countries and just beginning to emerge in the South – the Fundraising Consultant or consultancy organisation. These may specialise in major appeals, event organising, direct mail campaigns or corporate sponsorship. They can be quite expensive, as you are having to pay for their expertise as well as for their overheads. But particularly where you are developing a major initiative, they can provide an extremely useful input of experience and knowledge which can add value to your fundraising efforts. It is rarely the case that you will hand over all of the fundraising to an external consultant.

When you need to employ a fundraiser

If you decide you need to employ a fundraiser, the main consideration when deciding the right time to create this post in the organisation is a financial one.

Can you afford to? And what effect will it have on the administrative costs of the organisation? Not many organisations are lucky enough to obtain sponsorship for their fundraiser, so you will have to consider the costs involved.

On the other hand, can you afford not to? Will not having a person to do the work mean that you will fail to raise the money you need? Or fail to develop the support you will need if your organisation is to expand?

As a rough rule of thumb, to employ a fundraiser will require a full-time salary plus as much again in overheads – to cover such things as office costs, telephone, stationery and duplicating, postage, production of brochures, and so on. To justify such an expenditure, you should aim to generate at least five times as much a year in extra income as a result of this appointment – although it can take some years for the income to build up if you are just starting to fundraise seriously, and many organisations find that they cannot achieve a 5 to 1 return.

In the early days it may appear that the fundraiser is doing little more than raising the costs of his or her own salary. Those appointing a fundraiser for the first time should take a long-term view. It will take several years to develop the full potential of the fundraising effort put in. The appointment of a fundraiser should be seen as part of the organisation's longer term strategy, and targets should be set for the money to be raised in each of the first few years of the appointment.

In the event that you do not yet want to commit yourself to hiring a full-time fundraiser on a permanent basis, there are several other options. The first is to consider whether you have a volunteer with the time and skills to be trained up as a fundraiser. The next is whether a part-time appointment might be more appropriate. Alternatively, you might want to look at a fixed-term contract for, say, one year. You can always re-appoint or extend the contract if things are going well, but you will not be committed if they do not.

Recruitment of a fundraiser

Once you have decided to recruit a fundraiser, you should consider the following:

Objectives

What are the objectives for the fundraising post? Is it to develop alternative sources of funds to replace grants which are known to be coming to an end? Or to launch an expansion programme? Or to run a major capital appeal? Or to develop a corpus fund or endowment? Or to develop independent and local sources of funding? Or to create a large and active membership? Or to develop corporate support? Or to organise high profile events which will raise awareness as well as money? Or what? You need to decide quite clearly what your objectives are. This will help you write a 'job description' and a 'person specification', so that you recruit someone with the experience and capability of doing a good job for you.

It is also important to recognise that objectives should be set that are realistic – that recognise the fundraising needs of the organisation and the opportunities that exist, but which do not present an insurmountable obstacle to success. There will also be an inevitable learning process at the start when nothing much happens, whilst the fundraiser familiarises himself or herself to the work of the organisation and begins to build experience and contacts. But it is important too that results should begin to flow, even if the successes are quite small initially, as this will demonstrate that things are beginning to work.

Budget

As has already been mentioned, the budget for fundraising will be more than the salary costs of the fundraiser. A sensible budget needs to be set aside to resource the post and pay for all the promotional work that is needed.

Recruitment

So you've decided your objectives and written a job description. Where do you find this paragon you are looking for? You will need to identify someone with the right:

- **Experience** and **expertise**.
- **Personal skills** and qualities to do a good job.
- **Ethical values** and **commitment** to the cause.

Of these it is the last two which are really important – especially so in countries where there is not yet that much experience of fundraising except raising money from international donor bodies. Expertise can be acquired and experience gained, but the personal skills and ethical stance come with the candidate. The personal skills required in a fundraiser are discussed in some detail in *Section 2.2*.

When you decide to recruit someone, there is always a chance that the arrangement will not work out – that they will be the wrong person for the job despite having got through the job interview and selection process. You may want to have a 6 month probation period for the newly recruited fundraiser.

> **Where to recruit a fundraiser**
>
> - Circulate information about the job opportunity to your staff. This job might be something that a current member of your staff team could do well.
> - Circulate information about the job opportunity to your existing supporters and volunteers. They already have some commitment to the organisation. Someone might be just the right person for the job.
> - Advertise in the local newspaper, the business press and in marketing journals. These will reach the sorts of people you are looking for.

Induction

The fundraiser is 'selling' the organisation to donors. It is important that there is a satisfactory induction process, which might include:

- Meeting the **Management Committee**.
- Meeting **senior staff**.
- **Site visits** to projects to see the organisation at work.
- Discussing and agreeing **what the organisation stands for** and how it should be projected to the public.
- Discussing **'no go areas'**, where the organisation is not prepared to solicit support.
- Agreeing the **fundraising strategy** and the targets for the first year, and sketching out what might be achieved over the first three years.
- Reviewing **existing donor support**, identifying problem areas and opportunities, and being introduced to any key contacts.

Management and motivation of fundraisers

Fundraising is a tough and demanding job. And often a lonely one. With all the difficulties in raising money, and with a steady flow of rejections, it is easy to get downhearted. Proper management of the fundraiser's job means:

Keeping in touch with the work of the organisation

The fundraiser should keep in regular touch with those doing the front-line work of the organisation, visiting projects to see the work, talking to project workers and beneficiaries to get a feel of the need and the quality of the work being done, and to understand the issues and the particular approach and ethos of the organisation. This interchange of ideas also has the effect that those spending the organisation's money learn more about the fundraising process and begin to recognise the concerns and interests of the donor.

Setting targets and monitoring progress

Targets should be agreed with the fundraiser rather than imposed. And progress should be regularly monitored. If targets are not being met, then this will need to be discussed and the causes identified. Perhaps they were over-optimistic in the first place. Perhaps a particular fundraising approach or technique is not working well enough. Perhaps things could be done better or there was a mistake to learn from. One idea is to create a small fundraising advisory group who will take a particular interest in the fundraising with whom the fundraiser can discuss issues or refer problems.

It is also important to keep track of the time and effort put into each fundraising initiative. There is a tendency to spend a lot of time chasing after sources which are marginal or unlikely, and too little time developing those which are really important to the organisation and its future. There is also the problem of organising fundraising events which take up a lot of time but may yield little in terms of money raised. So it is important to find out whether you are using your time effectively – since your time is usually the biggest fundraising cost you will be incurring.

Giving fundraising due importance

It is important that fundraising be recognised in the organisation as an important function, and that the fundraiser be given the support that is needed to do a good job. Fundraising which is just delegated and forgotten about will rarely work well. Fundraising which is starved of resources – it will always take money to raise money – is also likely to fail. So the Executive Director and the Management Committee need to have confidence in the fundraising process and the abilities of the fundraiser, and then provide support for the fundraising and the fundraiser in whatever way is appropriate.

Finding out about what others are doing

A fundraiser should try to find out how other similar organisations are raising money, and how successful their fundraising is. Here are some simple things to do:

- Write and ask to be sent a copy of their latest annual report and accounts. Then see how much the organisation is raising, make a note of their major sources and their major donors (these are often acknowledged), and see how their fundraising is growing.
- Scan the newspapers for mentions of their work.
- If they have produced an appeal brochure or fundraising literature ask to be sent a copy. See if you are then put on their mailing list.
- Telephone to ask about their work – and see how well they answer your call.
- Where you can, participate in their fundraising events. For example, get yourself invited to a gala dinner, participate in a sponsored walk. See how well the event is being run, and how successful it is in raising money.
- Make friends with fundraisers in other organisations. Go on fundraising courses to share experiences.

Recognising success

When a fundraiser achieves success, this should be recognised by the organisation. How this is done is up to you. Some organisations offer incentives to fundraisers in the form of some form of commission or performance bonus based on the amount of money raised. This is not always wise, nor might it be the best way of motivating a fundraiser, and it can sometimes lead to a conflict of interest.

Training and meeting other fundraisers

There are now courses on aspects of fundraising being run in most countries, and the International Fund Raising Group runs active training programmes worldwide (see box) as well as annual conventions. These are good places to brush up on basic skills, to share ideas and experiences, and to meet and network with others doing a similar job.

Free time to think

Some of the most creative fundraising comes from thinking about what you are doing, chatting to people about your ideas, meeting people and talking about your work (with no immediate intention of asking for money, but to develop a contact and a relationship). With the pressure to raise money, it is often this 'creative time;' which gets lost. The successful fundraiser will make sure that he or she has sufficient time to do all of these things by building this into the work schedule.

The International Fund Raising Group

The International Fund Raising Group (IFRG) was founded in 1981 to establish a forum so that fundraisers from different countries could come together, exchange ideas and learn from one another. The result was the first ever **'International Fund Raising Workshop'**, which was held in the Netherlands in October 1981 and was attended by some 35 delegates from Europe and the USA.

From that small beginning, the annual International Fund Raising Workshop in the Netherlands has grown to become a truly unique, international event of exceptionally high quality. It now attracts each year around 500 delegates from more than 30 countries.

The tremendous growth of the NGO sector (also referred to as the 'voluntary' or 'not-for-profit' sector) worldwide meant that fundraising training was also in increasing demand in Africa, Asia, Latin America and Central and Eastern Europe. So, in collaboration with a group of international donor agencies, IFRG launched its **'Worldwide Programme'**. Through this programme, fundraising training workshops now take place annually in ten regions of the world (East Africa; West Africa; Southern Africa; South Asia; East Asia; South-East Asia; South America; Central America and the Caribbean; Central and Eastern Europe; and the Middle East).

In each of these ten regions, IFRG helps organise workshops working closely with local partner organisations, which bring together fundraisers from a wide variety of organisations and from several countries. During each of these events, which generally last from three to four days, around 150 delegates have the opportunity to discuss a wide variety of fundraising issues and to exchange ideas on and learn practical skills in specific fundraising techniques.

In addition to the publication of this handbook, another recent development in IFRG's Worldwide Programme has been the development of a series of in-depth

training courses. Each course focuses on a particular facet of fundraising and is designed to help 30 or so participants acquire the necessary knowledge, confidence and skill to put particular fundraising techniques into practice in their own country.

Through the International Fund Raising Workshop and the Worldwide Programme, IFRG is playing its part in developing a stronger, more self-sufficient and more independent voluntary sector worldwide. A voluntary sector able to fulfil its role in building a better world for all.

For more information, contact IFRG, 295 Kennington Road, London SE11 4QE, UK. Tel +44-171 587 0287; Fax +44-171 582 4335; e-mail wwp.ifrg@dial.pipex.com

2.4 Equipping a fundraising office

In order to succeed as a fundraiser there are some items of equipment which will help you in the job. Not all are essential by any means, and you should be able to find some way of organising the fundraising whatever the resources available to you. The following are some of the things to consider getting. You may not want to rush out immediately and spend large sums of money. Once the fundraising has started to develop, this may then be an appropriate time to invest in the equipment which will make the work easier.

1. Word processor and database. To write fundraising letters and keep records of donors and their support. This is at the heart of successful fundraising, and there are now some specialist fundraising programmes available commercially. If you know nothing about computers, talk with someone who does and seek their advice, or visit some organisations of a similar size which have active fundraising programmes. If there are power cuts, you may also need equipment to regulate voltage levels and to provide back up if the electricity goes off.

2. Desk Top Publishing (often referred to as DTP). To design simple leaflets and communications material in your office, rather than sending it out to a design studio. Now that the software is available, and if you already have a computer, it is worth getting this design work done in house. Using computers for wordprocessing, database management and DTP is covered in more detail in *Appendix 3*.

3. Telephone. The telephone is an essential tool. It can be used to find out names, job titles and confirm addresses of the people you are writing to; to follow up on an application letter to see if it has arrived and whether more information is required; to check the progress of the application; to thank donors for their support, or to see whether you can change their mind where you have had a rejection; to inform donors of progress; and in many, many more ways.

4. Fax. In a modern office, a fax is becoming a really useful piece of equipment, particularly where postal services are uncertain, and speed of communication and certainty of arrival are important.

5. Photocopier (and a supply of paper). If you are in the business of writing to hundreds or thousands of donors, you will definitely need some photocopying capability – either your own or access to a local copy bureau, or perhaps even an agreement with a local company that you can use their facilities.

6. Annual reports, brochures and other project information. Most of the institutional donors, such as aid agencies and foundations, which you are approaching will want to see a copy of your latest annual report and accounts. The annual report should be carefully written and nicely, though not necessarily expensively, produced. You should also have a simple brochure, perhaps a single letter-sized sheet of paper (A4) folded once or twice, which gives basic information about your organisation, and includes a 'reply coupon' so that people can respond. You may also want to produce some simple information sheets on the various projects your organisation is involved with and for which you are seeking money.

7. Books and practical information on fundraising. Including handbooks and technical information on tax and giving which you should be familiar with, but also grant guides for government sources, foundations and listings of major companies.

A simple fundraising brochure

How you can help:	Name of Organisation
1.	photo
2.	
3.	
4.	Mission statement
page 4	page 1

About the organisation	A case study
	photo
six facts about the need	photo
	"endorsements and quotes about your work"
page 2	page 3

8. Tax exemption and permission to receive foreign funds (where this is required). It is also important that all the legal requirements for fundraising are complied with.

9. Cash collection facility (usually a bank account). So that you can receive funds and advise donors as to how to pay you. If you are holding substantial cash balances, then you will want to place your funds on high interest earning account, both to protect against inflation and to earn a return. You may also need such things as collecting boxes for house-to-house collections, and procedures for opening them and counting the money (to avoid temptation and fraud).

10. Letterheads and compliments slips for correspondence. These could state the name of your organisation, its logo, its legal status, any charity registration number, the names of the Committee Members and the Executive Director, any affiliations, and even a slogan or 'strap line' explaining your 'mission' in a short sentence. It is up to you how much information you provide. But make sure that it's nicely designed. Your letterhead may be the first point of contact with your organisation for many of the people you are approaching, and it should give the image of a lively and successful organisation. You will also need a short and nicely designed explanatory leaflet illustrating the work of the organisation, which you can include with your correspondence (see point 6 above). You might even consider the possibility that all your letterheads and literature carry a brief appeal for support and some response mechanism. This could generate some return, but it will also indicate to everyone you are writing to that you are actively seeking support.

11. Display equipment for exhibitions. Exhibiting at fairs and conferences can be an effective way of introducing your organisation to a wider public and meeting new supporters. Creating an attractive display so that people notice you and want to come and find out more will enable you to profit from the time and trouble of exhibiting. A short video showing the work of the organisation can also be useful.

12. Furniture. A desk, a filing cabinet, chairs and a table for meetings – just the basic furnishings that any office requires. And why not a display of photographs of the organisation at work on the walls, so that any visitor to your office can see what you are doing?

Setting up an office can be expensive. Asking suppliers or supporters to donate equipment may be an effective way of getting what you need. Borrowing what you need is another option. If you have to buy something, then always ask for a discount. Try asking the following:

- Your **Management Committee members** and your **volunteers**, who might have just what you need.
- **Local companies**, who might provide furniture and equipment that they no longer need, donations of their products or a discount on list price, or use of their facilities.

The most expensive items are likely to be the computer and associated software, fax and photocopying equipment. These are difficult to get donated or buy cheaply second hand. So you will just have to budget for what you need and find a donor prepared to pay for it.

If you are supported by a major donor, then you might present all of the above as 'an investment package' to help you develop your fundraising, arguing that it is in their interest to get you established in fundraising as this is a first step to reducing your dependency on them.

2.5 Engaging a fundraising consultant

There are a number of people with experience of running an NGO or who are experienced fundraisers who have set themselves up as independent fundraising consultants, available to advise organisations with their fundraising in return for a fee. There are three main sorts of work that such freelance consultants might do for you:

1. Make an **appraisal** of a particular area of your fundraising and advise you on what to do about it.
2. At the same time, be involved in the **implementation** of the fundraising programme.
3. Help you **write and design** effective brochures and other fundraising literature.

You must decide what sort of help or advice you really need. Each consultant will have their own particular strengths which you need to identify. Some have specialist skills, such as expertise in corporate giving, sponsorship, direct mail, advertising, promotion, design and print, producing annual reports or videos. Others will have more general skills, or managerial and strategic experience to offer.

Since consultants are expensive you need to be sure you are going to get good value. If at the outset, you are not certain what value a consultant (or consultancy firm) can bring to you – or of how much you can afford to pay them – you might suggest a feasibility study first. This should be a short, paid investigation of the major issues involved and a preliminary indication of what might be achieved by the consultant. Such a study would involve no further commitment on your part.

Payment by results

Many charities think that it is desirable to hire a consultant on a commission or payment by results basis. Although this is done from time to time, it is not generally considered a sound basis for remuneration.

Beware of fundraisers who offer this sort of deal. Particularly where the commission levied is high, they will be remunerating themselves at your donor's expense. For most consultants there is sufficient incentive to succeed without linking pay to results. And from your point of view, selecting the best person is what is most likely to lead to success.

Selecting an adviser

Whoever you decide to choose, there are a number of steps to go through:

1. **Be absolutely sure of what your problem is** and what sort of service you actually need. Do you need someone to help you devise the strategy only? Do you need both the strategy and help with its implementation? Or do you have some specific task you need done, and require someone to do it for you? Or do you just need advice?
2. Write a **good brief and clear job description**. This should cover what needs to be done, the timetable, and the specific objectives.
3. Wherever possible, make sure you have a **good selection** of people or companies to choose from – so as to ensure that you choose the best.
4. Agree the **basis of remuneration**. Is the budget acceptable? What control over success and failure will you retain? How will expenses be charged? How much notice is required to terminate the arrangement if you are dissatisfied?
5. Get **references** and follow these up to find out the quality of their work for other similar organisations. If you do not get good – or indeed any – references, proceed only with the greatest caution.

See *Appendix 4* for Guidance Notes for organisations taking on a fundraising consultant.

3. Fundraising strategy

3.1 Developing a fundraising strategy

Your fundraising strategy is the backbone of your fundraising. Getting it right demands a good deal of attention at an early stage. Not thinking through what you are doing can waste your time and efforts.

Outlining the needs

The starting point for any fundraising strategy is to define the needs of the organisation. This can be done at three levels.

1. Just to keep going

What are the financial requirements if the organisation is to continue its work programme at the present scale of operation? How much money is already assured and how much will need to be raised to meet spending requirements?

These calculations will usually take the form of annual and rolling budgets for the short and medium term (say, up to five years ahead).

2. To expand to meet growing need

Most organisations will say that they are only scratching at the surface of the problem, that if they had more resources, they could do much more to meet the need. And alongside this, the need may be growing or the problem getting worse. Starting with the human or societal needs being addressed by the organisation, you might ask the following questions:

- What exactly is the current level of **unmet need**?
- What are the **consequences** or **implications** of this for the future if nothing is done?
- How are the needs growing and what changes do you foresee happening over the next few years?
- **Who else is doing anything** to meet the need?
- What should you be doing to **respond to the challenges** of the future?
- How does what you plan to do **fit in with what others are doing**?
- Is what you propose to do an **effective way of addressing the need** given the limited resources that are likely to be available?

All these questions should be asked and answered. Future plans should be discussed and developed. Is it just a question of expanding what you are doing? Or will you need to develop different mechanisms for addressing the problem? If the need is not important and your role not clear, then developing a good fundraising 'case' can become very difficult.

3. The future development of the organisation's work

Most organisations do not stay still. There is often a momentum to expand and develop. Success with one project not only gives the organisation a feeling of confidence, but it will also throw up ideas for other things that the organisation might do, and it brings greater credibility with funders and public bodies who might wish to create closer working partnerships.

What developments will you want to consider for the future? What new services or projects will you want to run? Will you want to export your work into other regions? Will you want to enter into major collaborations with your funding partners to extend your work? Will you want to enter into partnerships with governmental authorities, working with them on a much wider scale to address the problem?

Then, if you are a development organisation, there is the relationship with the people you are helping. Are you empowering people to help themselves? And if you are, how will you be planning to operate once local people have the structures and skills to organise their own development? Will you extend and develop your work and maintain your development role? Or will you develop a withdrawal or exit strategy?

The future of your organisation starts with what you want to do. It is up to your Chief Executive to plan this, with an input from other senior staff and from you. And then it is up to you, the fundraiser, to get the resources that will be needed to put the plans into action.

How the organisation itself will develop

Besides funding the work, you will also need to fund the organisation and its future. There are several factors to consider:

1. Capital developments

What are your capital requirements for the future? Will you be developing a training centre or a school? Will you be buying land or acquiring property? Will you be extending or improving your existing facilities?

2. Corpus funds

Many organisations plan to develop a corpus fund or an endowment – that is a capital reserve which can be invested to produce a regular income for the organisation. Some approach major donors for contributions to this fund. Others set aside some of their income each year to be accumulated for this fund. Either way, this will impose a short and medium-term fundraising need on the organisation.

> **The development of 'corpus fundraising'**
>
> One recent trend in India has been the development of 'corpus fundraising' to create an endowment. Examples of this are: PRADAN, a rural development agency headquartered in Delhi, which had been able to raise a corpus from its US funder; and SEARCH, a training and information agency based in Bangalore, which has moved towards a more commercial basis for providing training and consultancy to NGOs and community organisations, and has been allowed by its funders to accumulate any surplus income into a corpus fund.

3. Reducing dependency and developing independent sources of funding

There is a fundamental difference between an organisation that receives all its money from one source, and an organisation which has developed a wide range of sources each contributing towards the total requirement. Too much dependency on one source can give too much control to the donor to dictate how the organisation should be working and where it should be going. It can put great pressure on the organisation to meet the agenda and objectives of the donor, rather than stand up for what it wants to do (where this is different). It can create a risk of failure – that the organisation will not be able to survive if the grant is cutback or withdrawn.

It is for this reason that many organisations seek to extend their fundraising base, bringing in other major donors and developing new sources of funding. You need to decide whether your organisation's funding base is too narrow, and if it is, then how you are going to broaden it. You will need to think about all the possible sources of funding, and decide which are the most sensible for your organisation to develop.

4. Developing a membership and a supporter base

This is another aspect of financial independence, where the organisation attracts large numbers of individual supporters. This not only brings in money, but it also strengthens the organisation by:

- Creating **a constituency** of support (the numbers of people who support you matter).
- Building **a local base** for your organisation (the relationships with the local community will be different if the funding is drawn from it rather than obtained externally).
- Creating **opportunities for further fundraising**. Each donor can be asked to give regularly and to give more generously. They can also be asked to recruit other donors, to volunteer their time and skills to help the organisation, to donate items of equipment, or even to leave a legacy when they die. The more people who support you, the greater the opportunities.

5. Long-term sustainability

One way of looking at the development of your organisation is to see the funding as an 'investment' in your future, and to plan to organise your future such that your organisation can run itself without major external funding after the development phase has been completed. The organisation and its core work is then sustainable – it will not collapse if external funding is withdrawn. And any fundraising can be used to invest in new developments.

This approach is in contrast to the more normal approach of using fundraising to cover running costs. It requires the organisation to plan for a sustainable future, which can come from:

- Designing services which pay (either wholly or very largely) for themselves.
- Creating income generating initiatives which will fund the organisation's work.
- Developing partnerships with governmental bodies (such as education services, forest departments), where the programme is paid for from taxation.
- Developing a corpus fund or an endowment.
- Developing independent and assured sources of funding (such as a large membership or a successful fundraising event which can be repeated to produce an income year after year).
- Developing self-help solutions and more economical ways of working, which require less professional support.
- Using volunteers and donated technical help to work alongside the professional staff that are being paid.

Sustainability

Stan Thekaekara, Director of ACCORD, a community development project working with tribal people in South India, says: "We should be talking about the sustainable community, rather than the sustainable NGO. This means developing plans which invest in the community to give it a secure future, and not simply pay for processes or services or support. Donors are not used to giving capital; they prefer to pay for projects, and have developed elaborate systems to deal with this task. And communities are not being asked to develop plans which ensure a continuing life for the community organisation and the community institutions were the funding to be withdrawn."

The development of sustainable funding strategies is an area where much more creative thinking is required. This might include:

- **Seeing aid as investment** in a development process, rather than a subsidy for work done.
- **Using aid to build income generation** into the community, so that it will have more resources of its own eventually to invest in its own future.
- **Building institutions** and other capital investments in the community, which give the community control over resources and an ability to generate income.

Looking at the progress towards financial sustainability made by ACCORD in Gudalur will illustrate these points:

- They are beginning to fund their health programme (including the running of the hospital and the employment of doctors) through a commercial insurance scheme linked to an insurance company, where the local families pay regular small contributions. This is very similar to the mutual aid health schemes which emerged and flourished in the UK prior to the introduction of a National Health Service.
- They are negotiating with government to give the community a role in both education and forest conservation, and the resources to back up this role.
- They have set up families in agriculture so that they are no longer forced into low-wage and uncertain day labour, and especially introduced tea growing, which is a lucrative crop.
- They are looking at adding value to the tea growing activity, and within the community organisation they have set up a tea nursery, joined the tea planters association collectively marketing their crop, and are looking at purchasing a tea estate for the community (provided that they can raise the capital). They are also considering direct marketing of the tea to Europe.

Identifying the sources

In constructing a fundraising strategy a useful starting point is to identify your likely funding sources. These might include:

- Support from individuals through **membership** or **donations**.
- **Major lifetime gifts**, and **legacies** receivable on death.
- Support from **fundraising events** such as public collections, entertainment events, participation events such as sponsored walks.
- Support from individuals giving their time (as **volunteers**).
- **Gifts in kind** (by individuals or from companies).
- Income generated through **fees, charges and sales**.
- **Investment income** from corpus funds or the interest on cash deposits.

- A grant from a **central government department**.
- A grant from a **nongovernmental agency**.
- A grant from a **local authority** (town or city, district or province, region or state).
- A **contract** with one of the above to provide services.
- A grant from an **international or national donor agency**.
- A grant from an international or a local **foundation** (or from another source).
- Support from **companies** (by donation or through sponsorship, by providing you with skills and expertise or facilities).

Assessing the opportunities

The above is a fairly comprehensive list of the sources of money that might be available to you. In deciding which to develop, some of the factors to take into account are:

- **Past experience**. The results of your fundraising so far provide a good indication of where you are likely to succeed and what is likely to be less successful.
- **Your natural constituency of support**. Who do you think should be funding you? Who has a stake in the problem you are addressing? Government? Business? Local people? A religious network? Can you get them to share in the solution by becoming an investor in your work?
- **The type of organisation you want to be**. Do you want to be membership based? Or supported by prestigious international donors? Or linked closely to business? All this affects the style of your work and how people perceive you.
- **The style of your work**. Are you radical or conservative? Young and fresh, or established and mature? Innovative and at the leading edge? Every organisation will be able to identify individuals and institutions which share its vision and outlook.
- **The resources and skills available to you**. If you have a good event organiser, then that's a good reason for organising an event. If you have lots of volunteers prepared to do house-to-house collections, then that's something to consider. If you are already experienced in direct mail, then why not develop that source of income further. If you're small and under-resourced, then you will have to acquire the skills and resources you need.
- **Your existing funding base**. Starting from where you are and building on the sources you are currently dealing with is a priority. They already know about your work and have demonstrated their interest in and commitment to you. You need to assess how your donors feel about you, whether they would like to become more closely and more substantially involved with you, what their current interests and priorities are. It is always far easier to build on your existing support than to develop new support. Talk to your existing donors. Share your ideas and plans with them. Identify areas of common interest. See how you can extend their support and increase their commitment. And with your supporters, conduct some simple market research to see what they think about the organisation and its work, whether they would like to become more involved, and what is preventing them from doing so. This can be by questionnaire or through interview, or just by chatting to the people you meet.

- **The opportunities that are available to you.** A major company expanding in your area. A new government programme. A chance meeting with the director of a major foundation or aid agency who seems interested in your work. If there are particular opportunities available to you, then seize them!
- **Who you know.** Contacts are important. If you know prominent philanthropists, prominent industrialists, prominent politicians, the stars of screen and media personalities, then you will find access to grants that much easier. Some people have a knack of developing contacts and forming relationships with the people they need to help them succeed. But all organisations have some contacts which could be mobilised. It is worth sitting down with your Management Board, staff and volunteers to see who you know or who you can reach who might be useful to you.

The importance of a long-term perspective

Some sources are essentially short-term, whilst others can develop into long-term relationships and partnerships. If your organisation is going to continue for the long term, then you will need money not just for this year, but for next year, the year after that, and into the future. If you raise short-term money, you may meet this and next year's fundraising targets, but you will be looking at a deficit after that.

It is sensible when fundraising for your future to consider the long-term potential of each source of funding:

Short-term and long-term sources

Short-term	Long-term
• A foundation grant for a project	• A long-term funding partnership with a donor agency
• A donation from a company	• A major fundraising event which can be repeated each year
• Business sponsorship	• Membership subscription income
• A house-to-house collection	• An annual appeal to your supporters
• A time-limited grant from a government source	• A long-term contract from a government agency to provide a service

- If you receive a major grant or are involved in a contract to deliver a service, can you negotiate a long-term arrangement for continuing support (subject to meeting performance targets)?
- If you are attracting support from individual donors, how can you develop regular and increasing support from them? It will not be just a question of soliciting support, but of managing the donor base that you develop.
- If you are organising a major income-generating event, can you plan to organise it again next year? And the year after? And do it better and better each time you run it? To raise more and more money from the event.

Clarifying the constraints

There will always be a number of constraints on what you can do. Some stem from the nature of the organisation and what it stands for. Some are internally generated. Some are externally imposed. However they arise, you need to take them into account in planning your fundraising.

National or local

Are you a national or a local organisation? And if you are local, is what you are doing of national significance or importance? Most national and international funding sources will want to support national projects or what they consider to be the best local projects – work which is innovative or at the leading edge. They are unlikely to respond to requests from local projects they've never heard of.

Local sources will usually support local projects in their own area. Local people will certainly be more interested in supporting projects on their doorstep. And companies will only want to support local projects in those areas where they have a business presence or some connection or where they are planning to start up.

Appropriateness of the source and 'no go' areas

Some sources are completely inappropriate because what the donor stands for goes completely against what the charity stands for. The most obvious example of this is a cancer charity receiving support from a tobacco company or a peace initiative funded by an armaments manufacturer. Every organisation should decide what sources are inappropriate to them – either for ethical reasons or because they will cause controversy amongst supporters – and then designate these as fundraising no go areas. Ideally, this should be discussed with the senior management of the organisation and a policy agreed with the Management Board before you set about asking, rather than creating problems for yourselves afterwards. Remember that whenever you turn down a donation (or decide not to approach a particular company) you are depriving your beneficiaries, and this has to be set against the problems that you will create for your organisation if you do accept the support.

Many companies use charitable support to enhance their image. Oil and mineral extraction companies, for example, are active supporters of environmental projects. Yet these companies also have an impact on the environment through their operations. You have to decide whether an association with them is appropriate, and perhaps even see an opportunity of influencing their behaviour through your association with them.

The attractiveness of the cause

Some causes are instantly attractive to donors; some have to work hard to make themselves attractive. And some will appeal only to certain types of people who share your outlook and your approach. A good example of the is the Medical Foundation for the Victims of Torture based in London. This is a 'world class' organisation doing invaluable work. Its instant appeal is only to those with a concern for human rights. But, through clever presentation of case studies and clearly explaining what it is doing, it can appeal to anyone concerned with fairness and who admires people who have the courage to stand up against injustice. But it will never have the glamour of a large hospital appeal or a children's rescue charity.

You need to think about whether you are radical and campaigning, or whether you are safe and conservative. Most companies and many 'establishment' sources will not want to support anything that is 'too political' or too controversial. This can impose a constraint on who to approach, or a constraint on what you can do if you accept money from a particular source.

The scale of your need

If you need large amounts of money, there is no point approaching someone who can only give a little – unless it is a major campaign where you intend to recruit large numbers of small donors. Nor is it sensible to spend a lot of time organising a fundraising event which will only generate a small sum. Equally, if you are just looking for some modest support, there is no point approaching a huge international foundation. Horses for courses!

The resources available to you

The resources available to you determine what you can and you can't do. You will need to decide whether you have:

- The **people** to organise the activity.
- The **skills** and experience you will need.
- The **money** to invest in the activity.
- The **capacity** to respond to requests.
- The **contacts** with prominent people or star personalities that might be needed if you are to succeed.
- The interest and **commitment of supporters** to get involved.
- The **credibility** as an organisation for people to want to be associated with you.
- The **time** available and sufficient lead time to organise the particular fundraising activity.

And then you can decide what sorts of fundraising activity are possible, and which are completely inappropriate.

What other organisations are doing

It is important to see what other organisations are doing – rival organisations doing similar work to you, as well as major fundraising initiatives which are likely to draw away support and media coverage from you. A major hospital appeal, for example, might involve all the leading businesses who might not want to get involved in any other major initiative for the time being.

Legal constraints

Are you able to receive foreign funds? Are you registered as a charitable organisation so that you can receive tax exempt donations? Will gift tax be payable? There are a whole range of legal and taxation issues which need to be sorted out before you apply. Some will determine who you can receive funds from; others will ensure that you get the best tax advantage from any support you receive.

Determining your strategy: some simple techniques

The strategic planning process enables you to think through your options, make informed decisions on the best approach, plan the next steps, and carefully consider the resource implications. There are a number of simple techniques that you can use in strategic planning. Here are four you might find useful:

The Ansoff Matrix

This allows you to consider ways of developing new audiences and using new techniques. Techniques are placed along the horizontal axis and audiences on the vertical axis. The possibilities then divide themselves into:

- **Continuation**: continuing to use existing methods with existing audiences.
- **Market development**: developing new audiences using existing techniques, such as expanding your direct mail programme to lower income groups or specifically targeting it to lawyers and doctors.

- **Product development**: developing new methods and techniques for raising money from your existing audience, for example asking your membership to become major supporters of a new development or to leave a bequest in their Will.
- **Diversification**: developing fundraising methods which involve new audiences and new techniques. This is the most risky as you will be using an untried technique to attract people with no current involvement with your organisation.

The Ansoff Matrix: ways to develop your fundraising

TARGET AUDIENCE	FUNDRAISING TECHNIQUES	
	EXISTING	NEW
EXISTING	**Continuation** safety area expand existing fundraising	**Product development** try new techniques with existing supporters
NEW	**Market development** extend known techniques to a new audience	**Diversification** danger area try out new ideas with new audiences

SWOT analysis

A SWOT analysis identifies the **strengths,** the **weaknesses**, the **opportunities** and the **threats** to the organisation and its fundraising. By doing this you will be able to develop:

- Fundraising approaches which build on your strengths.
- Avoid those areas of weakness or find ways of compensating for them.
- Seize the opportunities that present themselves.
- Develop ways of dealing with the threats that appear on the horizon.

SWOT analysis

S trengths	W eaknesses
O pportunities	T hreats

Here are some examples of strengths, weak-nesses, opportunities and threats that a SWOT analysis might generate:

Strengths
- An established and active supporter base.
- Good contacts with local industrialists.
- A well respected organisation.
- An active group of volunteers who are happy to run fundraising events for you.
- Good relationships with a major company and an important international foun-dation.

Weaknesses
- No existing fundraising experience.
- Nobody available to do the work.
- Poor promotional material.

Opportunities
- A major company has just located in your area.
- A new funding programme is due to come on line.
- Your twenty-fifth anniversary.
- A TV documentary on your work is about to go out.

Threats
- Your major supporter is beginning to re-focus priorities on other types of work or other areas.
- Structural adjustment will lead to price rises which will affect your supporters.
- You are in confrontation with the government, which is leading to adverse publicity.

Developing a Fundraising Strategy: a case study

The following shows how the fundraising consultants to the UNESCO/Bolshoi Theatre partnership developed a fundraising strategy in Moscow.

Until quite recently there was no modern tradition of charitable giving in Russia as the regime made this unnecessary by providing all the required funds. There is also a general distrust of "charity" and some are perceived as corrupt.

Strengths:
- The beauty and popularity of the theatre, its importance to the culture of Moscow, and its international recognition.
- Pockets of extreme wealth in modern Russia, and particularly Moscow.
- The fundraisers' will to succeed.

Weaknesses:
- Lack of fundraising and marketing experience and resources.
- No tradition of charitable giving among the newly rich.
- An unrealistically high expectation by the Bolshoi management of instant results.

The fundraisers also undertook a stakeholder analysis, a PEST analysis and established their selection criteria for the fundraising strategy.
They then renewed the potential target audiences for fundraising:
- The Russian public.
- Newly rich Russians.
- The expatriate community.
- Local companies in Moscow.
- Foreign owned companies in Moscow.
- The media to run an appeal targeted at the general public.

The fundraisers also considered the range of possible fundraising activities.
- **A mass appeal via the media**. Despite the popularity of the Bolshoi Theatre, the fundraisers had limited access to the media, and the poor postal and banking services made it nearly impossible for people to reply with a donation.
- **Social fundraising**. Activities like sponsored walks and coffee mornings are unknown in Russia. To organise such events among the expatriate community,

though culturally more feasible, would have little financial impact.
- **Trading**. The Bolshoi has a small, well-hidden shop with a limited range of goods. The fundraisers felt it would be great fun to develop this, but the logistics, poor infrastructure, lack of capital and limited potential returns made this an unrealistic fundraising option.
- **A Big Gift Campaign**. This would capitalise on Moscow's civic pride and the love of ostentatious display among the newly rich. Local and expatriate companies as well as individuals could be targeted, but there would still be need to convince the donors of the benefits of donating.

Limited resources would allow only one activity to start with, so a Big Gift Campaign was chosen, to be launched with a Gala Evening at the theatre. Trading activities and a media appeal could be developed later if the resources and infrastructure made this realistic.

These conclusions took the fundraisers several days, much coffee and even a little vodka. A Big Gift Campaign seemed like an obvious choice but having done a thorough strategic review they also knew it was the right one. It also offers them a clear direction for future activities and the skills needed to reassess the situation when this is required.

Source: Karen Culver, Fundraising Consultant.

Stakeholder analysis

Stakeholder analysis identifies those funders and agencies with an interest in your organisation's work, and explores reasons why they might be interested in assisting with funding or through the provision of other resources or through some form of partnership.

You need to think as creatively as possible. For example, for an organisation working with tribal people in a forest area, potential stakeholders would include the governmental body charged with preserving and protecting the forest. They would be interested in income generation projects and projects which sought to develop forest resources on a sustainable basis, both of which would reduce the need for local people to cut down the forest; and also in schemes for protecting the forest, which involved the participation of local people as 'forest guardians'.

Identifying stakeholders and understanding the reasons for and strength of their interest is a good starting off point for developing some form of relationship. It seeks to answer the two questions:

- Who do you think should be funding you?
- What is their interest in doing so?

PEST analysis

PEST analysis is used to explore the environment in which the fundraising takes place, in order to analyse external factors which may impact on the organisation or on the fundraising effort. PEST examines the Political, Economic, Social and Technological environments – for example:

- Political changes: Will elections next year bring a change of government? If so, what impact will this have on NGOs? Will the NGO bill currently going through Parliament make fundraising easier? Or more difficult?
- Economic changes: What effect will the next round of Structural Adjustment have on our fundraising? What will be the impact of current major economic

expansion, and what opportunities will this create for our fundraising? What will be the impact of our country joining the regional trade network next year? What will be the impact of the predicted 15% decrease in government-to-government aid spending from North to South?
- Social changes: What impact will the predicted growth in tourism have on our country and on our fundraising? What impact will the growth in the urban population have?
- Technological changes: What opportunities will arise when the banks introduce electronic cash transfer systems? What will be the effect of the major changes in the postal system? What opportunities will the expansion of satellite television and local radio in rural areas have?

All of these factors will affect the organisation and its fundraising. There may be little we can do about some of them, but we must take these factors into account when we are developing our longer-term strategy and constructing our fundraising programme.

Deciding your funding mix, planning your future

Having read through this Chapter so far, and considered all the factors and related them to the circumstances of your organisation, you are now in a position to start sketching out your plans for the future.

One useful tool for doing this is to display the percentages of your funding coming from different sources on a bar chart, and then show how these will change over a three or a five year time span. This will then illustrate:

- **The major sources**, which is where you should be putting a large part of your fundraising effort
- **The major changes**, where you will need to focus your time and energy to make sure you succeed.

The diagram in the box below shows how this can work.

Some other strategic principles

Be cost conscious

Everything possible should be done to save money both in the organisation and in its fundraising. For two good reasons: you will be asking supporters for only what is really necessary; and as much as possible of what you raise will go to support the work of the organisation. Anything you can beg or borrow, any discounts you can negotiate, any ways of saving money

---

Deciding your funding mix: an example

You are a research and campaigning organisation working to reduce child bonded labour. At present, 90% of your funding comes from international donor sources, with the balance of 10% coming from sundry gifts and donations. You decide that you want to move away from so much dependency on large international grants, and develop your own fundraising. Ideally you would like to generate at least half your funds in your own country through developing a strong membership base which will contribute to your work, through local community fundraising in the town where you have established a training project for the children rescued from bondage, as well as from the sundry income you will continue to receive. This can then be displayed as follows:

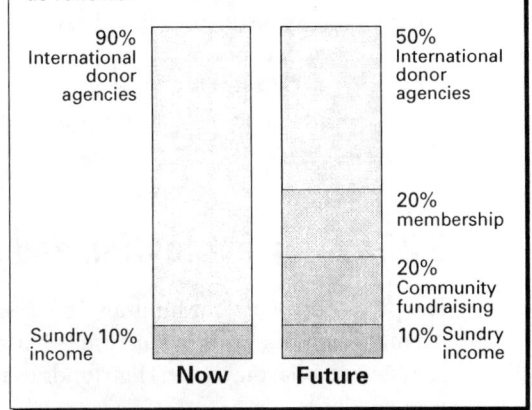

Now:
- 90% International donor agencies
- Sundry 10% income

Future:
- 50% International donor agencies
- 20% membership
- 20% Community fundraising
- 10% Sundry income

such as through hand delivery of newsletters by volunteers, will all ensure that you are running 'a tight ship'.

Relate your fundraising effort to your priorities

If you have a grant from one source which accounts for 70% of your annual income, you must invest time and effort in developing good working relations with that source, doing more than just complying with any reporting requirements which are a condition of the grant. There is a tendency for fundraisers to concentrate on finding new sources of money, and to spend a lot of time on fundraising efforts which are quite marginal to the overall budget. You must relate the importance of the income to you to the amount of effort you put in, not just in securing it in the first place, but also in ensuring that it continues.

Be cost-effective

All fundraising activity should adhere to some cost-effectiveness ratio. What is acceptable will depend on the technique being used. Selling Christmas Cards will obviously cost more than soliciting a major donation or winning a contract with a public authority. Getting repeat support from donors who have already supported you is far more cost effective than finding new supporters. But for most fundraising you should try to aim at a cost ratio of between 10% and no more than 25% of the amount raised. The subject of cost-effectiveness in fundraising is covered more fully in Section 3.2.

Avoid risk

Some fundraising is high risk. For example, if you are planning a gala evening at the local arts centre, you may have to pay for the venue and the performers, pay to publicise the event and lay on a reception. The expenditure for all this has to be committed before you see any money coming in. If nobody attends, then you will lose a substantial sum. This does not mean that you should not run the event. If you think it will work, then do it. But can you find some way of reducing your exposure to risk? Get a local business to sponsor the whole evening. Or find ten supporters each of whom will guarantee to bring along 20 people. Or include a cancellation clause in your contract with the venue, so that you have the option of calling it off if things look as if they are going badly.

Someone has to pay

Remember for everything that your organisation does, somebody has to pay for the cost. It may be the beneficiary paying for or contributing something toward the service; it may be an external funder or sponsor; it may be volunteers giving their time and effort free of charge. Or it may be a mixture of all of these. If you are to continue the work you are doing, you need to continue raising the money to support it. That's your job as fundraiser.

3.2 Testing, evaluation and control

Keeping control of your fundraising is essential. Donors, supporters and Board Members will scrutinise your results periodically and want to know why your results were what they were. High fundraising costs can be the worst advertisement for new donors.

Fundraisers must know exactly what is going on and how they can improve their performance. Control of fundraising centres on the need to generate the maximum funds whilst consuming the minimum of resources. Ideally your fundraising strategy should consist only of those elements which are going to be most cost-effective. The first issue then is to identify which fundraising methods are actually going to prove most cost-effective for you. This is where testing comes in. Demonstrating what is cost-effective requires some measure which relates the effectiveness of one form of fundraising against another. Finally you have to keep track of what you are doing and compare your performance with what you achieved in the past and how others are doing.

Measuring fundraising effectiveness

There are a number of measures of effectiveness that you can use. The most important measure is the fundraising ratio. This is simply the income raised by a particular fundraising idea or method divided by the cost of doing it. Costs include any direct expenditure on the fundraising, but also the cost of your organising time as well as an appropriate share of the organisation's overhead costs (rent, electricity, telephone and management costs). This gives the best indication of the costs needed to raise a given amount of money. The higher the ratio, the better the method. Many organisations use a guide ratio of 5:1. This indicates that if all income is raised at this rate, 80% of income will be available for the organisation and 20% to meet the cost of fundraising. It is a useful measure since it relates directly to what appears in your accounts. The actual ratio you aim to achieve will very much depend on your organisation and cause. If you are starting up a fundraising programme, the ratio you achieve may well be lower the 5:1 guide ratio, as it is harder to raise new money than it is to get existing supporters to continue giving. If you have a large endowment generating an income, a well-established legacy income flow or large government grants, then you would expect a much higher ratio.

An alternative approach is to use the net income measure. This is the amount you actually receive from your fundraising initiative. A mailing to a small group of people may have a good fundraising ratio, but produce very little money. On the other hand, a successful event may have higher fundraising costs but produce a substantial income. Which is better? It is only the net income you have raised which is available to support the work of your organisation. Simply concentrating on achieving a high ratio may produce only very little income,

> **Measuring your success**
>
> The following are some ways of measuring the success of your fundraising:
>
> **1. The fundraising ratio**
> The ratio between the income raised and the cost of raising it. Donors do not like to see a low fundraising ratio.
>
> **2. Net income raised**
> The amount you actually raise after all the costs of fundraising. This is what is left for your organisation to spend – and you need to achieve your income targets for the year.
>
> **3. Response rate**
> The percentage of those you approach who actually respond. The higher the rate, the more supporters you recruit.
>
> **4. Average donation**
> The amount given on average by each donor. The total raised will depend on the response rate *and* the average donation.
>
> **5. Recruitment cost**
> The cost of recruiting a new supporter, and this is then compared with the expected stream of income from this donor whilst they continue to support you.

although it has been raised very efficiently. But concentrating only on net income may lead to inefficiency and show your organisation as having a high fundraising cost in its annual accounts. The net income measure may be more appropriate in certain circumstances – for example – for trading in shops and local activities, where it is deemed that local fundraising costs are not really within the control of the charity anyhow, and only the net income from the activity appears in the accounts. Organisations which use both measures to assess each part of their fundraising will be able to make a judgement as to the effectiveness of the fundraising and the value of the income generated to the organisation.

When assessing your cost-effectiveness, it is always worth considering the value of the efforts put in by your volunteers. Although this does not show up in your costs, it is a resource, and you need to be sure you are using their time effectively. There may be other things that your volunteers could be doing which would use their time to raise much more money for you.

For mass fundraising campaigns, you are likely to need two other measurements. The first is the response rate. For mailings, house-to-house calls, collections and other fundraising methods where you are asking a large number of people to help, it is important to know how many of those people respond positively. The response rate is simply the numbers responding divided by the numbers approached.

This will help you decide whether your approach is better than last time, and if you can improve this, you will also improve the amount of funds you receive. But your success also depends upon the amount each respondent gives. This measure is the average donation. The two figures together can be satisfactorily combined into the yield, which is simply the money raised divided by the number approached.

For situations where you are more interested in getting people to support you over a number of years, you should consider the cost per new donor. For a mailing to people who have never supported you before (a cold mailing), for example, the cost ratios you will get are usually very high. This does not mean that the fundraising method has no value. Far from it, it means that you are measuring the present value of something that is expected to have a future benefit – perhaps yielding a stream of support over many years, and even a legacy on death. Ideally here you should also have a measure or estimate of the average lifetime value of a supporter. This can then be compared with the investment needed to find such a person. Even if you cannot accurately estimate their lifetime value, you should attempt to measure the effectiveness of this sort of fundraising on a cost per new donor basis.

Controlling your fundraising effectiveness

Controlling the effectiveness of your fundraising requires two pieces of information. The first is a realistic plan. Control then centres on ensuring that you stick to your plan, that the costs are as budgeted and that the sums which appear in your bank account are what you predicated they should be.

Clearly the first essential ingredient in this is to have a budget for both your costs and the income you plan to generate. Fundraising budgets should be based on past experience as much as possible. If you do not have the experience, you should ask the advice of other fundraisers rather than expose your organisation to the risk of getting your predictions completely wrong. You should also be cautious in estimating the yield from new fundraising methods not tried by your organisation before, or seriously think about testing out the method before investing large sums in it.

Annual budgets should be broken down into monthly budgets (quarterly for smaller organisations) which take account of inflation, growth of the organisation and the support it is attracting, new developments, and any seasonal elements (such as the Christmas period in Christian communities). Projected income and expenditure should be shown separately for each period. Results should be produced for each period and compared against the original budget. If there is a problem, this should be discussed, including the reasons for the poorer than expected performance or higher than budget costs, and action taken accordingly.

If you are running any large-scale operation, you will want to know whether perhaps there is some other organisation that is doing its fundraising much better than you yourself are doing. The easiest thing to do is to get hold of a copy of their annual accounts and try to do a rough comparison of their figures with yours.

For more detailed information on Testing and measuring the effectiveness of your fundraising, see *Appendix 1*.

4. The sources

This chapter sketches out the main sources of funding – individuals, government sources, international sources, charitable foundations, companies and a miscellany of other possible sources – describes their characteristics, identifies the main opportunities for the fundraiser, gives practical advice and identifies the skills you will need to be successful.

4.1 Individual donors

There are a wide range of potential donors to your cause – each with different characteristics, each having a different motivation, each preferring a different way of giving, and each having a different pathway by which they can be reached and communicated with. It is important for the fundraiser to have a clear idea of who they plan to approach and how they propose to attract their support. The range of potential donors includes:

- The **institutional donor** as well as the **individual**. Institutions might include Rotary Clubs and other similar philanthropic groups of local business people, schools and colleges, trade unions, etc.
- The **less well off** as well as the **rich**. It is often said that the poor are more generous, and K S Gupta who runs an eye hospital in Delhi has set out to target the professional classes rather than the seriously rich.
- The **young** through to the **elderly**, and everyone in between. People have different interests at different stages in their lives. When they are young, they may be more concerned with the environment or AIDS. When they are elderly, it may be medical causes (such as cancer) which will attract them more.
- Those that are **affected by the problem** or in some way involved with it to those who are only mildly interested. A parent of a disabled child will have a different interest in disability than a member of the public who has no such direct contact.
- The **general public** – everyone through to those with a particular perspective (such as lawyers or doctors or scientists or teachers).
- The **whole of the country** to those living in a **particular city** or **region**.
- **Family and friends** of existing supporters. Many people support charity simply because they are asked. And if they are asked by someone they know well, it becomes quite hard to refuse.

The more clearly you can specify who is likely to be interested in your cause, the more successful you will be in reaching them. To find out about your organisation's potential for attracting support you can:

- See who is already supporting you – perhaps carrying out some simple market research to find out why they support you.
- Test different audiences to see what the response is. You may be surprised to

find that a wider range of people want to support you and for different reasons from what you imagine.

The different ways of giving

There are not only different audiences, but there are also different methods of obtaining their support. A donor can support you by:

- Giving a **one-off donation**. Incidental support is not so important to you, because the cost of getting it will often outweigh its value. What you want are donors who are...
- Giving **continuing support** on a regular basis, perhaps through some form of commitment, such as a membership scheme. A useful measure of your effectiveness as a fundraiser is to measure the total support you will receive from a donor with the cost of obtaining that donor and keeping in touch with them whilst they are supporting you.
- Making a **major gift** to an appeal or towards a project.
- Leaving a **legacy** to you when they die. This is the only form of giving that does not cost the donor anything! It is paid from the donor's estate.
- Making a **gift in kind**. This can be anything you need, from offering you office space to giving you items to sell at a charity auction.
- **Purchasing a gift item** (such as greetings cards) or promotional material (such as tee-shirts or posters).
- Supporting a **charity fundraising event**. And there are many types of event which can be used to raise money successfully for charity.
- Participating in **lotteries and raffles**, by purchasing a chance to win a prize (although many organisations are reluctant to accept the proceeds of gambling for ideological or religious reasons).
- Raising money from **family and friends**. This is the basis on which most sponsored events (such as sponsored walks) are organised.
- Giving time as a **volunteer** to help you (doing anything from simple administrative tasks, delivering newsletters, helping organise fundraising activities, through to assisting in the organisation's core activity). Many organisations benefit very substantially from the time and effort put in by their volunteers – which can often be more important than the fundraising.

Why people give

If you can understand why people will want to give, then it will be easier to get their support. It is difficult to generalise about why people give. Different causes and different organisations benefit from different motivations. Possible motivations include:

- **Concern**, which is probably the single most important reason why people give. This will embrace the person who is worried about the environment, whether this is the increasing levels of pollution in cities or the continuing destruction of the countryside and the natural habitat. It will cover the parent who is horrified at the sexual harassment of children and wants to make some kind of response. And it will describe the individual who sees the pitiful faces of starving refugee children on the television news and telephones in to make a donation. Giving provides someone with the opportunity to do something significant for a cause they believe in.

- **Duty**, which probably comes a strong second as a motive for giving. The idea that we are rich and they are poor. Or the feeling that life has been good to us, who have a house, a job, an income and a comfortable life. People may want to respond to their good fortune with some charitable act (giving their money or their time). Many religions promote the concept of charity. Some even recommend that their members allocate a certain share of their income to charity.
- **Guilt** is another motivation. But unlike duty, if people give out of a sense of guilt, then this will not often lead to long-term relationships. Guilt encourages the donor to give in the hope that the problem (and you) will go away.
- **Personal experience.** Those people who themselves or whose families have been hit by cancer, heart disease or some other illness are likely to be especially motivated to give. Likewise, those who have children at school will want to support the school or anything that helps develop their child's education. All research indicates that personal interest is one of the most powerful motivations for giving.
- **Personal benefit** of some sort. Many people like the status or recognition that comes with giving when their generosity is publicised. They may like to be associated with any prominent people involved in the organisation – access to people and social ambition are important to some people, and giving to charity can be one way for them to achieve these personal objectives.
- **That they are asked**. The main reason for most people NOT giving is that they are never asked. Research demonstrates this again and again.
- **Peer pressure** is also important, where people know that their friends and colleagues are known to be giving and that they have not yet given, or where friends and colleagues are asking them to give. It can be hard for one member of a group to refuse if all the others are giving. One way of asking that exploits this principle is to get people who support you and who have already given to ask all their colleagues and contacts to contribute.
- **Tax**, and in particular the ability to save tax on gifts made for charitable purposes. Tax is not usually the prime motivator for giving, but can be an important factor in encouraging people to give and to give more generously. The tax concessions on gifts for charitable purposes vary from country to country, and the subject is discussed again in *Appendix 2*.

It is important to be able to understand why people want to give, and more particularly why the particular person you are approaching might be interested in giving to you. This requires an understanding of human psychology, but also some good research before you approach particular individuals for support. This will then enable you to tailor your message and create an approach which makes it much harder for them to refuse.

It is equally important to understand why people might not be interested in giving, and reasons may include that they are just not interested in your organisation and what it stands for, or the fact that they have given substantially to something similar recently. Bad publicity can affect people's inclination to support you; people are often worried about high levels of administration costs or have the idea that little of what they give will actually reach the poor. The problem may be so big that it appears hard to make any impact. People may feel that it is the government's job to do something, and that the matter should not be left to private charity. And then there is the fact that some people are by nature generous, whilst others will always be looking for an excuse not to give.

Your Concern is Our Concern...

Share your concern for the socially and economically deprived with us. And we'll make it possible for you to reach out and touch their lives and futures.

You can participate in any one of our fundraising schemes. Or you can simply contribute your skills, expertise or even your spare time.

Every little bit counts. Because every little contribution adds up to make a big difference. Here are some examples of how a small amount can amount to a changed life:

- Only Rs300 per month provides complete day-care for a young child, which includes nutrition, health care and education.
- Rs1,200 can educate a child for a whole year.
- Rs1,500 a year pays the fees of a young man or woman's vocational training.
- Rs180 sponsors the education and training of a mentally disabled person for a month.

What is most precious to us is not the size of your contribution, but the start of your involvement with our cause. We see it as the start of a lifetime of changing our concerns into opportunities.

Source: leaflet produced by Concern India Foundation

Getting in touch

To be successful, you need to do four things:

1. Identify likely supporters, then...
2. Create the right message that is likely to appeal to them, and then...
3. Direct that message to that person, and...
4. Support your promotional work with **good public relations**.

The right people are those who fit the picture you have constructed of your potential supporter, whose background and motivations indicate a likelihood that they will want to support your cause. Careful thinking, and possibly also some research, will help identify such people and their characteristics.

The right message is the one (and there may be several) that: builds on the motivation of the potential donor; starts from their understanding of the cause; and takes account of their natural hesitations or reasons they might have for not giving. A good understanding of your cause and its appeal will help; but some simple market research can also be helpful here.

Equally important, you will need to find the right method of reaching your target audience. In a sense you can only define a target audience if at the same time you can define a way of reaching it. For example, if senior business people are your target, then there are all sorts of channels you can use to reach them, including the business press, obtaining address lists of major businesses and writing to the names on this list, working through Rotary Clubs, Chambers of Commerce and other associations of businessmen, using businessmen to invite other businessmen to small receptions where you can give a presentation or ask them to ask their colleagues directly for support.

And finally, people will be more likely to support you if they have already heard about your organisation, its work and the importance of the need you are

Some tips for PR

- Keep a list of media people to send your promotional material to.
- Make friends with journalists, including journalists on local papers and radio, keeping them in touch with what you are doing.
- When you have a 'success', publicise it by sending out a press release. Follow this up with a phone call to encourage their interest.
- Use your beneficiaries to talk about your work, either through interviews or by quoting them in your press releases.
- Issue a press release with your annual report, and try to get publicity for it.
- When you win a substantial grant, or if you get support from a government body or from an important company, try to get publicity for this. You might be able to get the cheque hand-over photographed.
- Use 'stunts' to generate PR, especially those that illustrate the need or demonstrate the support that your cause is attracting. A stunt is an event specially designed to attract publicity – for example, going on hunger strike to draw attention to poverty or starvation, or throwing money into a crowd to protest corruption.
- When you produce and publish research on the cause, try to get a feature written about it to coincide with publication. Or make it newsworthy so that journalists will want to cover it, and issue a press release highlighting its news value.

addressing. This is where Public Relations comes in. It is often said that good PR is an essential ingredient of successful fundraising. So you need to spend some of your effort promoting your organisation and publicising its work – see *Section 8.8* for advice on getting publicity.

The chart below is adapted from the *Charity Household Survey* in the UK. It shows how people in Britain rate the various causes that they might be presented with. The greater the number, the higher the importance they give to that cause. In Britain, causes which relate to helping people – including children and people with handicaps and disabilities – appear to rate the highest. Arts, education and the environment are much less popular causes. The culture and circumstances of other countries will be different, but in every country there will be causes which generate an extremely positive response and causes which are less attractive. The less attractive the cause, the more important it is to target your appeal at those more likely to support it.

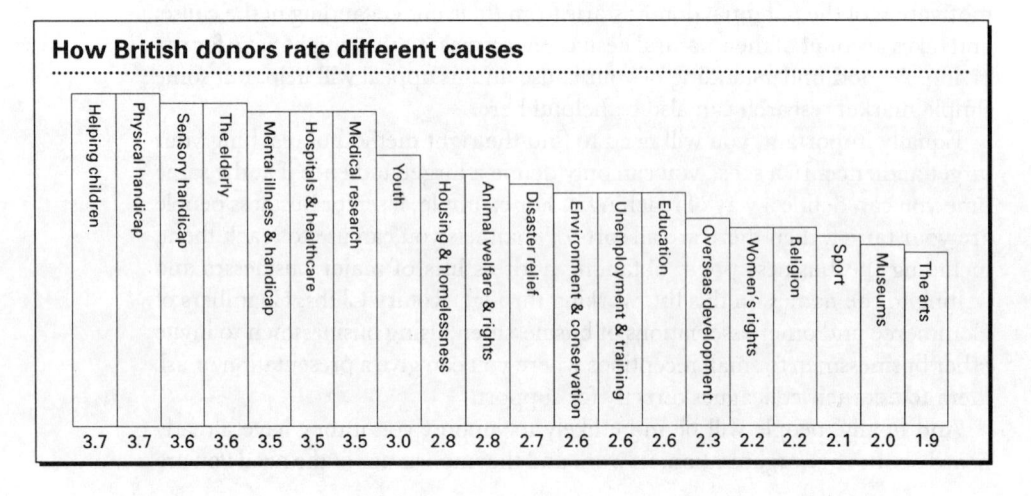

How British donors rate different causes

Cause	Rating
Helping children	3.7
Physical handicap	3.7
Sensory handicap	3.6
The elderly	3.6
Mental illness & handicap	3.5
Hospitals & healthcare	3.5
Medical research	3.5
Youth	3.0
Housing & homelessness	2.8
Animal welfare & rights	2.8
Disaster relief	2.7
Environment & conservation	2.6
Unemployment & training	2.6
Education	2.6
Overseas development	2.3
Women's rights	2.2
Religion	2.2
Sport	2.1
Museums	2.0
The arts	1.9

Five good ideas when fundraising from individuals

1. In approaching individuals, always try to identify clearly and precisely **how much money is needed**, and show how their contribution can play an important part in what you plan to do. You should not suggest an unattainable figure, but you should make people feel proud to have done something significant to help you.

2. In making the appeal, try to **express the need in human terms**, giving graphic images of the problem and how your work actually helps individuals. Try to avoid giving abstract statistics describing the global importance of the problem unless you are trying to emphasise the point. It is said that:

One hungry person next door to you is equivalent to...

One hundred hungry people in a nearby town, who are equivalent to...

Ten million hungry people in some far off country.

The nearer you make people feel to the problem and to how it connects with their concerns, the more successful you will be. If they feel that by helping you they are helping to solve a real person's problem, they will be much more likely to give than if asked to support a general cause.

3. Ask for exactly what you want. Prospective donors will not know the size nor the nature of the contribution expected of them. One way of doing this is to suggest a range of levels for a donation, asking them to choose their own level of giving. Sometimes you can show what the different amounts can achieve, linking the amount to outputs (to feed or educate one child for one year) or to outcomes (redeems one child from bonded labour and returns him or her home).

4. Repeat the message that you need their help, and that with their help you can do something. Repetition reinforces the message. It is good communication practice to:

Tell them what you are going to tell them. Then...

Tell them. Then...

Tell them what you have told them.

5. Target your appeal as carefully as you can, and make your message as personal and relevant to the prospective donor as possible. If you are approaching existing supporters, then refer to their generous support and what you have been able to achieve with it. If you are approaching doctors, tell them about your work from a medical perspective. If you are approaching local people, show the local benefits that will be achieved by your work. The more closely targeted the message, the more successful you will be. People will feel that you are speaking to them personally, and they will respond far better when you engage their interest. And you will have already identified those categories of people that are more likely to want to support you.

Getting started

It is far easier to develop donations income from a base of existing supporters than it is to start from scratch. An existing donor is probably ten times more likely to support you than someone who has never given. But many organisations are in the position of having no existing donors. If that is the case for you, then what can you do? Here are some possibilities:

1. **Produce a simple leaflet** that explains your work and shows that you are looking for money. This should have a 'reply coupon' with space for anyone interested to fill in their name and address so that you can 'capture' them on

your database. To find out their interest, you could ask them to tick a number of boxes (these could show their interest in giving money, becoming a member, volunteering their time). This need not be anything more than a letter-sized sheet of paper (A4) printed in two colours and folded to make a four-page leaflet. It should include photographs of the organisation at work.

2. Get **press coverage**, perhaps a feature written about your organisation in a newspaper or a magazine, and make sure that it includes a reply address for anyone who is interested to write to.

3. Think about **exhibiting** at a fair. At the Zimbabwe International Book Fair, various library development projects, women's writing workshops and other projects take stands. This is an opportunity to create interest and win support. But you do need to have an interesting display, leaflets on your work available for people to take away, and the stand staffed by outgoing people who are prepared to enter actively into discussion with visitors and capture their interest.

4. Find an appropriate **mailing** list which you could send a simple appeal to – for example, your leaflet and a short covering letter could be sent to doctors and health workers.

5. Think about **house-to-house collecting**. Remember that most people say that they don't give because they haven't been asked. House-to-house solicitation is an excellent way of asking. Try to have some form of **membership scheme** so that you can enrol those who are interested. A personal approach will always work better than a written appeal, but obviously takes more time and effort. You need to strike a balance between ease and effectiveness.

6. And once you have recruited a donor, **try to keep them** for life. Getting the most from your donors and supporters is covered in more detail in *Section 7.4*. And also beyond the end of their life. Getting legacies is covered in *Section 6.7*.

4.2 Government grants

Government funding includes:

- Being funded **nationally** by central government
- Being funded **regionally or locally** by regional or local government

For some organisations government funding is the mainstay of their work. For others it is marginal or just one of several sources.

The scale of the funds available from government sources is potentially extremely large, and is likely to increase steadily as government moves away from providing services directly to the purchase of services from another body (often under some form of contract). This process of 'privatisation' of service provision, pioneered in Britain under Mrs Thatcher, is now an accepted mechanism in many countries for the delivery of a wide range of services, including social welfare programmes, environmental conservation and community development.

Voluntary organisations as part of civil society

The availability of funding from government for voluntary organisations depends in part on the relationship between the two sides:

- Government may see voluntary organisations as a **threat**, since some exist to expose need and failings in society and to campaign for change. As such, their objectives may run counter to government.
- Government may see voluntary organisations as a **mechanism for delivering services efficiently** and with the added benefit of drawing in outside money. As such the voluntary sector may become a valued partner, with government seeking to create an environment where voluntary organisations are able to thrive.
- Voluntary organisations may be seen as being **part of a 'civil society'**, whether or not they criticise or show up the failings of government. In India the strengthening of local democracy through the 'panchayati raj' reforms which encourage organisation at the village and community level and the establishment of a government-voluntary sector forum at national level are both manifestations of the civil society dimension.

Often the relationship between the two sides is complex, perhaps containing elements of all three approaches.

National government

National government will relate largely to national organisations in a number of different ways:

- It may want to offer funding to support **national organisations** dealing with issues of concern – for example population, environment, rural development, watershed management. In this way it will benefit from the energy and ideas that voluntary organisations will bring to discussions on policy.
- It may wish to bring voluntary organisations into **policy formation** – to draw on their expertise and their experience of mobilising people and creating change.
- It may seek to deliver **national development programmes** using the voluntary organisation to undertake the delivery – as a matter of expediency (because the structure is there) or of efficiency (they are more cost effective).

Local government

Local authorities will be responsible for the delivery of a wide range of local services, whether at state, regional or city level. The functions for which local and regional government is responsible will vary from country to country, but are likely to include health, education, social services, recreation and leisure services, transport and housing.

It is in the areas of their own particular responsibilities that they are most likely to make grants for many of the same reasons that national government supports voluntary organisations. Giving support may also provide good publicity for government and a feeling 'that something is being done' about an issue of public concern.

Support might be given in a number of ways, including:

- **A grant**. The local authority may have an established programme of offering grants to voluntary organisations.
- **A fee for a service** provided under a contract. Here the money is related to the work done, which is work that the local authority is responsible for, where

it has decided that it is more cost-effective to pay a voluntary organisation to undertake the work programme.
- The giving of services or **support in kind**. Local authorities can assist in many ways, for example through the provision of premises or property.
- Some form of **partnership** with the voluntary service being run alongside a statutory service adding to it or complementing it – for example, a cultural education programme for tribal minorities provided alongside the mainstream curriculum education in schools.

The five stages of a successful application

> **Government grants: 5 steps to success**
>
> **1.** Do your research to find out current interests and priorities and to refine your project idea
> **2.** Find out application procedures and deadlines
> **3.** Write and submit a good proposal
> **4.** Lobbying and publicity to try to influence the decision
> **5.** Success – and if you succeed, say thank you and keep in touch

The process of getting a government grant is often slow and extremely tortuous. It can often take years (or longer) to succeed. The outcome can depend on a whole range of factors, some of which will be outside your control such as the time of year, the political climate and the state of the economy. To get a grant, you will probably need to go through the following stages.

1. Research
- Research the **structure and responsibilities** of government. You need to know who is responsible for what, and how decisions are made before deciding your approach.
- Find out about **current policies and priorities**, and how your work can advance their agenda. This includes official policy, published reports, and statements made by government and politicians on particular issues.
- Find out what's currently on offer and what sort of **funding** has been made to voluntary organisations in previous years. Identify and match possible funding programmes with various aspects of your organisation's work. In some countries, directories of government funding are produced. You can also talk to 'umbrella organisations' operating in your sector.
- Find out what, if any, **links** you have had previously with any statutory authorities, and whether any of your trustees or members have good personal contacts with any likely funding sources. Approach possible funders to discuss their requirements and how you might be able to meet their objectives cost-effectively.

2. Application procedures and deadlines
- Find out about the **application procedure**: when you need to apply by (there may be an annual cycle for the submission of applications, and if you miss the deadline you will have to wait until the next year), and how to apply (whether there is an application form, what information you will need to supply, how the work will be evaluated, and what referees you will need).
- Find out **who is responsible** for making the decision, and get to know as much as you can about how they function.

3. Submit your proposal
- Write a **confident and well argued** proposal in the format that is required.
- Be as **factual** as you can.
- Show that you will be effective and efficient in the use of their money – they are publicly accountable to see that it is well spent.

Advice on writing an effective fundraising proposal is given in *Section 8.1*.

4. Lobbying and publicity
- Back up your application with **lobbying**. Government and politicians respond to pressure. Make sure that everyone important knows about your application and the benefits that it will bring. Get experts and important people on your side. Try to reach everyone who will play a part in coming to a decision on your application.
- Get **media coverage** for your organisation, its work and the ideas behind your proposal.

5. Say thank you
- If you succeed in getting support, then say **thank you** enthusiastically and frequently.
- Give them as much **good publicity** as you can for the support that they have given you.
- **Report back** regularly, and be accountable for the money you are spending. Sometimes this will be specified as a condition of grant.
- If you fail, then **don't give up**. Think about how you might approach them next time, and what you could do to improve your chances of success.

Four good ideas for statutory funding

1. Don't be shy about **making friends** and chatting up the people who will be making the decision on your application. But make sure you chat up the right people. Who you know (and what they know about you) can be extremely important.

2. Consider whether it is a useful ploy to ask for **funding on a matched basis** – that they will support you if another funder contributes a proportion of the total funding requirement. The matched sum could even come from your own organisation out of its existing resources or against the volume of the volunteer time put in. Matched funding can be an attractive proposition to funding bodies.

3. Make your applications **relevant to funders**. Link them to themes of current interest and concern to the funder, and show them how your work will help solve their problem. Get hold of their priorities and show how your work fits in with these. Show how cost effective you are in doing the work – you may be able to show that they can achieve much more by working with you than by going it alone. They are particularly interested in performance figures – how much work you will do for what amount of money. But remember that cost-effectiveness is not the only criterion. The quality of your work is also important.

4. Publicity is important. Government departments and agencies are sensitive to political pressures. So if you can mobilise public and media support it can help your cause. But beware of appearing to put extreme pressure on funding bodies through your media coverage, as they sometimes they will react against it rather than respond to it.

4.3 International grant aid and development funding

International grant aid falls into several categories:
- Support from **international development agencies**.
- Support from **overseas government aid programmes**.
- Support from **overseas NGOs** which raise money from the public for development and often act as delivery agents for international aid programmes.

Many Southern countries receive considerable amounts of overseas funding, which can be the largest single source of funding for development projects. In order to gain access to this source of money, you need to:

- Understand the **issues**.
- See whether there are any **legal requirements** necessary to receive foreign funds (e.g. registration as a charity, or permission to receive foreign funding), and ensure that you meet such conditions.
- **Research** what is available and for what purposes, and whether it is available directly to NGOs on application or whether it is channelled through government or some other agency. You will also want to find out about the application procedures, whether counterpart funding is required, and any other strings that may be attached.
- Develop **contact** with the grants officer or field officer who will be assessing your application. If you are intending to apply for a major sum, then allow a lot of time to build the relationship and to enable them to visit you to see your work.
- **Apply** in the required way.

Issues in international funding

The primary focus of this book is the generation of national resources from governmental bodies, charitable foundations, the corporate sector and the general public (all discussed in the following sections). However, whilst pursuing and developing national resources, it is important to understand how international support might assist or could undermine your attempts to raise support nationally. If the key issues are understood, then international assistance could make a real input into your overall funding strategy. There are also some fundamental questions to ask yourself before you start:

Does the funding come with a political agenda?

'Political' aid in this context refers to aid given by governments to other countries very often under the banner of 'helping the world's poorest'. Allocation is often decided by a geopolitical agenda. The two countries which for a long time now have received the largest percentage of the US government's international aid are Israel and Egypt – not because they are the poorest countries in the world, for very clearly they are not, but because of the strategic interests of the USA in the region. On the other hand, the Scandinavian countries of Norway, Sweden, Finland and Denmark are generally considered with regard to aid allocations to be the least political. Whether or not there are a strong geopolitical priorities, humanitarian concerns sometimes impinge on the consciousness of governments, particularly where there is public pressure through media reports and from pressure groups. An example of this is the large amount of money channelled into the Horn of Africa during the famine years of the mid-1980s and to Rwanda in 1993-94 as a result of the sufferings of millions in the conflict.

There is another factor, which is difficult to 'prove' but appears to be the case, that governments and NGOs in 'receiving' countries do not invite assistance from the economically stronger countries, but are on the receiving end of 'offers of assistance'. And with the offers come 'conditions' – trade linked to aid, pressure to vote in a certain way in a United Nations debate, to 'open up' the economy, to receive an expert, to work in a particular way.

In comparison to governmental aid, which may be clearly 'political', support given by the international non-governmental donor agency system is perceived to be, and is, much less political, and is based more on 'humanitarian' concerns. But the situation is not quite that simple, as agencies have other influences that affect their decision-taking. They naturally reflect the attitudes and ideologies of their founders, their current leaders and their supporting public – and strong links to countries with their 'colonial past' are common. Support to predominantly Christian groups in particular countries (whether Catholic, Protestant or Evangelical) is another example of the influence of 'mandates'. And often with large-scale disaster and emergency aid, which a number of international NGOs specialise in, their own funds (raised from the public), will be supplemented by government funds, as the agencies may represent the most effective way for a government to deliver its support.

> **Some questions to ask when considering international funding**
>
> - What **criteria** seem to be used in deciding which countries and regions get support?
> - What **forums** are there in your own country for discussing development priorities?
> - What links are there between development and anti-poverty work in the North and the work being supported in the South? And are these links all one way?
> - What is the **gender and racial balance** of the donor agency's board and staff?
> - If the donor agency has representatives and **staff in your country**, where do they come from? And is there a decision-making Board in your country to decide priorities and grants? And if there isn't, why not?
>
> Questions like this are not often asked, but they should be. Besides these questions, ask for a copy of the agency's latest annual report and funding criteria. Do you fit? Do you want to fit? Too many people just see that money is available and apply for it. Such questions and the dialogue that might ensue could become an important step towards what is grandly called a 'partnership'.
>
> Some of these issues are discussed in: *New Internationalist*, a magazine dealing with global aid issues on a regular basis and in a readable way. This is available from 55 Rectory Road, Oxford, UK.
>
> By Murray Culshaw, former Director of Oxfam India.

Remember too that almost all the international NGOs set policies, establish procedures and make decisions in their home country, or on the advice of the representatives they have placed in 'receiving' countries. There is usually little or no widespread or public discussion in the countries they have decided to assist on what the priorities and approaches for spending the money should be.

International aid and development funding is 'complex'. It is important that you understand how it works – and what conditions are attached – before proceeding. This means asking questions – and getting answers that satisfy you.

Do you want to be supported by overseas funding?

You may feel that your country should try to support its own development rather than rely on outsiders, and find ways of mobilising local energies and resources.

The issues of dependency and sustainability

These issues should be considered and discussed carefully. Here are some possible responses:

- Build into your development plan a strong element of **public communications and fundraising**. This will not only raise money, but it will also generate public support for what you are trying to do.
- Ask the donor agency to **invest in your fundraising strategy** over a number of years, either to help you become less dependent by diversifying your sources of income, or as part of an agreed phase out strategy.
- Get the donor agency to support **'capital' developments** as well as paying for the running costs. This way, there will be something left when the money runs out.
- Suggest the idea of **matching funding** for your local fundraising efforts.

On the other hand, international aid money is there, and it can become an important component of the funding of your work.

The receipt of large sums of overseas funding can limit your local fundraising work (simply because overseas funding may be simpler to obtain, you may not put enough energy into developing local fundraising, and this may create a long-term dependency). The relatively easy availability of large amounts of money from overseas can mean that you grow too large and create an unsustainable organisation. International donors are not based in your country, and their interests may change rather more quickly than you might imagine. The funds that are readily available now might not continue to be available into the future. What will you do then?

Another problem is that the donor agency funding relationship is almost private. You get the money and the work is done – and hopefully some people benefit. If you are forced to fundraise in your own country, then you have to go out to the public, raise public awareness of the problems and the need for change, explain the issues and why things remain as they are, before you can get support. This public education and mobilisation of public support is important if you are to build real pressure for change in your own country.

Multilateral aid

Multilateral aid mainly refers to aid channelled through the large UN agencies (*see page 63*). It is called multilateral because many governments contribute to the costs of the programmes of these agencies. Each agency may also be seeking bilateral funding from particular countries for particular projects they are interested in promoting.

Usually multilateral aid is channelled to government programmes in your own country. But increasingly these international agencies are looking to cooperate with NGOs. Thus an NGO which works alongside a government programme and can obtain strong government endorsement for its work may be able to get funding from one of these agencies – either directly or channelled through the government.

Approaching an international agency is not easy and can be time consuming. If you are interested in exploring the possibility, make enquiries through a visit or a short letter to the specialist agency working in your field of interest (eg. WHO for health matters, FAO for agricultural matters, UNESCO for literacy, etc. – *see page 63, for list of UN agencies and their fields of work*). The agency may well have an office in your country. Obtain the address from the Telephone Directory for your capital city. If the agency has no office, then approach the UNDP, which may serve as the focal point for all UN agencies working in your country.

Each agency has its own particular relationship with the NGO community. For example, UNHCR on the whole has a very positive relationship because of the need for active cooperation in refugee situations; whereas at the opposite end of the spectrum, the World Bank has a more complex relationship because many NGOs are critical of the Bank's economic and development policies, and are often fighting the consequences of Structural Adjustment Policies. So before you start, do some homework. Find out about programmes in your own country, visit some of the projects that have been supported, meet NGO people who know something of the work being done. Once you know the background, you can decide whether it is worth proceeding.

Some United Nations agencies

Food and Agriculture Organisation (FAO), promotes farming, forestry, fisheries, water and land management and rural development. FAO, Via della Teme di Caracalla, 1-00100 Rome, Italy.

International Labour Organisation (ILO), supports projects that promote income generation for the rural poor, vocational training and manpower development. ILO, Route des Marillons 4, CH-1211 Geneva 22, Switzerland.

United Nations Children's Fund (UNICEF), supports formal and non-formal education programmes, and maternal and child health programmes. UNICEF, 866 United Nations Plaza, New York NY 10017, USA.

United Nations Development Programme (UNDP), supports rural development and infrastructure projects. UNDP, 1 United Nations Plaza, New York NY 10017, USA.

United Nations Educational and Scientific Cooperation Organisation (UNESCO), promotes education, science and culture, and supports literacy, libraries, educational and cultural development. UNESCO, 7 Place de Fontenoy, F-75700 Paris, France.

United Nations Fund for Population Activities (UNFPA), supports family planning, maternal and child health, and population policy. UNFPA, 220 East 42nd Street, New York, NY 10017-5880, USA.

United Nations High Commissioner for Refugees (UNHCR), is responsible for welfare and aid to refugees. UNHCR, Palais des Nations, CH-1211 Geneva 10, Switzerland.

World Bank, the major institution channelling loans for development. The small grants programme supports policy analysis, dissemination, publications and conferences. World Bank, 1818, H Street NW, Washington DC 20433, USA.

World Food Programme runs food for work projects and provides food to vulnerable groups. World Food Programme, Via Cristoforo Colombo 426, 00145 Rome, Italy.

World Health Organisation (WHO), promotes health development and prevention work. WHO, Avenue Appia, CH-1211 Geneva, Switzerland.

These are some of the main agencies of the United Nations making support available for development work. They work largely through national governments, but some operate grants funds which support NGO work.

Overseas government aid programmes

Most Northern governments make aid available to the developing world. The suggested norm is 0.5% of gross national product. Most countries fall well below this norm, although the most generous country per capita is Norway. The most significant aid giver is USAID, the aid agency of the United States government – although recent political changes in the US and the ending of the Cold War are bringing into question the purpose, direction, objectives and scale of US aid. Government aid is:

- Often **government to government**, where all aid is routed through the national government. An NGO wanting to receive funding will have to get approval from its national government.
- Sometimes **tied to trade**, particularly in the case of major infrastructure projects.

The British Overseas Aid Programme

The British government has seven priority objectives for its global aid programmes:
- To promote economic reform.
- To enhance productive capacity.
- To promote good government.
- To undertake direct poverty reduction activities and programmes.
- To promote human development, including better education and health, and children by choice.
- To promote the status of women.
- To help countries tackle environmental problems.

A recent trend is to acknowledge that problems can only be solved with the participation of the people involved. This means that mechanisms for developing programmes in partnership with local people need to be designed; and this in turn means that government agencies need to work closely with NGOs and People's Organisations, which means developing partnerships, supporting empowerment and economic development programmes, etc.

A second trend is to make support available directly to NGOs. This can be done in one of four ways:

- As part of the government's aid programme. For example, in India much more direct support is planned by the ODA, which is moving the administration of its Indian aid programme from London to New Delhi.
- Through major foreign NGOs acting on an agency basis. For example, the UK government might work through Oxfam or Save the Children to channel disaster relief to Rwanda or Somalia.
- Through foreign NGOs, co-funding their projects, usually by putting up half the funds.
- Through small grants schemes run through the embassy. For example the British High Commission in New Delhi and the Deputy High Commission in Bombay both make small grants to voluntary projects. This helps keep staff 'in touch' with what's happening in society, as well as providing opportunities for good publicity and photocalls for the High Commissioner.

European Union Funding

Fifteen Western European countries are now members of the European Union, which has a co-financing programme for supporting initiatives in the developing world.

A primary aim of the programme is to promote local self-development, rather than support welfare or relief oriented programmes. So the beneficiaries (who should include women) should be involved in all stages of the project's planning, implementation, management and completion. The projects must be sound economically, financially, technically, sociologically and culturally, and priority is given to projects which are able to continue once the aid has ceased. There should be clearly defined objectives attainable within a timetable of up to five years. Projects should be development rather than welfare or relief oriented.

Project proposals must be submitted by an NGO in a European Union country, which is a partner in the programme and has to find the balance of the funding (normally 50%). The European Union's maximum contribution under the scheme is in the region of £100,000 a year depending on the length of the project. There is a minimum of around £10,000. Beneficiary projects cannot apply directly, but have to work through a recognised and respected European charity. Most of the larger European donor agencies now employ specialist staff to deal with the EU. If you are interested in this source, first contact the country office of the agency you propose to work through. They will help you prepare a suitable proposal and take you through the procedures. The process takes a lot of time, and if you are successful, the reporting requirements are demanding.

If you are in Brussels and you think that your work is particularly interesting or innovative, then it will be worth your while trying to arrange an appointment to meet Commission staff, as this point of contact can be useful later on in getting support for your project. The 'General Conditions for the Co-financing of Projects Undertaken in Developing Countries by Non-Governmental Organisations' are set out in a booklet of this title, which can be obtained from Department VIII/B/2 (NGOs), Directorate-General for Development, Commission of the European Communities, 200 Rue de la Loi, B-1049 Brussels, Belgium (+32-2-299 9861).

Besides the co-financing programme and funds available for emergency aid and disaster relief, the EU has a few specialist budget lines – for such things as refugees, financial assistance to the West Bank and Gaza territories, aid to NGOs in Chile, South Africa, Vietnam and Cambodia, for ecology and rainforest projects, and for AIDS control. The Commission publishes a 'Digest of Community Resources available for Financing NGO Activities in the Fields of Development Cooperation and Humanitarian Aid', which gives a comprehensive listing of all sources of funds available from the European Commission for these purposes. A copy of this digest can be obtained from the address given above.

The European Commission maintains offices in the capital cities of most Southern countries. Other useful points of contact are:
- The Secretariat of the Liaison Committee of Development NGOs to the European Communities, 10 Square Ambiorix, B 1040-Brussels, Belgium (+32-3-736 4087).
- Euro-Citizen-Action-Service (ECAS), 1 Rue Defacqz, 1050-Brussels, Belgium (+332-3-534 5166). ECAS documents budget lines, publishes a directory of European commission funding sources, and can provide advice to NGOs.

The member countries of the European Union are: Austria, Belgium, Denmark, Finland, France, Germany, Greece, Ireland, Italy, Luxembourg, Netherlands, Portugal, Spain, Sweden, United Kingdom.

Overseas NGOs and donor agencies

There are enormous numbers of foreign donor agencies, which might be divided into the following categories:

- **Volunteer sending agencies** such as Medecins Sans Frontieres (France), Voluntary Service Overseas (UK) or the Peace Corps (USA). When these programmes started the aim was to send usually younger people overseas to 'give service'. Today, many of these agencies now send people with those specialist skills that are requested by local NGOs, who are often required to contribute something towards the cost of the assignment. An interesting scheme from the UK is BESO, which provides retired executives looking for a new challenge. There are also a number of agencies which send young people on short-term assignments, where the benefit is likely to be more for the young person than for the receiving organisation. Typically, these are 'gap year schemes' for young people after they have left school and before university or a job.

- **National and global charities** which raise money from the public to support development projects in 'the third world'. In Europe, these include Oxfam, Save the Children, Christian Aid, ActionAid, Brot fur die Welt Stommestiftelsen, Radda Barnen, Aide et Action, etc. Some of these are generalist agencies, some have a particular perspective (children or the elderly), some are connected either closely or loosely with a religious denomination. They will usually have a country office or even a regional infrastructure in the countries where they provide support, whose function it is to identify 'project partners', assess project applications, account to head office for the money that is donated, offer technical and infrastructural support to their project partners alongside the financial support that is being provided, participate in policy analysis and development. The support given to project partners is often long-term. Sometimes there is child sponsorship, community sponsorship or project sponsorship, where the individual donor providing funds to the donor agency ties their support to a particular project, a particular community or even a particular family or child, and where the donor expects to be kept in touch with progress.

- **Specialist charities** which are dealing with such things as intermediate technology, leprosy relief, blindness, deafness, family planning, water management.

- **Smaller specialist charities** usually set up through the vision and enthusiasm of one individual to pursue a particular idea or address a particular need. Organisations such as Farm Africa, Send a Cow, Tools for Self Reliance, Book Aid International, Arid Lands Initiative, Green Deserts, Action on Disability and Development show the diversity of the sorts of initiatives that are being developed. Typically, these organisations will have no fundraising base of their own, but will be raising money from foundations and international aid sources for their work. Their work will usually be confined to one or two projects, simply because of their small size. But these will be used as 'demonstration projects' to demonstrate new approaches and possibilities.

- **Support groups for local projects**. These are often set up by someone visiting your project or a volunteer who has worked with you on their return home. They set up a fundraising initiative to support your work by raising

money and channelling it to you. This may start as a fundraising committee, but can develop into a charitable institution. For example, Mother Theresa in Calcutta has many local support groups raising money for her work across the world. And the Karuna Trust in the UK supports an orphanage in Pune. One strategy for raising money is to get enthusiasts to set up support groups for you.
- **Denominational initiatives**. Many religious denominations channel support to the developing world through their affiliate churches and religious institutions across the world. The money can come from the religious body itself and the foundations it controls, or it can come from public subscription. Sometimes this aid is purely for welfare, education and development. Sometimes there is an evangelistic agenda or religious objective behind the provision of the aid.

A good source of information is the *'Directory of Non-Governmental Environment and Development Organisation in OECD Member Countries'*. The **OECD** is the organisation for the world's richest countries. This directory, published in 1992, covers 650 agencies which support environment and development programmes around the world. It is available free from OECD, 2 Rue Andre Pascal, 75755 Paris Cedex 16, France. *See also the Third World Directory in Useful Publications.*

How new donor agencies start

There appear to be several stages in the evolution of a development agency. As a wild generalisation this would start in the Gambia (or next year's fashionable tourist destination), where an individual or group would go on holiday. There they would see the high levels of unemployment and poor living standards from their hotel balcony, and talk to Gambians about the problems and challenges they face. This would lead in turn to a realisation that the local school was not able to teach for lack of basics like pencils.

On their return, our holiday makers would rally support in their own community to send a package of pencils and school books. This would lead to more requests. Once a second package had been sent off, and a third, our holiday makers begin to realise that it needs more than just pencils, and the next step might be skills training to address unemployment in The Gambia. It is only a matter of time (and sustaining their enthusiasm) before the holiday makers are transformed into a development agency.

By Will Day, Africa Grants Director of Charity Projects until 1994, adapted from The Third World Directory, published by the Directory of Social Change

How donor agencies raise their money

Many donor agencies recruit regular supporters who make a commitment to give a certain sum each month. Donor agencies are much more likely to find supporters if they can link the supporter's contribution with a particular aspect of their work. There are two main ways of doing this. One is through 'project sponsorship', where the support is linked to a particular project, and progress on this project is then reported back to the supporter. The other is through 'child sponsorship', where the supporter is linked a particular child, and can chart his or her progress over the years through progress reports received from the donor agency and correspondence with the sponsored child. This form of support has its critics, but is extremely powerful in mobilising support – as people feel that their money will really make a difference to someone. PLAN International is one of the major users of child sponsorship. with over 830,000 sponsors around the world, helping more than 8 million people in over 30 countries. This is how PLAN International recruits support:

How a nurse from Guildford gave a boy in Kenya the chance to go to school...

When Helen Taylor decided to sponsor Ben, an 8-year old boy from Kenya, she didn't realise how much difference her help could make. Now with the help of PLAN International sponsors, Ben's village has a school where he's learning to read and write. And a mobile clinic where every child can be immunised against disease. PLAN International have also helped the community to improve their own farming methods, so that the land is more productive and no one need go hungry. For Helen, sponsoring Ben has been one of the best and most satisfying things she has ever done. She knows from the regular reports she receives from his village, how much difference her help has made.

Children like these need your sponsorship today...

Diabe Cisse, age 11, Senegal. The village where Diabe lives lacks even the most basic health care. Neither Diabe nor her brother and two sisters can read or write. The Cisse family live in a mud compound which they share with relatives. It consists of 20 huts, along with a cookhouse, granary and animal shed. The Cisses rely entirely on their own resources. The soil is poor, if the rains fail the crops fail too.

How PLAN International appeals to UK donors, asking them to sponsor a child.

"We know that we cannot really help the world's poor by giving them handouts, or imposing preconceived 'Western solutions' on them. Our approach is to help people solve their problems in their own way."

Dealing with a donor agency – twelve steps to success

The following are twelve recommended steps in identifying, approaching and attracting funding from donor agencies. They have been developed in discussion with Murray Culshaw, former head of Oxfam (India), and now a fundraising consultant working closely with the South Asia Fund Raising Group.

1. Research

To find out about donor agencies that might be interested in receiving an application from you, you could:

- Consult a **funding directory** if one has been produced in your country (for example in India, the Voluntary Health Association of India has produced and published a directory of funding agencies supporting health development programmes).

- Identify a **similar organisation** to your own, and then find out who they are receiving funding from. These might lead you to one or two sources you had not previously considered.
- Ask your **existing funders**. There may be an informal network of donor agencies, and they might know which other funders might be potentially interested in supporting you, and even 'put in a good word for you'.
- If you belong to a religious network, **ask around the network**. If you are interested in receiving money from a particular country, ask their Embassy for any contacts that they have.

From all of this research, you will want to get the name of the donor agency, its address and telephone number, the name of the person to write to with job title, and a brief description (if you can get it) of their funding policy.

2. Finding out more

At this stage you will want to find out as much as you can about them to see whether it is worth your while approaching them. Write a short letter of no more than a page. It is better to write, as donor agencies are being plagued with people phoning or faxing. This not only creates annoyance, but they have no capacity to deal with these enquiries. On the other hand, a letter gets put into the system and will be dealt with in due course. If you don't get a reply within a month, then try phoning.

In your letter ask for a copy of any statement of policy that they have for supporting development work, and for a copy of their latest annual report.

3. Selecting a number of donor agencies to approach

At this stage you will want to draw up a short list of donor agencies which you plan to approach for funding in a systematic and professional way. This shortlist should take into account the donor agency's:

- **Origins, motivation and bias** (political and religious). You will want to know if the organisation has religious affiliations, for example, and any implications for you if you accept money from them. If you are a democracy organisation, then you will want to know the motivation and political viewpoint of the funder before accepting support.
- **Size**. You will need to know the level of their grant-making, and whether they have the capacity to support your application.
- **Interests**. You will want to know their grant policies and focus areas, the types of organisation they support, the types of grant they give and the sorts of project they like to help.

4. The first approach

At this stage, it is best to send a letter, even though you might have had no previous contact with them. The last thing that any donor wants is someone turning up at the door asking for money. And if you were to ring in, they would only tell you 'to put it in writing'. A letter allows the donor agency to respond within its administrative constraints. Donor agencies are always looking for good projects to support, so they will want to hear from you.

Your short introductory letter should not be more than two pages (one page is even better!). Do not send a long and detailed proposal at this stage. You want to introduce yourself and see whether there is any interest in your work, and

therefore whether there is any point in your investing a considerable amount of time and effort into developing a full project proposal for them to consider. In your short letter, you will:
- **Introduce the organisation**.
- **Describe the project.**
- **Highlight any special features** of your work or your plans, and anything you are planning of an innovative nature.
- **Indicate the approximate scale** of your financial need, the contribution that you will be making to the project (including funds at your disposal and that you can mobilise, any technical skills and expertise, assets and equipment that you bring, partnerships with others, etc.) and any other funding sources that you plan to approach.
- **Endorsements** for your work or for the project. If you are known to an acknowledged expert in the field, then it is worth mentioning names. Most donor agency staff are generalists, so a commendation from a specialist in your field will carry weight.
- **Any previous funding**. Oxfam found that when their project partners approached other donors, they stood a better chance of getting support if they mentioned that they had received funding from Oxfam. This provided a point of reference for checking on the quality of the work, and also some assurance that the work was worth supporting. Many donor agencies belong to an informal network of donors, where they can share thoughts and 'find out the gossip' on organisations they have not had contact with before.

5. Wait for their reply

The donor agency should reply within a month or two, indicating whether your project falls within their mandate and current focus, and whether they have the resources to support you. The funds available to most donor agencies are limited and even declining. The donor agency will indicate whether it is worth your while submitting a proper application, and any deadline for receipt of this. They will also tell you whether they require you to complete an application to a prescribed format, or whether you can submit a proposal in your own preferred style. Sometimes they will arrange to visit you or send a representative to check you out first. If you have not heard within six weeks, then send a reminder or possibly ring up.

6. Prepare a project proposal

This will set out your proposal in detail, and will be the basis on which your project will be assessed. It should be prepared with great care – far too many shoddy applications for often quite large sums of money are received by donor agencies.

Typically your proposal should run to between six and twelve pages plus attachments. Details of how to write an effective application are given in *Section 8.1*. The following are some important things to consider:
- **A needs assessment**. Nobody wants to support something that is not needed! They may require evidence of participatory research, participatory appraisal, baseline studies, and other 'fashionable' techniques for needs assessment.

- An indication that the **community and project staff** have been involved in shaping the proposal, and that it is not just a good idea submitted by the Director.
- An indication that support has been obtained from experts during the planning stage, where **specialist expertise** is important.
- Clearly defined objectives which appear to be **achievable**.
- A commitment to **monitoring** and measurement of results and outcomes.
- A degree of **creative thinking** about the problem, or innovation in the way you are attempting to tackle it.
- A solid **evaluation of your past work** and a **knowledge of other programmes** of a similar nature to what you are proposing.
- A long-term **strategic framework** for the project, with thoughts about its longer-term financing – or for a time-limited project, an indication of the period over which the project will run and be completed.
- Some evidence of a **capacity to raise public funds** or to build a constituency of **local community support**.

You will then attach:

- Your latest **annual report** plus an audited statement of accounts.
- A copy of your **constitution** or anything else which confirms your charitable credentials and legal status.
- **References**, where appropriate.

You will type your application neatly (a word processor helps, as this enables you to send similar applications to several donor agencies, each tailored to that donor agency's particular needs). And then send it off, within any indicated deadline for its receipt.

If you are a small organisation or do not have sufficient experience of project preparation, then it could just be worth hiring a consultant to help you.

Remember too that most agencies prefer to make substantial grants rather than scatter their money in lots of small grants. They also want to 'invest' in the project over the long term, and even to put in more money if the work is going really well (they like backing a winner).

7. Project assessment

The donor agency will then want to consider whether they want to proceed with dialogue and assessment of your proposal, or whether they want to reject you at this stage. If you have done your research well, then you should not fail here.

Their assessment procedure will almost always require a project visit from a project officer or from a consultant. Much will depend on the size and staffing of the donor agency, your location and whether they can easily reach you, and whether the proposal calls for specialist knowledge that they do not have.

8. On the visit

The following are some tips for handling the assessment visit:

- **Plan** the visit carefully, but be flexible enough to respond to their needs and interests.
- Show something of your past **successful and unsuccessful work**. What most people do is try and avoid showing the mistakes of the past. But assessors

can sense when something is wrong – they are visiting so many projects that they get an instant 'feel' for your work. Be honest about failures, don't be defensive. If you are prepared to learn from experience and generate new ideas from work which has not succeeded, they will respect you all the more.
- The Director should stand aside to allow other members of **staff and community representatives to take part in the discussion**.
- **Invite Board Members** to be present, and brief them first. This provides evidence of a participating and strong Board.
- Ceremonial displays and welcomes are *a real bore*. **Show them your work**; you are not there to entertain them.
- Everything should be **tidy and ordered** – but then it should always be. If you appear sloppy and disorganised, this will create the wrong impression.

9. Awaiting a decision

The assessment process will normally take between four and six months. How the decision is made and the speed with which it is made depends on the size of the proposal, whether it is central or peripheral to that agency's main interests (the more unusual it is, the longer the decision period will be), and the agency's decision-making procedures. Most agencies have the discretionary authority delegated to their project staff to make grants within certain guidelines.

10. Saying thank you

If your proposal has been supported, then:
- Send a short, courteous **letter of thanks**. No frills and no gimmicks!
- Read and understand the **terms and conditions** of the support. Many donor agencies will send a contract for signature confirming your acceptance of the conditions of grant.
- **Accredit the donor agency** as required by them. For example, PLAN International support some major projects in India, which then have to be described as a *"PLAN-Deepalaya Project"*, for example.

11. Reporting back

You will be required to report back at least annually – some donor agencies require a quarterly report of progress. You will need to:
- Set up a **schedule** for coping with the reporting obligations.
- **Make someone responsible** for seeing that this reporting is done, and done to time. There will also be an expectation that you turn up at partner meetings organised by the donor agency, attend certain seminars and 'free' training events that they organise for your benefit and to enable you to network with others, and entertain donors and visitors that they send your way.
- Ensure that your organisation's **financial reporting** system is able to cope with the financial information that you are obliged to provide. And it is standard practice that your accounts should be professionally and independently audited. You will also need to report any variations on budget and any changes in plan which require the funder's approval. Most donor agencies want to know before significant amounts of money are shifted from one budget head to another. As a general rule, variances within 10% are normally not a problem; above 10% then you need to consult with them first.

There is a danger that the original proposal becomes a rigid framework for the project. Circumstances may have changed; you may be learning from experience as the project proceeds. Nobody minds changes made for good reason. If development was an easy process, then all the world's problems would have been solved by now.

Donors on the whole are becoming more demanding in their reporting requirements. This is a direct consequence of the increasing competition that they are faced with in fundraising and maintaining good relationships with their donors, who are becoming more sceptical about the efficacy of development aid, more aware of the problems of poverty and distress in their own countries, more informed and aware of the wider issues. You need to show evidence of success to assist the donor agency raise more money.

For this reason reporting back can become a major burden on your organisation's resources, and the implications of this should be considered in the context of the budget you submit for the project, so that you are not out of pocket. Try to give facts and figures in your project reports, rather than writing whole pages of generalisations; and try to measure performance against the objectives you originally set for the project in your proposal. For large projects, you may want to build some form of external evaluation into your project plans, both at mid-term and at the conclusion of the project work, and the cost of doing this can be built into your project budget.

12. Maintain good working relations with donor agency staff

Remember that donor agency staff are human beings who are (usually) genuinely interested in you and your work. A project officer will typically be dealing with 10-20 projects, usually in one geographic area rather than on a thematic basis – but this is now changing as development work becomes more technical. The project assessment work involves constant travel, often in difficult conditions and with continuous work pressure. Some may have done a great deal to ensure that your proposal got supported in the first place, and will be as committed as you are to its success. Remember too that distributing money is not an easy job. Difficult choices have to be made, and it is the personal relationships with project staff and tangible evidence of progress and success that make their job worthwhile. So do make sure that you:

- **Keep in regular contact** with donor agency staff.
- **Give evidence of success** and achievements, not just to agency staff, but also for inclusion in the supporter

---

What donor agencies like to see

- **Proper accountability** for the money given, and up-to-date reporting of income and expenditure.
- **Monitoring and evaluation** of progress, as agreed when the grant was made.
- **Evidence of achievement and success.** They are particularly interested in innovative ideas or ways of working that you are developing.
- **Impact on the community** in creating real and lasting change for the better.
- **Evidence of enthusiasm** from the community for what you are doing.
- **Case studies** that demonstrate how you are succeeding.
- **Newspaper and media coverage** of your work.
- **Mobilisation of financial support** from government programmes and from the community to add to the funds they are providing.
- Progress towards operational and financial **sustainability**.
- Your own **continued enthusiasm** for the work you are doing.

newsletters – both in your own country and in the country the money has originated from. Getting to know newsletter editors, sending news releases when there is news to report, providing photographs with captions are all ways of getting news about your project into print.
- **Be honest about failures**, or where the project is not going quite according to plan. If the project is proceeding more slowly than expected or in a different direction, then seek a meeting to discuss progress and what to do next.

If you visit the donor agency's own country:
- **Make a visit to their office**, to meet project staff but also to meet fundraising staff, to tell them about your work and your successes.
- Tell them three months in advance that you are coming, and **offer to speak to supporters** or at fundraising meetings that they might organise for you. If you can spare a week, or whatever time you have available for this, it will be much appreciated. They should be able to cover your out-of-pocket expenses during this time. These meetings are not opportunities to ask for money, but a time to describe your work and to say thank you. If you can, prepare a video which shows the work actually being done.

4.4 Foundations

Foundations are independent grant-making bodies, deriving their income from an endowment or some form of continuing fundraising. They come in all shapes and sizes, including the very large foundations established by successful business people and large companies, to smaller foundations linked to religious institutions or established by a family to pursue the philanthropic interests of members of that family. Each will have its own policies and priorities, and its own mechanisms for considering applications.

Foundations (sometimes also known as 'trusts', as many are established with the legal format of a trust) can be a very important source of support, as they are set up with the express intention of giving their money away for charitable purposes and community development. Much will depend on whether there is an established tradition of foundation giving in your country, and whether your work is the sort of thing that they are interested in supporting.

One role that some foundations adopt is the promotion of innovation and new ideas. Many emerging organisations owe their existence to the support from the outset of clear sighted and progressive foundations who were prepared to shoulder whatever risk there may have been at that stage of the organisation's development.

Background information

Foundations come in all shapes and sizes:
- From **very large** institutions such as the Ford Foundation to **tiny bodies** with just a few hundred pounds or dollars a year to distribute.
- With an **international** remit (such as the Aga Khan Foundation), or a national remit (such as the Rajiv Gandhi Foundation) or just operating **regionally or locally** (such as the Bombay Community Public Trust).
- Supporting a **wide range of activities** (many are set up for general charitable purposes) or **specialising** in providing support for a particular type of work (such as bursaries for tertiary education).

The structure of the larger foundations is highly professional and likely to include a Secretary or Director (the title varies), who is in executive charge of the grants programme, possibly with administrative staff and, for the very large foundations, a team of specialist or regional grants officers. They will report to a Board of Trustees, who are ultimately responsible for policy and for seeing that the foundation operates effectively. The Trustees will usually take or ratify the final decision on where the grants go, basing their decisions on the recommendations of their professional staff. There may also be local advisers or experts in the specialist areas who will be asked to assess the larger grant applications.

Smaller foundations are often run by the family or the individual who set them up. They may be administered by a firm of lawyers or accountants. They are unlikely to employ professional staff to assess grant applications. Many have difficulty in distributing their income – through lack of expertise or energy, or simply because they do not receive enough applications from organisations looking for support. With the smaller foundations, good contacts with their trustees or some form of personal connection is extremely important.

National and local foundations

In every country there will be some local foundations which give support for national or more local projects. These may have been set up by a prominent industrialist in the colonial era (such as the Beit Foundation, which operates in countries of Southern Africa). They may have been set up more recently (such as the National Foundation for India and the India Foundation for the Arts). They may have on-going public fundraising programmes (such as CRY – Child Relief and You, which funds child relief programmes in India).

There may be a tradition for individuals to establish foundations to support public institutions such as eye hospitals or orphanages, or to support some religious project (a temple or mosque, and associated good works). And in recent years with the growth of many economies in the developing world and the emergence of a 'super-wealthy class', many successful individuals and families may have established a foundation either personally or through their company.

Establishing a foundation will usually require registration, and procedures

---

How a foundation works

The donor
The money for a foundation can be provided by:
- A rich individual.
- A legacy that establishes the foundation on the donor's death.
- A company.
- A public collection or appeal.
- Continued fundraising to top up the endowment or increase the annual income available for distribution.

The trustees
This money is then invested, and the income from the investment is distributed in the form of grants to the beneficiaries. The trustees are the group of people who are responsible for:
- Managing the foundation's investments.
- Distributing the foundation's income in the form of grants.

The beneficiaries
The foundation will have a constitution which sets out who can benefit. This is known as the foundation's 'objects'. It may also state the geographical area where the money can be spent. This is known as the foundation's 'beneficial area'. The trustees decide on the policies and priorities of the foundation. However, they are not permitted to support activity that falls outside the objects or takes place outside the beneficial area of the foundation.

The applicants
Most foundations decide on who to support through having written applications submitted to them. There is no point applying to a foundation if your work does not match the foundation's current policy and priorities, or if you fall outside the beneficial area.

will vary from country to country – in most countries foundations will register nationally. But registration does not imply that there is a central bank of publicly available information on foundations. And in most countries there is no published information on foundations – although in some there are attempts being made to compile information for use in fundraising. Where there is no ready source of information, you will find out about foundations:

- Through personal knowledge and contact.
- By finding out how other 'rival' organisations are being funded.
- Through keeping your eyes open – there may be articles in the press for example which refer to the support of foundations or the philanthropy of rich individuals.

International foundations

At the other end of the geographic scale are the international foundations. Most of the larger ones are situated in the US (including the Ford Foundation) and in the UK (including foundations with a remit to give support in the Commonwealth), but there are many in Europe and a few in Japan which give internationally. The main sources of information are:

- The literature produced by the foundations themselves. But only the largest publish **reports or guidelines for applicants**, and these may not always be in a language that you understand; and
- A number of published **grant directories** produced by information and documentation centres (*see box*).

Raising money from an international foundation is difficult, unless they have a specific focus on giving grants in your country, where they will have developed a mechanism for receiving and assessing applications, or where you have a good personal contact. You are a long way away, and they may not even have heard of you – even though you are a reputable and successful organisation in your own country. Their view of the world and their priorities may be completely different from your own (there are a large number of US foundations, for example, promoting 'democracy' defined in different ways according to their political stance). And they will prefer to give in their own country to organisations they know, even if the purpose of the grant is to provide help in your own country. But there are opportunities:

- Undertaking **work which they are particularly interested in**, where you can demonstrate your track record and expertise. For example, Warren Buffett, the highly successful US investor is keen to support innovative projects that address the world's population growth.
- Where there is an **international dimension** to your work. There may be many people interested in supporting the intellectual property rights attached to tribal and traditional medicines in face of the attempted patenting of such remedies by the multinational drug companies. Equally rainforest preservation has attracted support from around the world.
- A **bilateral or multilateral** project, comparing approaches and practice in different countries.
- A **joint venture** between you and an organisation supporting similar issues in the home country of the foundation. They will have heard of your partner organisation, who can then act as a conduit for the money, a source of

technical and other aid, and even a guarantor of the project's success, as they will be ultimately accountable for the grant. This is certainly a sensible strategy if you are serious about getting support from a US foundation, as most grants given by US foundations for international purposes go to US-based organisations.

Five don'ts in dealing with overseas foundations

1. **Don't assume** that because they are rich and philanthropic they will want to support you. They have plenty of other calls upon their resources.
2. **Don't write a begging letter out of the blue**. You either will get no reply at all, or a certain rejection.
3. **Don't ask for money for your existing work**. Try to find a project which has some international aspect or dimension and which they should be genuinely interested in.
4. **Don't leave it to the last moment**. You will need plenty of time to make contact, discuss your ideas with them, even meet, before submitting a full proposal.
5. **Don't assume that they have heard of you and your work**. You will have to build your credibility with them. Getting world renowned experts to endorse your work can help. Good literature clearly explaining the problem and how you work will help. Meet people at international conferences, and follow up on these contacts. If you travel abroad, set aside some time to develop contacts with larger foundations in that country. Just telephone or fax them in advance and ask to visit, or even telephone them on your arrival to try to arrange an appointment.

Many of the large international foundations produce newsletters and annual reports outlining their policies and programmes. This bulletin in produced by the Ford Foundation's New Delhi office.

Fundraising from overseas foundations: some lessons from experience

The following advice is given by Nilda Bullain of the Civil Society Development Programme in Hungary following a US fundraising trip when a group of CSDP staff visited 12 foundations in four cities during a three week period, and succeeded in raising a major part of CSDP's budget:

"We found it vital to have good references and to be well informed about the foundation. During the trip, we prepared carefully what we would say and how we would say it – about our project and about ourselves. Among other exercises, we practised our introductions and the presentation we had prepared. We measured the time this took and helped each other with constructive observations. We also had to be aware of the weak points of our proposal. We brainstormed the possible questions that might arise and allocated who would answer each question. We tried to put ourselves into the foundation officer's shoes and imagine how they would see our proposal from their standpoint and what questions they might want to ask. We also prepared our own list of questions so that we could get all the information we needed about procedures, deadlines for applications, the possibility of further contact, etc. We knew exactly what we wanted to accomplish at each meeting, and were usually successful in sticking to our agenda. We always made sure that there was some subsequent follow up (a telephone call, etc.). For us it was well worth the time and cost of meeting donors personally, and it is part of our fundraising strategy to develop and keep good working relationships with programme officers in foundations."

Information on international foundations

United States

The Foundation Center publishes a wide range of grant directories, including an *'International Funding Directory'*. You can turn up at their offices (or at any of the documentation centres they run) and access information on particular foundations, including grants lists from previous years and current policies and priorities. Note though, that most US foundation funding for international purposes goes to Central and Southern America, and more recently to Eastern Europe and the former Soviet Union. They are not big funders in Africa and Asia (although there are exceptions), and they will have their particular interests and priorities. For example, they are much more likely to want to give support in South Africa than to the other countries of Southern Africa. **CAF America**, an affiliate of the Charities Aid Foundation in the UK, publishes *'The Guide to Funding for International and Foreign Programs'*. This prepares grant-seekers for an informed grant search with up-to-date information on over 600 foundations and corporate giving programmes.

The Foundation Center: 79 Fifth Avenue, New York NY 10003-3076, USA.

CAF America: 90 Park Avenue, Suite 1600, New York NY 10016, USA.

United Kingdom

With its historical links to Commonwealth countries, the UK is potentially an important source for funding in South Asia and Africa. International funding is largely directed towards those countries where there has been some historical connection, although more recently media interest in famines and disasters has drawn attention to the needs of countries such as Ethiopia and Rwanda where there was no colonial

---

Some major UK foundations supporting work in other countries

Aga Khan Foundation (UK): supports innovative, cost-effective and replicable projects in child development and education, family health and nutrition, rural development, skills training and professional exchanges in low income countries of Asia and East Africa.

Charity Projects: supports projects in Africa which empower indigenous peoples through rights and building participatory institutions, small-scale trading initiatives which promote fair trading, education, training, literacy, improved communication and networking within Africa and projects addressing the needs of those suffering the effects of long-term disruption (e.g. from war, AIDS and drought).

Gatsby Charitable Foundation: supports projects mainly in the Cameroon and East Africa which assist farmers, artisans and small business.

Paul Hamlyn Foundation: policy under review; up until now the bulk of the support to the developing world has gone to the Indian Sub-Continent to support dissemination of the 'Jaipur Foot' an artificial limb and other disability aids.

Joseph Rowntree Charitable Trust: promotes corporate responsibility, racial justice and disarmament issues in Southern Africa.

connection. A particularly interesting foundation is Charity Projects which funds in Africa, as its funding is drawn from a highly successful television fundraising spectacular called 'Comic Relief'. Good documentation on international funding by UK foundations is provided by the **Directory of Social Change**, which publishes: *'Peace & International Relations'*, covering UK and overseas foundations with an interest in peace, security and international relations.

The Directory of Social Change: 24 Stephenson Way, London NW1 2DP, UK.

Europe

'US Foundation Support in Europe', published by the Directory of Social Change, details US foundations with significant grant programmes in Europe. The **European Foundation Centre** in Brussels keeps information on European foundations and can provide informal advice. Just as the UK directs much of its overseas support to Commonwealth countries, so projects based in Francophone countries will have equivalent close links to France and French foundations, and projects based in Lusophone countries to Portugal and Portuguese foundations.

European Foundation Centre: 51 Rue de la Concorde, B-1050 Brussels, Belgium.

Commonwealth

There is no published grants guide to sources of Commonwealth grants, but you may be able to get advice from the **Commonwealth Secretariat** based in London.

The Commonwealth Secretariat: Marlborough House, Pall Mall, London SW1Y 5HX, UK

Other countries

Other countries, such as Australia, Canada, Japan and South Africa have 'foundation centres' which act as focal points and publish information on foundations operating in their country. For further information on foundations in Canada see the *'Canadian Directory of Foundations'* from Canadian Centre for Philanthropy, 1329 Bay Street, Toronto M5R 2C4 Canada. For information on South African foundations, see the *'Donor Community in South Africa: a Directory'* available from the Institute For International Education, 809 UN Plaza, New York, NY 10017-3580 USA. And for Japan, contact the

---

Commonwealth foundations supporting travel, exchanges and community service

The Commonwealth Foundation
Marlborough House, Pall Mall, London SW1Y 5HY
Annual grant total £2 million. The Foundation gives bursaries for short-term study, refresher courses, advisory visits and training attachments; and travel grants for attendance at conferences, seminars and workshops. Applications should be made in writing at least three months in advance.

The Commonwealth Relations Trust
28 Bedford Square, London WC1B 3EG
Annual grant total £200,000. Offers programmes of fellowships and travel bursaries. Details of award schemes are available from the Secretary.

The Commonwealth Youth Exchange Council
7 Lion Yard, Tremadoc Road, London SW4 7NQ
Annual grant total £160,000. Promotes reciprocal exchanges to develop contact and better understanding between the young people of the UK and other Commonwealth countries. An application form is available, and applications should be submitted at least 9 months in advance.

The Prince's Trust
18 Park Square East, London NW1 4LH, UK
Annual grant total £5.2 million, most of which is spent in the UK. Grants are made to organisations which enable young people from the Commonwealth to undertake long periods of community service for the benefit of local communities. Applications in writing.

Some major international foundations supporting work in other countries

Ford Foundation, New York, is the most important US foundation making grants overseas and has regional branches and grants programmes in many Southern countries

Rockefeller Foundation, New York, and **The John D and Catherine T MacArthur Foundation**, Chicago, are two important US foundations with substantial international grant programmes

These are very major foundations with wide-ranging grants programmes. Details of what they do can be obtained from one of the international foundation directories. There are also many smaller foundations especially in Europe and North America which make grants for international purposes.

The Aga Khan Foundation

The Aga Khan Foundation is a private, non-denominational development agency promoting creative and effective solutions to selected problems that impede social development in the low income countries of Asia and Africa.

Founded by the Aga Khan, spiritual leader of the Shia Ismaili Muslims, the Foundation encourages initiatives in health, education and rural development. Grantees are selected without regard to race, religion, gender or political persuasion on the basis of their ability to address important issues related to improvement in the quality of life in their communities.

Established in 1967, its HQ is in Geneva, Switzerland. There are branch offices in Bangladesh, India, Kenya, Pakistan, Portugal and Tanzania, and independent foundations in Canada, the United Kingdom and the United States.

Although the Foundation is decentralised, its units pursue common objectives. The majority of grants are to grass roots organisations interested in testing innovative approaches in a variety of settings, which if successful offer the possibility of replicability. The heart of the Foundation's approach is the cross-fertilisation of ideas amongst these grass roots projects, often linked closely with national and global resource organisations operating in the same field that can offer training, research, networking opportunities and the possibility of disseminating any results.

Foundation Library Centre of Japan, Elements Shinjuku Building 3F, 2-1-14 Shinjuku, Shinkujuku-ku, Tokyo, Japan.

Religious foundations and missionary work

In some Southern countries much of the early development of health and education was undertaken by missionaries with support from church bodies and religious foundations, and this influence has often continued after independence.

A distinction needs to be drawn here between:

- **Evangelism**, which is the promotion of religion; and
- **Development work** carried out by a religious body, where the work is to do with social or educational provision rather than religion, and which may be for the benefit of everyone or just for co-religionists.

Some religious foundations are only interested in funding evangelistic work, whilst others support the social development work carried out in the name of their religion. There is usually a close link between the country and the project. For example, German foundations will be closely linked to projects run by the German Lutheran church, and Norwegian foundations to projects established by Norwegians with Norwegian support.

How foundations give

Foundations are constrained by their founding constitution and by a requirement to support charitable work. This does not mean that they have to give to organisations that are constituted and registered as charities, but that the work they support must be of a charitable nature (for example political campaigning will normally be excluded).

Most foundations simply make cash

donations. These can be a one-off grant or a regular grant over a number of years. Even if a one-off grant is obtained, it is possible that the same foundation may be willing to support another aspect of your work in future years.

Most foundations do not want to be committed to supporting a particular project indefinitely. So it is important for the fundraiser to be clear about the long-term goals and funding strategy of the organisation, and to show how the grant proposal fits into this. Where the proposal is for a building or to purchase a piece of equipment, the application should try to show how the facility will be used and how the running costs will be met. Where it is towards running costs, the application should try to show what will happen when the grant runs out.

Beside grants, some foundations may be prepared to make interest-free or low-interest loans. But this will require an ability to repay the loan at some future date, which can only happen if there is some return expected from the project.

Every foundation has a different approach to grant-making. Some prefer giving start up money, whilst others prefer to support the development of more established projects. Some preclude money for capital projects, while others will only provide support for these. Some prefer to support safer, more conservative work, whilst others are radical and pioneering. Some want to make a large number of smaller grants, whilst others prefer to concentrate on a few major projects. The least popular area of support is towards salaries and the overhead costs of the organisation (core funding, which is often what most organisations require); and most foundations prefer to support specific 'projects' and 'initiatives', where they can feel that their support is having some impact.

All this can be ascertained from the foundation itself (either by speaking to the director or by reading its literature – if it publishes anything). It is extremely important that you use all available intelligence to ensure that you send only appropriately targeted appeals to foundations, which match:

- **Their policies and priorities**. There is no point sending an

> **What foundations like to fund**
>
> On the whole, foundations like to fund 'projects' – which are particular aspects of an organisation's work that they can identify with and feel that they are having some impact. Here are three projects supported by the Rajiv Gandhi Foundation, which demonstrate different sorts of project which are likely to be attractive to a foundation – one is a rather interesting way of delivering health care, one is to do with new approaches to the welfare of the disabled, and one is a pilot project with enormous potential if it can be made to work successfully.
>
> **Lifeline Express Camp**: Lifeline Express is a mobile train hospital consisting of three restructured coaches containing an operating theatre, a sterilisation room, a diagnostic centre, wards and a 12-bed post-operative care unit. It is a modern, sophisticated hospital providing diagnostic and surgical treatment for those afflicted with polio, cataract and hearing defects. Camps are run in areas where medical facilities are scarce. So far 56 camps have been sponsored, each lasting 5-6 weeks and benefiting around 3,000 people.
>
> **The National Co-ordination and Liaison Unit for Disabled People**: The Unit promotes employment opportunities for disabled people, by working with potential employers who are interested in being socially responsible. For example, with a watchmaker, a repair business was established employing disabled people in an economically viable way.
>
> **Model Village Libraries**: The project develops a self-sustaining model for a rural village library run on professional lines, but supported by contributions from villagers and village funds. More than 450 such libraries have been set up to date, and the project is being documented to promote its wider dissemination.

application to a foundation which has no interest in that sort of work.
- **Their scale of grant-making**. There is no point approaching a tiny foundation for a large grant. Or a major foundation for a small item of expenditure.
- **Their ethos and approach**. You will have the greatest success with those foundations that share your outlook and values.

Getting started

1. First of all, find out what if any **previous approaches** you have made to foundations previously, and whether any have been successful. And for those that have failed, try to establish reasons for your rejection. Those that have supported you once are more likely to want to support you again – especially if you have done a really good job with their money. Those that have turned you down are also likely prospects for future support. You have already identified them as being potentially interested in your work – but as yet, you have failed to convince them of the value of supporting you. Try to find something really interesting for them to support, and present a better case. Most foundations work on an annual grants cycle, which usually means that you can approach them each year.

2. Then find out whether any of your trustees or members have good **personal connections** with any likely funding sources. Personal contact can be an important ingredient in your success.

3. Do your **research** to identify and match possible funders with various aspects of your organisation and its work. The more you can match what you want to do with what they want to support the better.

4. Remember that foundations are unlikely to give a very large grant to organisations they have never heard of. If you are looking for large sums, it may be more sensible to **apply for something small** now, and then when you have made a success of that, then go back for something more substantial. Another strategy is to work in partnership with a larger well-established and well-known organisation. Their partnership with you will, in effect, vouch for your credibility.

Making contact

Getting in touch with trusts should be a several stage process. It might include the following:

1. General PR to make people aware of your organisation and its work, so that when you approach trusts, they have already heard of you and understand the importance of what you are doing. Some ways of doing this include: sending out copies of your annual report or relevant publications well before you intend to raise money; getting coverage of your work and achievements in the press, and sending photocopies of any articles that are printed to people who you think might be interested; and being asked to participate in radio or TV discussions.

2. A phone call to establish contact. This can determine whether there is a best time in the trust's year to apply, whether a trust is able to support your type of work, and the procedure for applying for a grant. You may also be able to get a clearer picture of the sort of work that the foundation is likely to want to support. An important thing to find out at this stage is whether an application form is required. There is nothing so maddening as having written a 'perfect application' only to then find that they require all applications to be submitted on a standard form.

3. A **written application** setting out your request. Paper is the medium in which most foundations deal, and how your request will initially be judged. Make sure that you attach a copy of your latest accounts, and an annual report (if you have one) or some other description of your organisation and its work. See Section 8.1 for advice on writing a fundraising application.

4. You might then **telephone** to see whether your application has arrived, and to ask whether any further information is required.

5. You might try to arrange to **meet a representative of the foundation**. This could be either at your premises, if there are people or things to see, or at their offices, or on neutral ground. This encounter can seal the fate of your applications, so try hard to get to meet your potential funders face to face.

6. If you have **contact with a particular trustee** or with the Chair of the trustees, then you can try to discuss your proposal with them and enlist their support before the matter comes up for discussion.

How to be more successful in fundraising from foundations

1. Thoroughly **research** your application from the available information and by making contact with the foundation concerned.

2. Present a concise but complete **written proposal** setting out your needs. This should include an introduction to your organisation and a background to your proposed work; what you intend to do and how you intend to set about doing it; how the work will be effective and cost-effective, and what long-term impact it will have; the budget you require, what support you are requesting from the foundation, and how you plan to organise the funding of the project after the grant finishes; and any references or other information which will build the credibility and show the success of your organisation.

3. Ask for an **appropriate amount**. You can find out from your researches typical levels of grant that the foundation makes.

4. Try to get representatives of the foundation, whether they be staff or trustees, to **visit** you. It will considerably enhance your chances if someone has visited the project. But make sure that everything is working well, that the premises look well kept and well used, and that they meet some of your clients and beneficiaries who can speak enthusiastically about your work and the help you have given them.

5. Remember one **picture** is worth a thousand words. Have photographs taken of your project at work, showing people and not just buildings.

6. Very often foundations will back the **ideas and energy of a key individual** in your organisation. If you have such individuals, make sure that their strengths are clearly being promoted in your proposal, include a CV, and try to get that individual to meet the foundation.

7. Invite foundations to consider **matching** their support to that of another foundation, company or individual. For example if you are seeking support to produce a brochure, getting the foundation to pay for the design and paper costs, and getting a printer to donate the printing might be an attractive way for both to give their support. Many donors warm to the idea of their gift effectively being worth double its face value. There is of course a risk that the second donor will not respond and you lose the first donation: but this is quite unusual.

8. If you find you have raised more money than you need as a result of approaches to several foundations, **be truthful** and go back to them with alternative suggestions. Offer to extend the project or improve it rather than have to repay the grant. They will almost always agree.

4.5 Company giving

Why companies give

There is no particular obligation for companies to give their money to charity or to support projects in the local communities where they operate. But they do give. The main reason for their giving is often said to be enlightened self-interest, rather than pure altruism. And the following are some of the reasons for giving:

- **To create goodwill**: to be seen as good citizens in the local communities where they operate and as a caring company by society at large. But also to create goodwill amongst employees, who will get a good impression from the good works that the company supports.
- **To be associated with certain causes**. Mining and extraction companies often like to support environmental projects, pharmaceutical companies health projects, banks economic development projects, and so on. This may be to enhance their image, but it could also be to find out more about matters that interest them from another perspective.
- **Because they are asked** and it is expected of them. They also don't want to be seen to be mean. If a major bank supports an important cultural project, then other large banks might also want to give their support, and to be seen to be generous in how much they give.
- **Because the Chairman or other senior managers are interested** in that cause (and perhaps support it personally). There is also the Chairman's wife who can play an important part through her interests and influence.
- **Tax**. Giving to a charity or similar organisation can often be done tax free. This will be an added benefit for the company, but seldom the determining factor.

It is the shareholders' funds that are being given away. For privately owned companies or companies that are largely owned and controlled by a family, giving by the company is little different from personal giving. But for public companies, the company will always want to be able to justify the support by being able to give a reason for it. And this is something that you can do when approaching them – tell them not just why you want the money, but why it would be interesting for them and in their interest to support you. And also tell them what they will get out of it in return for their money.

Companies always appreciate thanks, recognition and good publicity for their support. And you can provide this by acknowledging their support in newsletters and in your annual report, and by trying to get press or media coverage for the activity they have supported, mentioning their support of course.

The sorts of project that companies like to support

Companies support all sorts of projects. But the following are the sorts of activity that they might be particularly interested in:

- Important **local projects** in the areas where they have a significant presence.
- Prestigious **arts and cultural events**.
- **Sporting events** and competitions, especially those that attract keen public interest.
- **Activities that relate to their product**. For example, an ice cream manufacturer might want to support children's charities.
- **Economic development projects** – because a flourishing economy will benefit business.
- **Environmental projects** – because these days everyone loves the environment.
- Initiatives which have the **backing of very prominent people**.

Looked at from the fundraiser's point of view, this can provide an interesting insight as to the sorts of company to approach and how to make that approach.

> **Company support in India**
>
> ActionAid has carried out a survey of corporate giving in India, when they asked companies to spell out the issues and causes they particularly liked to support, the four most popular causes were:
> 1. **Rural development**, including adoption of surrounding villages, 48%
> 2. Support for **the disabled**, 33%
> 3. **Education**, 31%
> 4. **Health and sanitation**, 25%
>
> The fifth was medical benefits and welfare of employees, which was seen as a philanthropic activity.
>
> The main reasons for choosing an area of support included:
> 1. **Concern** for that particular group, 49%
> 2. To build **corporate image**, 24%
> 3. **Family tradition**, 21%
> 4. **Company tradition**, 19%
>
> When asked what benefits they expected in return, they gave the following main reasons:
> 1. Satisfaction of fulfilling **social responsibility**, 45%
> 2. Improved **credibility**, 28%
> 3. Increased confidence amongst **staff**, 19%

It is also important to know what companies are unlikely to want to support. Surveys suggest that most companies will not give to:

- **Local appeals outside those areas** where they have a business presence.
- **Purely denominational appeals** for religious purposes, although this does not preclude support for social projects run by religious bodies.
- **Circular appeals**, which are printed and sent to hundreds of companies. These usually end up unread in the bin.
- **Controversial causes** which might bring them bad publicity. They prefer to play safe, and they are seldom interested in supporting active campaigning bodies.
- **Overseas appeals**, although some do support emergency and aid appeals on the basis that this is the sort of thing that the staff would like to see supported.

What companies give

There are a variety of ways in which companies can support charities:

- **Cash donations**.
- **Sponsorship** of an event or activity.
- **Sponsorship** of promotional and educational materials.
- **Joint promotions**, where the company contributes a donation to the charity in return for each product sold in order to encourage sales.

- Making **company facilities** available, including meeting rooms, printing or design facilities, help with mailings, etc.
- **Support 'in kind'**, by giving company products or office equipment that is no longer required. Giving things rather than money is often easier for a company.
- **'Secondment'** of a member of staff to work with the charity, where a member of the company's staff helps on an agreed basis whilst remaining employed (and paid) by the company.
- Contributing a senior member of staff to the charity's Management Board.
- Providing **expertise and advice**.
- Encouraging company **employees to volunteer**.
- Organising a **fundraising campaign** amongst employees.
- **Advertising** in charity brochures and publications.

> **British Airways collects money from passengers**
>
> **'Change for Good'**, an in-flight initiative with the UNICEF, was launched in 1994 at the suggestion of staff, and has raised £2 million to date. An envelope is circulated to passengers, so that their small unwanted foreign currency can be donated, and the message is reinforced with an appeal on the in-flight video. Staff also donate and run local collections for the fund.

There are two points to bear in mind:

- There are very **many ways in which a company can help** you. This is an important difference from other funding sources, as most other funders can only give you money. So think carefully about the best way in which the company might help you. You may find that they don't give very much at all in cash donations, and that it will be far easier (and less costly to them) for them to support you in some other way.
- There is an important **difference between donation and sponsorship**. With a donation, the company gets nothing back except some form of thanks and acknowledgement. With sponsorship, the company aims to get a return for the money it is spending. This 'return' could be some form of publicity for the company, or it could be an opportunity to entertain customers and others (for example at a prestigious cultural event held in aid of charity).

The different sorts of companies that give

International and multinational companies

Multinational companies may well have an established programme of charitable giving in their home country. This will be particularly true for US companies (whose giving is documented by the Foundation Center) and UK companies (whose giving is documented by the Directory of Social Change). A trend in recent years has been for companies to extend their giving beyond their headquarters town and home country into the other territories where they have business interests, and also into countries where they are considering starting up (for example, American Express has been giving support to projects in Vietnam as a prelude to opening up for business in that country).

Some multinational companies have an international structure for managing their giving, with budgets set for each country and a common policy for the sorts of activity they are interested in supporting. This is the case, for example, with IBM. Others may give each country a small budget to spend on charitable projects of its choice. This has been the case with Microsoft up until now. With others it is a purely local decision.

Where multinationals give

If you look at the geographical breakdown of a multinational company's giving, you will find the following:
- Most money is spent in the **headquarters town or region**.
- Most money is spent in the **home country** of the company. For example, ARCO, one of the leading oil companies spends most of its budget in the USA, but it has a strategy of trying to spread its giving more evenly in those countries where it does business.
- The **North gets more than the South**. BP gives most in the UK and Germany, for example.

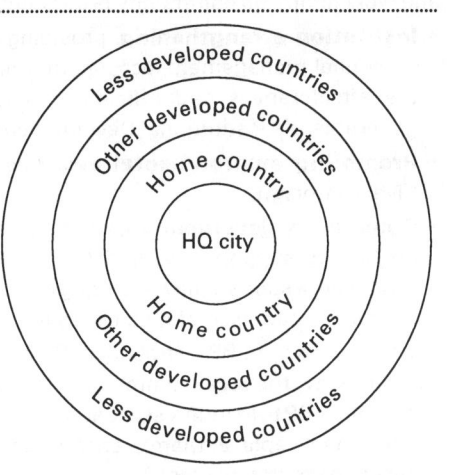

The circle of giving. The further out you are, the less you can expect to get.

Leading national companies

Most leading national companies will also be giving something to charity. This is partly in response to what overseas companies are doing, and partly because it often makes good sense to give. The first attempts are now being made in some countries to document the giving of top companies.

Larger local companies

In any city or region there will be large companies who are important to the local economy. These companies will often feel a responsibility to do something to support voluntary action and community initiatives in those areas, and value the good publicity that this will provide. If yours is an important project, it should be part of your fundraising strategy to develop some form of relationship with the larger companies in your area.

Smaller local companies

If you are mounting a general appeal, then you will want to approach smaller companies for their support. And they can often also be persuaded to give support in kind.

BP in Colombia

The British Petroleum Company (BP) spent $29 million (just under £20 million) in 1994 on community projects. Of this, 29% was spent in the USA, 39% in Europe, and 32% in the rest of the world. The main areas of expenditure are education (41%), community development (33%), arts (10%) and environment (excluding environmental programmes at BP sites, 8%).

BP's community relations policy states: "We value our reputation as a good neighbour and corporate citizen wherever we operate... Wherever appropriate we seek to use our expertise and resources to work in partnership with the community".

In Colombia, BP contributes $2.14 million, and also works in partnership with four other oil companies where it has established a foundation to pool resources and work jointly on community programmes. The three main areas of activity are:

- **Institution strengthening**, providing management training (which includes personnel management, accountancy and information technology) to improve the effectiveness and efficiency of government agencies as part of the government's Institutional Development Plan.
- **Promoting environmental awareness** in schools through the 'El Cusiana Viva' campaign.
- **Community development**, where the company adds resources to community projects to support local initiative. Projects include improving water supply, sanitation, a sports centre, fostering cultural awareness, health and environmental education, purchase of medical equipment and supplies.

"The foundation of BP's strategy in Colombia is a three-way partnership between the company, the local community, and local and central government agencies. This enables BP to identify essential needs, complement government responsibilities (rather than replace them), encourage community self-help and avoid any accusations of paternalism."

Who decides and who to write to

Practice varies from company to company. Many multinationals will have a manager who is given the responsibility of dealing with and deciding on charitable appeals – although the local top management may also have some say in what is supported. Sometimes decisions are made by an international donations committee based at international headquarters. For larger companies, the decision on what to support will usually be taken by the Chairman or Managing Director personally, or through some form of donations committee which meets regularly to consider applications. The larger companies may also employ specialist staff (rather like a foundation) to assess the applications that are received and make recommendations on what should be supported. Some large companies operate an independent foundation, where the foundation and its trustees will set policy and decide on applications.

With medium sized and smaller companies, it is nearly always the top person who decides. The important point to note is that you should write to the person who has the responsibility for receiving and dealing with charitable appeals, and to make sure that you have the spelling and job title correct. You don't want to write to the wrong person, let alone someone who left the company ten years ago!

Some questions companies are likely to ask... with some suggested answers

"Why is giving relevant to my company?"
- Business cannot operate in isolation from society.
- Having a social vision is integral to the success of the business mission.
- A social investment strategy is a must for any progressive company.
- Qualified professionals increasingly prefer to work for a company with a social commitment.

- Customers show preference for doing business with companies that are environment conscious and socially driven.
- Communities and government expect companies to be good corporate citizens.

"Why should I be doing it? Shouldn't the government be giving its support?"
- We already do receive substantial government support (if you do), and the money we are looking for is to enhance or develop our work.
- Government doesn't always have the capability or the resources to do everything.
- There are some things that are best done by NGOs and local people.
- There are some sorts of support and expertise that only companies can provide.

"How do I make sure that my money will be well spent?"
- Select a project that meets your criteria, has clearly defined objectives and the right development approach.
- Route your support through a credible development agency, if you think that this will be better than supporting the project directly.
- Insist on feedback.
- Even think about visiting the project.

"I don't have any spare money, so how can I contribute?"
- You can give material resources, such as old furniture and equipment or company product.
- You can provide technical know how, financial and management skills, media links.
- You can help implement schemes, such as the construction of low cost housing or toilets.

"I can't contribute the whole amount, so how will you make up the shortfall, or will my money be wasted?"
- We will find the balance from other sources, and your gift can be conditional on our doing that.
- You may be able to help us here by introducing us to other businesses who might be interested in providing a share.

"If I give to one project, won't I be flooded with requests?"
- Have a budget for the year and a stated policy on giving. That way you can support those projects you wish, and have a good reason for turning down the other requests.

Adapted from a 'tick list' for corporate fundraising prepared by the Concern India Foundation

Where to find out about company giving

There are two aspects of this:

1. Finding out **what companies there are in your area**. There are a wide variety of ways in which you can find out about local companies:
- Through the **local Chamber of Commerce** (if there is one).
- Through **other business and industry associations**.
- From the **local press**.
- By **knowing the area** you live in.

And nationally and internationally, there may be:
- **Business directories** listing the top companies, and for international

companies, *'Fortune 500'* and *'Forbes Magazine'* may be useful. These can be found in most business school libraries.

- The **national and international press**, especially *'The Economist'* which carries news on international business affairs.

2. Finding out what they are interested in giving to. To find out what a company gives to is not always easy. Large companies tend to have community affairs officers, who may be willing to meet fundraisers or to discuss their policies over the phone. But most smaller companies don't, and for these it is the interests of the Chief Executive or Chairman which are likely to be important. So if the Chairman is passionate about cricket, he may wish to sponsor a cricket competition for local schools. Or he may have an orphanage which he strongly supports. Any contact you have with the company at a senior level can be used to try to find out what they currently support and what they might be interested in giving to. Another possible way is to identify one of your supporters or volunteers who is employed by the company and ask them to find out for you.

Keep in touch with company news and events. This can often generate interesting ideas and opportunities. For example, if a plant is closing down or a new branch opening, then the company might want to support some sort of initiative which will benefit the community. Read the papers: the business press, the national press, the local press.

And finally, try to get hold of the company's annual report which will help you understand their business and identify their interests.

Getting support in kind

Giving things rather than money is often easier for a company. Here are some practical tips on how to set about getting support in kind.

1. Make a list of everything you need – this is called a 'wish list'. This can include services as well as products (such as the design for a leaflet you plan to produce).

2. Go through the list and try to **identify companies** that might have what you require. Personal knowledge is fine. But you might also want to use business directories.

3. Make contact. Writing a letter does not work well. It is best if you can make personal or telephone contact. State your request, saying that it is for a charity and indicating how well used it will be and how important to your organisation's future.

4. If they refuse to donate it, they might be able to give you a hefty discount (half price?). This is worth getting. And can be a fall back position in your discussions.

5. Be positive and enthusiastic. It can be very difficult for them to refuse if they know what you want and how important it is for you. It will always cost them far less to donate the item than it would cost you to purchase it.

6. Say thank you. Report back subsequently on the difference the donation has made. Send them your annual report. Try then to recruit them as a cash donor.

Getting companies to advertise in your publication

Companies are often prepared to support you by taking an advertisement in a brochure or a publication – possibilities include your annual report and programmes produced for fundraising events. This is known as 'goodwill advertising' as it is paid for to create good will for the company rather than sell more of its products. Companies like it because they can treat the expenditure as a business expense rather than as a charitable donation, because they get publicity in return for their support, and because they are being asked to give a specific amount that they can afford. Here are some practical tips on getting companies to advertise.

1. Prepare a **'rate card'** which gives the different rates for a full page, half page, etc., and calculate the amount you charge to be affordable to them, but to generate a good surplus for your work.

2. Outline the sort of **audience** that the publication will reach, and give some idea of the sort of benefits that the company can expect by advertising in your publication (reaching a select audience of decision-takers, or being distributed widely amongst your supporters, for example).

3. Approach companies that you think might be interested. These would include those that have advertised in your publications previously, your suppliers, local companies keen to associate with your organisation, and companies where there is some connection between their business and what you do.

4. Follow up your original communication by **telephone**, and tell them what other companies have agreed to advertise. Once one company does, then this makes it easier for others to decide to do the same.

5. Offer to design the advertisement for them. This is particularly useful if you are planning to approach smaller companies. You can make a small charge for doing this.

6. Always show them **a copy of the proof**, and get them to sign it as 'approved'. In this way, if there is a mistake, you cannot be blamed.

7. Send them **a copy of the publication**, with a note telling them on which page their advertisement has been printed.

8. Make sure you **get paid**... and **say thank you**.

Getting started

There are three things you should start with:

1. First find out what, if any, **previous contact** you have had with companies, and what previous fundraising approaches you have made, and with what success.

2. Through **research**, identify and match possible funders with various aspects of your work. In particular, try to find any local companies that are known for their generosity and might have an interest in supporting your cause.

3. Then find out whether any of your Board Members or supporters (or even your volunteers) have any **personal contact** with any of the companies you plan to approach.

Raising money from companies: a case study

The following is how the Botswana Red Cross set about raising money from companies.

"We started off by writing to larger businesses appealing to them to donate to us on an annual basis. We suggested P5'000 for the larger companies, and reduced the amount where we felt it necessary. We did not expect any of them to give at this level, but if you suggest a smaller amount, they offer an even smaller sum. But it did give them an idea of what we were looking for. Some actually did come up with the amount suggested. Overall the response was very pleasing. And most who made a commitment did actually pay up.

"We enjoy popular support in the community as the Red Cross Movement, which makes it easier to persuade people to part with their money. It really is essential to have their confidence and for them to be aware of what you are doing; and also to keep proper accounts, and to supply audited accounts on request if anyone wants to see them.

"It is not enough just to write letters to General Managers or Managing Directors. The personal approach has far more impact. It is more difficult to refuse if someone is sitting across the table from you. It also helps to invite people home and share a meal or a drink whilst discussing the issue.

"The Managing Director of one of our leading companies has always been a dedicated Red Cross fan. He decided not to give to us in response to our appeal, but instead to organise once a year a fundraising evening for our benefit, meeting the cost of this himself. He put on fantastic shows which were hugely popular, and charged enormous amounts for the tickets! He has now left Botswana, but the man who has taken over has continued with a similar idea, not putting on shows, because he says he has no talent for it, but as he is a keen golfer, once a year he organises a golf championship as a charity event to benefit the Red Cross.

"A corporate appeal can snowball if you have the right people receiving your requests. We raise around P70'000 annually, but some companies give to us in kind – for example, one wholesale company donates bags of mealie meal each month for our disabled training centre. The cost of running the appeal is almost nothing, as it mostly consists of stationery and stamps to remind companies if they happen to forget. Many companies take advantage of giving to us by promoting themselves in the media when they hand over cheques. We do not mind this; in fact, we welcome it, as it also advertises what we do. Other competitor companies in order not to be outdone decide also to give. More snowballing.

"The main lesson learnt is the need to gain the donor's confidence – making people aware of our rehabilitation and relief programmes, our training centre for the disabled, the work of our volunteers, and most importantly to convince them that the money they give us will be well spent, that we are working with the most needy and doing the best work. In Botswana, we have far too many organisations and societies appealing to too few donors. It is therefore our job to persuade people that they could do no better than support our cause because we will use the money the way that they would want it used."

Lady Ruth Khama, President Botswana Red Cross

Getting in touch

The personal approach is best, but often the most difficult to achieve. In smaller companies there is usually no staff member responsible for giving and therefore approaches have to be at Board level. As a first step you might telephone the company to see whether you can find out the following:

- **Who is responsible** for dealing with charitable appeals.
- Their **name**, correctly spelt, and **job title**, so that you get it right when you write to them or speak to them on the phone.
- What **information they can send you** about their company. They might have a brochure on their charitable support programme. They certainly will have a company annual report, which will tell you about their work.
- Any **procedure** or **timetable** for submitting appeals.
- Whether they might be interested in **coming to see your organisation** at work.

Visits are useful when discussing bigger donations with the larger companies, but are difficult to arrange for anything small. It is quite unusual to be able to persuade senior company executives to visit the projects that they are considering supporting. Business in the Community (BITC), a UK agency which promotes corporate giving, organises 'Seeing is Believing' days for senior businessmen and women. They find that when people visit projects and talk to project organisers and beneficiaries, they get really interested in the idea of giving their and their company's support. The interest and feeling of commitment that is engendered raises your chances of getting support, and any support that you do get is likely to be more substantial and longer term.

Almost certainly your appeal to them will be in the form of a letter. Make this as personal as you can. Circular letters suffer the fate of most of the thousands of appeals a company receives each month. They are put in the bin. Letters should therefore be directed to a named individual and written to them personally. Make the letter short and to the point. A brief letter of a page is much more likely to be read (and responded to) than a longer letter. Because companies receive too many appeals, their first instinct is to say no. They may not even read the letter. Many is the time when the sender of an invitation to an Open Day receives a standard letter of rejection – even though you have not asked for money – simply because the recipient has seen that the letter is from a charity!

Eight ideas for getting support from companies

1. Put yourself in the position of the company. Why should they want to give their shareholders' funds to you? Why should they choose your charity, rather than any of the other appeals they receive? Think about the benefits that they may get from supporting you. And mention these in your appeal letter. If you are looking for sponsorship, then these benefits will be at the heart of your proposal.

2. Suggest something specific for the company to support, which you think will be of particular interest to that company; and in your letter tell them why they should be interested. It is often best to think of something quite small if you are approaching them for the first time.

3. Use all the contacts you have in the company to help get your appeal supported. Do you know the Chairman, the Managing Director or any other senior member of staff? Or their spouses, who may be able to put in a good word for you? Or if you telephone, can you get into conversation with the Chairman's secretary or personal assistant such that he or she becomes interested and enthusiastic and will put in a good word for you. Do you have any volunteers who are helping you who also work for the company? They may be able to help you 'from the inside', and it will do you no harm if you mention their support for your organisation in your appeal letter.

4. Think of all the different ways in which the company could help. Cash might not be the best way for them to give their support. Might it be easier for them to offer staff time, perhaps giving you some expertise you lack? Or the use of a vehicle? Or access to company staff to circulate an appeal or to sell your New Year's cards to? It is likely that everyone else will be asking for cash. And the company may find it easier to give in kind. And once they have given in kind and got to know you and your work, cash support may become easier to obtain next time.

5. Consider whether there is a senior executive of the company (the more senior the better) who might become a trustee of your charity or serve on a fundraising or development committee to bring new ideas, good organisation and a wealth of business contacts to your organisation that will be worth many times the value of a donation. Such an invitation, even if refused, may be seen as flattering. If this level of involvement is too much, a request for advice may succeed.

6. Don't assume that every company will give. Make parallel approaches to a number of different companies.

7. Consider who might be the best person to make the approach or sign the letter. It may not be you. Often it is another senior businessman who has already supported your organisation generously.

8. Every time you buy anything from a company, ask for a discount. This will save you money, but it is also a way of getting them to support you.

4.6 Business sponsorship

Sponsorship needs to be carefully defined. It is not a jargon word simply meaning a gift from a company which is publicly acknowledged. It is an association between two parties with quite different interests who come together in order to support a particularly activity for two quite different motives.

The charity is looking to raise funds for its work. The sponsor hopes to improve its image or to promote its products or to entertain its customers – and thereby sell more of its products. The sponsor's contribution does not need to be money, though usually it is. It could also be a gifts of goods (such as a car), or services (such as free transport), or professional expertise (such as promotion or marketing consultancy), or staff fundraising (to raise money for the charity), or the use of buildings (such as an exhibition centre), or free promotion (in a newspaper or broadcast), and so on.

An additional benefit of sponsorship is the way in which the link with the sponsor can be developed subsequently – depending on how the original sponsorship goes. If all goes well and they get to like you and admire your professionalism, then you might look for further sponsorships on a larger scale, and possibly also for getting a donation from the company charitable budget, being able to use company resources and facilities (such as a training centre or meeting room) free of charge, getting employees involved in the work of your charity or senior management to sit on your management Board. These are all things you might expect to flow from a successful sponsorship.

One of the future directions of corporate giving is through sponsorship – as companies want to get more back for their money than a simple acknowledgement. In recent years, sponsorship has extended from sport and the arts into environment, education and social projects. Many companies will give much more as sponsorship than they would as a donation, if they can see the benefits that they can gain for themselves. Developing links with the major national and local corporate sponsors – even if this effort comes to nothing – could be an investment in your future well worth making now.

Who sponsors?

Most sponsors are commercial businesses, including state-owned industries. But government departments, public authorities, utilities, hospitals, universities and other institutions sometimes undertake sponsorship when they can gain some benefit by doing so. There are four main opportunities for sponsorship:

- Those businesses that are **anxious to promote themselves**, to create a better image of themselves, or to generate a public awareness in the local

communities where they operate. This includes those companies with an 'image problem' – for example, mining and extraction companies associated with the destruction of the environment who want to project a cleaner image by being associated with a conservationist cause.
- Those businesses with a **particular product or service** that they wish to introduce or promote. This could include a new brand of toothpaste or beer, or a supermarket opening in the area. Public awareness is important if a product or service is to get accepted. It is therefore easy to see why companies might be open to proposals that give a particular product or service more exposure.
- Those companies looking for **entertainment opportunities** to influence customers, suppliers, regulators, the media and other opinion formers. They may be interested in sponsoring a prestigious concert, theatrical event, art exhibition, horse race or sporting event, which would provide them with an appropriate entertainment opportunity and the opportunity to meet and mingle with celebrities.
- Finally those companies that are **committed supporters** of your organisation. They may find something that they would like to sponsor, even if it is partly for 'philanthropic reasons'.

> **Why companies like sponsorship**
> - It helps them **get their message across**.
> - It can enhance or change their **image**.
> - It can reach a **target audience** very precisely.
> - It can be very **cost-effective advertising** or **product promotion**.
> - Further **marketing opportunities** may develop from the sponsorship.
> - It generates **good publicity** for the sponsor, often of a kind that money can't buy.
> - It generates an **awareness of the company** within the local community in which the company operates and from where it draws its workforce.
> - Sponsors can **entertain important clients** at the events they sponsor.

Banks and financial services companies are particularly keen to sponsor, and often sponsor the prestigious cultural events. Foreign airlines and companies might be interested in sponsoring exhibitions and events that are based on their home country culture. Major international companies, and also those just expanding into your country, may have well developed international sponsorship programmes and can often lead the way, encouraging indigenous companies to think about sponsorship.

What can be sponsored

There is an extremely wide range of things that can be sponsored. In fact anything that can offer some benefit to a sponsor. The most popular things to sponsor include:

- **Cultural and sporting events**.
- **Mass participation fundraising events**, such as a marathon run.
- The **publication of a report or a book**, with an attendant launch.
- The production of **fundraising materials**, leaflets and posters, or the sponsorship of a complete fundraising campaign.
- **Vehicles**, where the acknowledgement can be painted on the side.
- **Equipment** such as cars or computers, produced by the company.
- **Competitions**, awards and prizes.
- **Scholarships**, bursaries, travel grants.

- **Conferences and seminars**, especially to specialist audiences (such as doctors) where promotional material can be displayed.

One company's sponsorship programme

British Telecommunications (BT) is the major telephone company in the UK. The objectives of its sponsorship programme are to demonstrate its commitment to improving the quality of life in communities throughout the country (as it provides a service to everyone). Its policy is to concentrate its sponsorship on the arts and the environment.

For **the arts**, BT sponsors touring companies rather than major national events, including regional tours of the Royal Philharmonic Orchestra and the Royal Shakespeare Company, which enables performances to be seen in more than 30 towns and cities around the country – many of which do not normally normally get live performances. The BT New Contemporaries exhibition takes art school graduate work to the Institute of Contemporary Arts and provincial galleries.

Local events are also supported, many of which have attracted national and even international interest. One such project is the Lake District summer music festival in Ambleside, which combines children's workshops, concerts and master classes, and allows top flight musicians to work alongside talented amateurs.

Young people are a particular target audience. BT sponsors Artswork, which encourages children to take part in a wide range of creative activity.

For **the environment**, the programme includes the sponsorship of National Environment Week and the Community Pride Awards scheme, both of which are organised by the Civic Trust, a national conservation charity. BT is working with Friends of the Earth on a city-wide recycling initiative in Sheffield, which is now being extended to other cities across the UK. Another 'demonstration project' is the joint venture with East Anglia police, the Square Mile project, which encourages teams of children to help clean up a square mile of their environment. Young people's involvement in other environmental activities is encouraged by the BT Young Environmentalists competition, and the Living Rivers scheme which aims to improve the condition of our rivers.

This is an example of a well developed sponsorship policy from one of the UK's major corporate donors. The overall aim of the programme is to enhance the company's image in the community and to be associated with innovation. Sponsorship policy will change and develop over the years. Before approaching a sponsor, it is worth finding out what they have sponsored in the past and what their current interests are.

Identifying possible sponsors

First you should decide what your proposed activity has to offer a sponsor. Is it a target audience? Access to public personalities? A prestigious event? Only when you have done this can you begin to define the companies who might be interested. They may be national companies looking for national publicity, or a major company located in your area or a purely local concern looking to develop local awareness. Remember that if you are looking for a substantial sum of money, only the larger companies will be interested.

You should draw up a list of potential sponsors that you plan to approach. You will need to do some research prior to submitting your proposal. Your research will include finding out what the company has sponsored before, what sort of sums it might be interested in providing, and its current interests and concerns which might be met through sponsorship. For example a construction company that has just completed a residential estate will be interested in marketing it. A new shopping centre that plans to open may need a promotional event to coincide with its opening. All opportunities for sponsorship.

The next step is to prepare the written proposal, which will outline the project, and highlight all the benefits to be gained by the company sponsoring it. It will also have a price for the sponsorship – which will as much reflect the value of the benefits to the company as your own fundraising need.

You will need patience. Sponsorship can take a long time to negotiate, and it is best to plan well in advance. Start discussions at least a year, and possibly longer before the activity takes place.

Sponsorship involves a close working relationship between the company and the voluntary organisation. This can create problems. It is one thing when a charity accepts or even solicits money from a company about whose activities it has some reservations; it is quite another when it actively seeks to promote the work of such a company, as it will be doing in a sponsorship relationship. It is strongly recommended that you develop a sponsorship policy before you apply for any sponsorship – agreeing in advance which types of company you are happy to approach and which you are not.

> **Sponsorship plan of action for a Royal Charity Golf Tournament in Malaysia**
>
> - Sponsors for each hole to pay RM5,000, and a placard with the name and logo of that sponsor to be placed at that hole.
> - An automobile company to sponsor the insurance cover for the 'Hole-in-One' prize.
> - Donors required for 27 useful and practical prizes.
> - A donor for the tonic drinks to be distributed to the 60 participating golfers at the Halfway House (after 9 holes) whilst the tournament is in progress.
> - Donors for golf balls and other items as gifts in Souvenir Slingbags.
> - Free printing of Sponsorship Cards
>
> In addition each participant was required to raise sponsorship of at last RM1,000 to be able to play. The net proceeds from the event amounted to more than RM100,000.
>
> *Source: Malaysian Red Crescent Society*

The sponsorship package

Before you make your approach, you will need to decide whether the nature of the company, its products, its ethos and its performance conflicts with your own work and ethos, and whether you are happy to work closely with that company in a high-profile relationship. If the answer is yes, then you will need to decide:

- The exact nature of **the project** or activity, and how it is likely to work.
- The **audiences** that will be reached and the publicity that will be obtained. These should be quantified as far as possible (how many column centimetres of coverage and in which newspapers can be expected, how many and what sort of people will attend the event, how many posters will be displayed, etc.). Remember that the company will be primarily interested in reaching those people who are its target audience for the sponsorship.
- The **geographical coverage**. Is it a national or a purely local activity?
- The **image** that will be projected through the event, and how this will fit in with what the sponsoring brand or company might be looking for.
- The **specific advertising opportunities** that will be available on poster hoardings, the sides of vans, in the event programme, on TV, in the press, and so on.

- Some of the **other benefits** that the sponsorship might confer on the company. The effect it will have on staff, on business contacts, and on government and other authorities.
- The **cost of the sponsorship** – and the value of the sponsorship benefits, and how they compare with other ways of reaching the target audiences or achieving the same promotional objective.

All this should be produced in a professional (though not necessarily expensive) way, together with photographs and press coverage from previous sponsored events, and brief background material on your organisation and its work.

Making the approach

Having identified a potential company and developed your sponsorship proposal, there are a variety of ways in which you can approach the company.

It is best to make an appointment to visit the company to give a presentation of your work and discuss the sponsorship opportunities. Only then will you be in a position to find out what the needs are of the company and how you might be able to meet them. You will need to make sure you are approaching the person who is able to make the decision. For product promotions, this will be the brand manager. For corporate PR, it may be a senior director.

If you are not able to arrange a meeting in the first instance, a phone call to the marketing department can elicit a wealth of information about who to send the proposal to, and what sort of sponsorships they are likely to consider. Then send a summary proposal to see if it sparks any interest. Follow this up with a phone call a few days later to try and arrange a meeting.

There may be an advertising agency or marketing consultant which will introduce sponsorship opportunities to sponsors. They will sometimes charge you a fee; more usually they will receive a commission from the sponsor. It depends who retains them, and in whose interests they are acting.

Contractual issues

Because sponsorship involves your giving something in return for the money you are receiving, it is advisable to agree terms through some form of contract, which can easily be done in the form of a letter. A number of important issues need to be included which should be settled when negotiating the sponsorship:

- **How long the arrangement will run**. Is it for one year, thus requiring you to find a new sponsor next year? Or can you get a commitment for three or more years? And what happens at the end of this period – does the sponsor have a first refusal on the following year's event? Most successful sponsorship lasts for several years, and the benefit builds up over the sponsorship period. But companies don't like being tied to sponsoring something indefinitely – their sponsorship programme could begin to look stale.
- **The fee to be paid**, and when instalments are due.
- **What benefits are to be delivered** in return for the fee – specified as clearly as possible, so that you know precisely what you are contracted to deliver.
- **Who is to pay the costs**. This is something that is often forgotten. Who pays for the additional publicity that the sponsor requires? There needs to be a clear understanding of who is responsible for what, so that you can ensure that everything is covered and there are no misunderstandings later on.

- **Who is responsible** for doing what. Who will do the public relations. Who will handle the bookings. Who will invite the guests. Whose staff will receive the guests. And all the other details that need clarifying.
- **Any termination arrangements** in the event of the activity having to be cancelled.
- **Who is responsible** for managing the relationship – on both sides.

If everything is written down in the agreement, there are less likely to be problems later – and it will ensure that everything has been properly thought through at the outset.

Joint promotions

For larger charities, commercial promotions which involve the charity in helping market a commercial product (often known as 'joint promotions') can be another way of working with a company, which can bring in large amounts of money relatively painlessly and expose the name of the charity to millions of people for little or no cost. The method can also be adapted for use by local charities through local promotions.

This type of fundraising is an arrangement that benefits both the charity and the commercial partner. It is rather like sponsorship, but the relationships are reversed – you are linked to the company's products, rather than they to your cause. Commercial promotions can include on-pack and licensing promotional deals, competitions and awards, the use of phone lines, and self-liquidating offers. What they have in common is that they present an opportunity to raise money for your cause and to project your charity to new audiences. But they require that you work with the company and on their terms to achieve this.

> **An example of a commercial promotion**
>
> **Save the World with World Savers**
>
> *"1989 has seen the launch of the Bank's biggest sponsorship to date – a guaranteed £3 million link with the World Wide Fund for Nature (WWF) over three years. Launched in January, the World Savers scheme offers accounts to children, paying a premium interest rate, which can be opened with a minimum of £5. A donation of £1 from the Bank's own funds will be given for each new World Saver account opened, and 0.5% of the total balances of all the World Saver accounts will be donated annually."*
>
> This joint promotion has been designed to appeal to supporters of WWF and anyone who wants to do something for the environment. The Bank reckons that if it can attract the savings of young people, they will continue to bank with the same bank for the rest of their lives. So they are offering an inducement to start an account, and a further inducement to keep money in the account. This is a classic example of the 'you buy this product and we give an extra £1 to charity' type of commercial promotion.

On-pack promotions

There are many variants of the on-pack promotion. They start with the need of a manufacturer to promote a product or service at a particular point in time – the promotion may be to the wholesaler, to the retailer or to the consumer. The basic mechanism is that with every purchase of the product through every label or coupon returned, the manufacturer agrees to give a specified sum of money to the charity, sometimes with an upper limit on the total that will be given as a result of the promotion.

Good practice requires that the amount to be donated is specified on the pack.

Manufacturers like this sort of arrangement as they can predict quite accurately what it is going to cost to achieve sales at a given level. Fundraisers like it, since it presents their cause to literally millions of shoppers, and because they can usually expect to raise a substantial sum.

Variations on this theme include the consortium promotion which includes a galaxy of well-known charities included together in one promotion. Local and smaller scale promotions are also possible. A local Indian take-away restaurant in London donates all the proceeds of the sale of a lentil dish each Friday to selected charities supported by the owner. Or a pizza restaurant chain, Pizza Express in the UK, created a special pizza (Pizza Veneziana), where a specified sum is donated to an Italian conservation charity (the Venice in Peril Fund) for each pizza ordered.

Licensing

When a charity has become a well-known household name, consumer goods manufacturers can become interested in developing an association with the charity to enhance its sales. It uses the charity's good name to endorse its product. Out of this is born the licensing deal. The promotion is likely to involve a fixed number of uses of the charity logo or name over a given period in return for an often substantial fee. Precisely how it is used will be set out in the licensing agreement. The outcome is then not directly related to the level of public support, but is agreed at the outset as a fixed fee.

Competitions

Another variant is the on-pack promotion that involves a competition. The competition is usually a prize draw, which is usually a game of chance rather than a game of skill (to encourage as many people as possible to enter) and may involve a tie-break question (for example, describe in 20 words why you like Brand X).

For the fundraiser, competitions offer several benefits. The promotion can be related in some way to the charity and its cause. If it's a charity working overseas, the prize could be a trip to that country. If a domestic cause, the competition questions could be designed to create a better understanding of your cause. Money will accrue to the charity, either through a contribution for each entry sent in, or from an agreed fee for the use of the charity's name.

Self-liquidating offers

The self-liquidating offer is the rather grand name for promoting one of your own products so that its costs are recovered from sales. You offer one of your products – say an attractive tee-shirt, with a design by a well-known designer – to a manufacturer to feature on the back of a pack. Consumers are invited to send in for this at the 'special offer price', which is set low enough to seem excellent value, but high enough to recover costs.

There are several advantages of such an arrangement. Depending on the pricing, you may end up making a profit on a large number of sales – something that charities do not often manage by marketing the same products themselves. Whether or not you do better than recover your costs, you can certainly expect to distribute a large number of items bearing your message. You should note the possibility of retaining the mailing list of purchasers as a suitable list for subsequent direct mail fundraising or trading. And finally, there will be an extremely large number of people who will see the promotion but not buy – which is additional publicity for the cause.

Getting started with promotions

Promotions of this kind are quite difficult to arrange. It is an area where professionalism will pay dividends, so you may want to talk about the possibility of your developing promotional links with companies with a marketing or advertising agency.

The first step is to decide whether you are the sort of charity which can expect a commercial link of this sort. Usually national 'brand name' charities and those addressing 'popular causes', such as helping children, are more likely to benefit from this area of fundraising than the less well know charities and those addressing difficult causes, such as torture or slavery.

Then you need to decide whether to wait until companies or their promotional agencies contact you (they may not), or whether to take the initiative yourself and contact companies you think might be interested. In order to do this, you need to be absolutely clear about the nature of your cause. The relationship is not one-way, so you also need to be clear about the extent to which you are prepared to associate your charity's good name with a particular industry, a particular company and a particular product.

Ideally, you need to research the industries, companies and products that are likely to make good partners for you. What are their marketing objectives? Who are their competitors? What might they gain through an association with you? With this information, it is worth trying to meet the marketing director to present the possibilities for working together and the advantages of an association.

It is preferable at this stage not to have too detailed a proposal in mind, so that you can react to what you find to be the company's own preferences and needs. You should take along examples of how other companies have benefited from an association with you – though this will not be possible if it is the first promotion you are arranging.

If you are approached by a promotional agency pitching for business, this does not mean that anything is certain. They may be working independently, hoping that a good idea that involves your charity can then be sold to a company. In nine out of ten times, these ideas come to nothing, and you may find you have put in considerable effort without getting any payback.

Issues

Commercial promotions business bring charities face to face with a range of dilemmas – just as with sponsorship, but more so since the relationship is that much more public. The charity will be seen to be actively promoting the products of the company, so it is important that there are no 'ethical problems' and that the product you are associated with is good value and does not fall to bits. As for sponsorships, you are strongly recommended to develop your own policy on what commercial associations you are prepared to enter into.

How much you should expect to receive from a commercial promotion is also a difficult question. Your name is effectively being sold to the company to enhance theirs or their product's. It may be worth a great deal to them to be linked with you. Any negotiation should start from what you think the association is worth to them and whether it is worth your while to enter into the promotion at that price.

4.7 Other sources

Giving by other institutions

There are many different institutions and organisations which might be interested in supporting your organisation in some way. These include:

1. Trade unions, especially where your work is to do with employment rights or some other matter of interest to them. Trade Union giving will normally be an extension of their political stance. For example, many unions contributed to the fight against apartheid by making donations to the voluntary organisations concerned with combating apartheid, in pursuance of resolutions at annual conferences. The structure of giving can be through the Congress of trade unions, a union HQ, one of the local branches or by being allowed to send your appeal to the membership at large.

2. Membership bodies such as the Women's Institutes, Young Farmers, Round Tables, Chambers of Commerce, Business and Trade Associations, Rotarians, Lions and the whole range of similar organisations (the sorts of groups that exist will vary from country to country) can provide important opportunities for fundraising. Usually they don't make large grants themselves, but will encourage their membership to support charity. This can be by adopting a particular appeal – such as literacy or health education. Or it can be by inviting different charities to address their lunches or dinners – when you have the opportunity to talk about your work and to circulate information about what you are doing and your need for support. So find out what organisations exist in your locality, make contact and suggest that you be invited to address them. Many organisations have been able to develop significant support from this source.

3. Religious bodies. A wide range of church, temple and mosque bodies give to charity. Many local congregations decide to allocate an annual collection to a particular cause – and that cause certainly does not need to be religious in nature. Groups within congregations often meet to explore particular themes and this will lead to them becoming interested in homelessness or poverty, and needing to find some way of developing that interest through practical action or giving. On a higher level, all religious bodies have governing boards who are interested in matters of social responsibility. Religious bodies also have extensive international networks that can be very useful in winning support from overseas sources – including the support of overseas congregations and from overseas foundations (including foundations set up by that particular denomination).

4. Embassies. Many embassies have small grants budgets to create goodwill, but also to create opportunities for their Ambassador or other senior diplomats to meet and greet people. This is in addition to any aid budget from that country.

5. Schools. Although schools will often be concerned to raise money for their own work, some will be interested in getting their pupils involved in charity – either as part of developing a sense of 'citizenship' or linked to their education in some way (for example, conservation charities have a natural link to geography).

If you can find or develop links between what you are doing and one of these bodies, then they can be a possible target for your fundraising effort. There are no clear statistics for the giving from any of these organisations, and their scale of giving is always going to be much less than from other sources. However, they do give you the opportunity to 'reach out' to other audiences. Raising money from schools and young people is covered in *Section 6.9*.

Rotary International

This is a worldwide organisation of businessmen and professionals who unite to provide humanitarian service, and build peace and goodwill. It has the following programmes:
- The Rotary Foundation to promote international understanding, grant education awards and sponsor international projects.
- The 3H Programme (health, hunger and humanity) supports immunisation and polio eradication.
- A youth exchange programme for secondary age children and ROVE, an overseas vocational exchange programme for people aged 18 to 25.

International Association of Lions Clubs

This is the global organisation for Lions Club members. The Lions Club International Foundation supports disaster relief including reconstruction of schools, hospitals and other institutions, vocational assistance and training, and projects that assist blind and deaf people – including glaucoma screening clinics, eye banks, rehabilitation institutes, auditory equipment for deaf people.

Tourism and tourists

For many countries, tourism represents an extremely important contributor to the national economy. And because of the structure of the international currency exchange system, the tourist pound or dollar can often go an extremely long way – so that what appears to be a modest sum of money to the tourist can have an enormous impact on your organisation. Some tourists are on tightly organised schedules and never stray from their group. Whilst others are more adventurous and may well be tempted to share in some interesting experience which you can devise for them. And then there are people who are already interested in what you are doing and make a point of visiting you – here you have a special opportunity to engage their support. Here are some ideas:

Visitors to your project. These can be people passing through who have heard about your work, or people coming on a tour organised by a donor agency for its committed supporters to see some of the projects they are helping. You have a chance here to show them your work, to engage their interest, and perhaps to get them to support you. They are clearly interested.

Attracting tourists to come and see you by arranging events and activities at your project (with transport laid on if required). Many tourists would like to do something 'out of the ordinary' during their stay which brings them closer to the life of the country they are visiting. Visiting local craftsmen at work (and perhaps buying some of what they are producing), seeing a rural development project, being shown round a museum with a talk from an expert. The opportunities are endless! What you can do is to arrange to have a display panel about your organisation and its work in local hotels, together with advance notice of events and activities you are organising.

You might even try to be extremely inventive by designing special events such as a cycle tour of the city, or a visit to see parliament in action, even where this bears little or no relation to your work – you will be doing something interesting that tourists want to participate in, and this will give you the opportunity to explain your work and to gain their interest.

Getting visitors to support your work

ACCORD is a tribal development project in South India supported by ActionAid. It runs a hospital and a community health service as part of its work. This is supported in part by an insurance scheme where families pay a small monthly contribution. It aims to be as self-sufficient as it can. But there is always a need for money to cover running costs, to purchase equipment or for new developments. ACCORD receives a steady stream of overseas visitors. They have developed a sponsorship scheme, whereby a visitor can sponsor the hospital and health work for one day at a cost of US$50. They will then write to you and tell you what happened on that day – what they were able to achieve with your money. How many babies were born, what operations took place, what lives were saved, etc.

Cold Comfort Farm played an important role in the struggle for independence in Zimbabwe. It is now the home of various craft projects including the Weya Women painters, and weavers, woodworkers and metalworkers. It is located some 10km outside Harare. Craft projects have a special opportunity, because visitors to the project often want to purchase something, which can be used to boost sales. Getting into the guidebooks (particularly the 'Rough Guide', the 'Lonely Planet' and the 'Spectrum Guide') and having displays at hotels encourages people to visit.

Attracting tourists in and exploiting tourism

The CAMPFIRE Association in Zimbabwe stands for the Communal Areas Management Programme For Indigenous Resources. Its aim is to use tourism and tourist income for the benefit of rural people and for rural development. Sunungukai Camp is the first eco-tourist project under the CAMPFIRE scheme started in 1994. Local people first identified the area's potential to host international tourists – it is next to a national park and in a lush and beautiful river valley. The camp takes in visitors who live in rondavels (traditional huts) and see the life of the village. They may meet a traditional healer, see local craftsmen at work, be shown round the village school, talk to a local smallholder about the state of agriculture, or participate in a church service. Although it is self-catering, tourists also purchase cooked food or fruit and vegetables from locals, thereby increasing their cash income. And they may hire guides for walks along the river valley or to tackle mountain trails or to see rock paintings. The project is owned collectively by the villagers who receive a dividend based on profits from the venture.

Returned volunteers

Many organisations have foreign volunteers working with them for a summer, for a year, or for a longer period. When these volunteers return home, they can be extremely helpful to you in your fundraising. They are already enthusiastic about your work, so your job is to build on that enthusiasm. You can do a number of things:

- Suggest that they **form a local support group** of interested people back home, who will fundraise for you. Give them a project to raise money for (or several projects). You will be surprised by how much money they can raise, and they will be surprised at how much you can do with it. A direct link between donor and project is a far more efficient way of raising money than working through an established aid agency (with its attendant overheads). Give them projects to fundraise for which have some real long-term benefit to the development of the community, which involve improving the lives of people, and where the results are obvious for all to see (for example providing a well or building a new classroom). You will need to keep in regular contact, so that they can see how your work is developing. They will need literature, which you could provide or which they could have printed. A set of photographs, or in today's world a short video, will also be extremely useful in helping gather support. You may find that a number of 'supporters' come to visit you or even volunteer to work with you.
- If they are going back to paid employment, they might like to make **a regular and substantial financial contribution** to your work. They may not have thought of that. So discuss the possibility with them before they leave.
- They may be able to **help you access sources of money** in their country, particularly from foundations. If you were to write to the foundation, you would almost certainly get rejected – not because your project is no good, but because they have no way of assessing your application from such a distance. If they write, then that provides a point of reference.
- They may be able to **link you with other organisations** – for example a school in their country which can adopt your project and fundraise for it; or a voluntary organisation which has just the expertise you need.

> **Creating a link between two communities**
>
> The Marlborough Brandt Group (named after Willi Brandt who produced a report on North-South issues) is based in a small town in England. The town through the group has 'adopted' a town in The Gambia. This involves a range of activities linking the two places and peoples, including: sponsoring students to train in England, fundraising, development education projects involving schools in both countries, sale of craft items made, etc.

Non-resident communities

With increasing globalisation in business, and as people travel through economic or political migration, and to seek out educational opportunities, there are more and more non-resident communities abroad. Whether it is the British or Indian expatriate community in Saudi Arabia or non-resident Indians in the United States (these are now so numerous that they are referred to as NRIs), or refugees in Germany from Sarajevo, they retain strong family links with their home country and culture. They represent an obvious fundraising source for charitable and development and relief work being done in their country of origin.

But how do you reach them, and what do you ask them to do? Helpage India tried direct mail to mobilise the support of NRIs in the Gulf States. But this did not work well. However CRY, an Indian development agency working with children, includes an appeal with bank statements sent to NRIs abroad who hold rupee accounts with selected Indian banks. This seems to bring good returns.

There are two possible approaches to consider. The first is general publicity to get your cause known to the non-resident community at large. The second is to find an individual who is interested and wants to help by organising the fundraising for you locally. Here are some ideas to consider:

- **Contact the Embassy** for details of business and community groupings, wives associations etc.
- **Use personal and family contacts**. It is surprising who you can get access to if you think about it or ask your friends. Many people when approached to do something useful surprisingly are keen to do it! So ask.
- **Go through your files and visitor book** to see if there are any addresses of people you can contact. if there are quite a lot, then you could even try to arrange a meeting for them to hear about your latest work and your plans for the future.
- **Undertake a preparatory visit** – not to raise money, but to make contacts and to see if you can find people prepared to help you. Bring along plenty of explanatory brochures, even a short video showing your work. Give a contact point so that people can get back in touch with you if they are interested. Follow up on every lead. Be persistent.
- **Organise cultural evenings** or similar events. Many non-residents are homesick and would welcome New year's parties or Diwali evenings when they could get together.
- **Get coverage in the émigré press**. There will often be newsletters or newspapers circulating that keep people in touch (with one another and with what's going on at home). Try to get your work covered in these, or write a letter asking if anyone is interested in helping start your fundraising initiative.
- **Publicise your work in the local press**, focusing on a local person who is doing something significant to help you.

5. Income generation

The arguments for income generation are in many ways the same as the arguments for fundraising:
- A question of **survival** (in an era when foreign donor funds are becoming less available, especially for smaller organisations).
- To **generate funds** for expansion and development.
- To **reduce dependency** on external aid and major grant sources.
- To **build a constituency** of support in your local community.
- To help create a **viable and sustainable organisation**.

Income generation means developing or participating in some form of commercial enterprise, with the intention of making a profit. The profits are then used to support the main work of the organisation. Put like that it sounds a simple and logical thing to do – and, in the right hands, and under the right management, it can be so. But the experience of many organisations suggests that successful income generation is more difficult than it seems, and that a lot of thought and preparation needs to be put into such an idea before the idea is put into practice.

If it was that simple to make money (for yourself – or for your organisation) then a lot more people would be doing so. It is quite possible for your organisation to become involved in an enterprise which not only makes no profit, but which becomes a drain on its resources and siphons off management and staff time which would otherwise be spent on the work of the organisation. This leads us to perhaps the most important warning for anyone thinking of developing a commercial activity: the enterprise is only a means of earning money for an end – which is to support the mission or main purpose of the organisation. If the enterprise becomes too demanding in time and resources, and if the income it generates is relatively small or non-existent, then stop.

Mixing up the mission in Ethiopia

An Ethiopian organisation which operated a rescue centre and hostel for street kids in Addis Ababa was always chronically under-funded, and living from month to month on donations and occasional project funding. A development agency offered it the chance to buy a small potato crisp manufacturing business with the intention that the organisation would run the enterprise as a business using the street kids as both employees, and as street peddlers of the packets of potato crisps. The organisation bought the business, and started the manufacturing cycle of buying potatoes, preparing them, cooking them, bagging them, and selling them. The management had never done anything like this before, and soon found themselves out of their depth in matters of quality control, health regulations, equipment breakdowns, and under-capitalisation. One of the organisation's main strategies with street kids was to try and get them into regular schooling, and this contrasted strongly with the idea of them selling packets of potato crisps on the street, even if they were good at doing this. The organisation's management spent more and more time trying to make a profit on the potato crisps and less and less time on looking after the street kids, to the detriment of both activities.

Keeping a clear mission in Indonesia

Yayasan Bina Swadaya in Indonesia is an organisation specialising in improving the lives of small farmers and fishermen through savings, credit, and the formation of cooperatives. Its early work was to encourage rural poor farmers to save their money and take out credit to expand their self-employment possibilities. The Yayasan (which means Association) charged a service fee for the credit which went some way to paying for the costs of the credit scheme. The Yayasan found that many of its customers wanted to raise chickens but that obtaining day old chicks was a real problem. It therefore went into the business of hatching and producing day old chicks and selling them, making a small profit, to its customers. It found that other people, apart from its target group, also wanted this service and so it also started to sell day old chicks in the marketplace. It started a small extension newspaper for its target group on improving farming practices, and found that this newspaper filled a need for a farmers magazine that existed beyond its immediate target group. It also geared up its production for the market place. It then found that its skills in and experience of running its original credit and savings program was at a premium for other development agencies, and that other organisations wanted to know how this could be done. The Yayasan started a consultancy service, offering its senior employees for short term hire to other development agencies. Everything it did to make money was a spin off from its original mission, based on skills developed in the course of activities connected to that mission.

There are a huge variety of enterprises that an organisation can become involved in, ranging from running hotels, through to selling handicrafts. Let us look first at the different kinds of enterprise that are possible, and the risks and opportunities involved in each.

5.1 The opportunities – different types of income generation activity

Supporting community economic development

This involves developing an income generating activity which is designed to improve the lives of people.

Let us imagine that the NGO's mission is to increase people's income by developing profitable avenues for self-employment. The NGO helps people start up an activity making something for which there is a local demand (e.g. baskets, farm tools, soap, or clothes) or for which there is an overseas or big city demand (e.g. craft items, or specialised foodstuffs). The organisation provides the credit and technical training, and advises on quality control and marketing, so enabling people to sell their products at a reasonable price and thereby make a better income for themselves.

If the NGO provides this help through a project which is funded from external sources, its ability to continue providing help depends on obtaining renewed grants from such sources. If, on the other hand, it charges a service fee on the goods that are sold, this then creates an income for the NGO, which will allow it to continue supporting the project on a continuing basis – and possibly also to accumulate reserves which it can use for other developmental purposes. The example of CORR -The Jute Works in Bangladesh illustrates how this can be done.

A very valuable aspect of this approach is that the enterprise acts as a reality check for the organisation. If the advice and the support it is giving is good, then the enterprise succeeds and the NGO succeeds. If it is bad or inappropriate, the enterprise fails and the NGO fails too.

Building income together in Bangladesh

CORR -The Jute Works started life in Bangladesh after the war of Independence in 1972 to offer some way of providing income to the large numbers of widows in the aftermath of the war. It capitalised on the local crop, jute, and the skills of village women in making pot holders (thika) from the jute fibre – a skill that was purely functional in the village context where such hanging pot holders were an essential part of handling liquids. CORR -The Jute Works saw an export market possibility in this skill, by buying the thika from the women for sale overseas as decorative plant pot holders. It arranged the women in groups and gave them training in new products and techniques, bought their output, and placed it overseas through alternative marketing organisations and a mail order catalogue. The sales of the craft work were divided: part of the income went back as a dividend to the producers (and this was used by the women's groups for a variety of useful activities like improved water supplies, or tree planting): part went to pay for the administrative costs of CORR -The Jute Works, and part was put into a reserve fund. From time to time, depending on the size of the reserves, CORR -The Jute Works would fund development activities for the women's groups beyond the craft operations – like latrine building. CORR -The Jute Works was living and expanding on the backs of the craft production work of the women, but was doing so in a way which enabled the organisation to be both self-sustaining, and a source of further funds. CORR -The Jute Works has not taken foreign funding since its third year of operations (1975). The most difficult aspect of its operation is keeping up with the buying patterns of the people in the countries to which they export, and feeding these product ideas back to the manufacturers. The enterprise (and the organisation) will only continue if they remain smart entrepreneurs who research the market and produce for it, being prepared to change as the market dictates.

The most important aspects of this kind of enterprise, where the NGO funds itself from a percentage of the income generating programme it has developed for its constituency, are:
- The **choice of products** or services to offer (how many of us have seen storerooms full of unsalable baskets or embroidery?).
- **Adequate working capital** to allow you to build up sales before your reserves run out.
- Close attention to **the customers and their needs**, and flexibility to change/modify product lines as customer preferences change.

- **Good costing**, to make sure that you are selling at a price which covers all the production costs, and possibly generates a surplus to provide further income to expand or develop the work being done.

It is also important that the requirement of the organisation for a sustainable source of income does not force it into the position of paying an exploitative price for the products of its target group so that it can sell them on at a big profit. If that looks to be a possibility, then the whole thing should be abandoned – the basic purpose of the organisation is to help the target group, not help itself.

Charging fees for services

This involves the beneficiaries paying for the services that the NGO is providing (and possibly was previously providing free).

NGOs usually claim to be working with poor people – if not the poorest, at least people with little disposable income. It has been customary in the past to offer such services free, in the belief that poor people could not pay for them. Experience, particularly in the health field however, has shown that even poor people are prepared to pay something, and that the provision of certain services need not always be a net drain on the organisation providing the service.

Where the organisation is offering a service to its constituency which is, in turn creating an income for them, then it seems entirely possible for a fee to be charged: but when the organisation is asking its beneficiary group to pay for a service that is not easily connected to increased income for them – like literacy or health, charging for that service seems, on the face of it, harder to justify. But experience suggests (see the example of PROSALUD) that people who, by definition have little disposable income, are prepared to pay for services if they are good, needed, and provided in a way that is accountable to the customers.

Where the service that is being provided assists income creation, there will usually be little difficulty in charging a fee – the most common example of this is the provision of credit. Here a handling charge or service fee, charged as a cost of providing the credit, can pay the costs of the credit programme. Even where a service charge is levied, the credit-providing organisation will almost certainly be offering a considerably better alternative to the other form of informal credit – the

Service Fee for Credit Programmes

A very large number of development organisations throughout the world operate credit schemes based upon peer group lending (i.e. loans are offered with the collateral of community pressure on the individual to repay rather than physical collateral). Many of these come from the long tradition of credit unions often exported around the world from the credit union movement of Canada. Another inspiration for many new credit operations is the Grameen Trust – the international arm of the Grameen Bank, the famous micro-credit organisation of Bangladesh. In nearly all these programmes, loans are offered to individuals which have to be repaid at the going official bank interest rates for loans of between 15-25% per annum. A further supplement (of perhaps 1%) is added to the interest rate which is the fee for the administration of the credit scheme. A well organised NGO which can keep its costs of managing the credit provision under strict control can cover the costs of the credit operation, and perhaps cover some part of the administrative costs of other parts of its operation from this 1% fee. A large number of loanees, and a simple management system enables such a fee to be an important aspect of the income of the organisation. The rural poor who are the usual target for such credit schemes do not seem to object to the supplementary charge – particularly when it is compared to the usual costs of money lenders of 12-15% per month (i.e. 150% per annum) or even more.

moneylender – and the customer will be quite prepared to pay a small fee to get access to non-exploitative credit.

Where the NGO provides other kinds of services which will lead to an increased income for its client group, again a fee for providing that service could be justified – but in such circumstances, it may not be able to get the fee paid up-front. If, for instance, an organisation offers vocational or entrepreneurship training with the intention that the trained person will then earn a higher income as a consequence of having been trained, then the organisation might charge a deferred fee, to be paid only once the person has achieved an increased income. This is possibly more difficult to collect, but experience from work with disabled people, or from hospitals which have handled rehabilitative operations, suggest that people who have been helped to become productive again are very eager to pay back the costs of the operation, but over a period of time.

The situation is more difficult where the NGO is thinking of charging a fee for services that do not result in an improved income for the beneficiaries, or that do so only indirectly. There is a lot of interest in cost recovery and selling of services amongst NGOs now, as donors and NGOs alike take on a more market-oriented philosophy.

The push towards cost recovery or charging fees for services provided comes from two directions: the first is pragmatism, arguing that services which are paid for are more valued, and that therefore it is more effective to demand some payment for services provided to the poor because they will value them more and use them more effectively. The second is more political, and assumes that the previous practice of offering free services came from a now discredited socialist perspective, and that payment for services should be the norm. There is a lot of pressure on, for instance, family planning organisations to sell their condoms or other family planning equipment, and for rural clinics to ask out-patients to pay for each visit.

It is true that no-one knows what the market will bear until it is tested, and it is undoubtedly true that the poor are prepared to pay for some services (in education, health, credit particularly) providing that they are good, reliable, at hand and provided by someone who they can hold to account for service failure. The final truth is, however, that the very poor may be prepared to pay, but they cannot pay very much – and so are not very likely to be able to contribute the full costs of the service. Again there is a possible clash between the need to generate an income to help pay for the service and the mission to help the poor and disadvantaged, who are only able to contribute up to the limit of their ability to pay. Some organisations make payment for services the norm, but offer the service free to a certain proportion (perhaps 10%) of their clientele.

Paying their way – but making allowances for the poor

In Zambia, the Government health services have introduced a fee paying structure since 1993 which contrasts greatly with the free services that the population received previously. Many countries under World Bank Structural Adjustment Programmes have faced the same kind of reorganisation. The Zambian NGOs in the health field have, for the most part, gone along with the new policy since they need the income just as the Government does. The Churches Mission Association of Zambia, for instance, which coordinates nearly all the health facilities run by religious organisations, has set up a fee paying system in its hospitals and clinics. Just like the Government, however, they have recognised that not everyone who needs the services can afford to pay for them, and so has developed a list of people who are not required to pay. These are pregnant women, children under 5, emergency accidents, and those classified as indigent by the Department of Social Welfare. At the margin, however, it is difficult to know how many people who need medical attention, but cannot afford the fees, are not attending a clinic or are doing so by forsaking expenditure on other important needs – like food, or schooling.

One advantage of charging fees for services is that it will soon become clear to the NGO which of its services people are prepared to pay for, and which they are not. The forces of the market place may well show the NGO that poor people are prepared to pay for health insurance, for instance, but not for literacy classes. Such market feedback is very valuable as many NGOs continue to deliver services for years without rigorous evaluation of their effectiveness and impact.

Self-Financing Health Services in Bolivia

PROSALUD's objective is to function without outside support, recovering its costs from the sale of health services and products. In the health sector, recovering costs by charging fees for health services delivered to low-income families is often considered impossible. Charging fees that are high enough to cover the costs of services appears to discriminate against the very poor, who live on the edge of subsistence and often have no money on hand to pay for services or goods of any kind.

This conventional wisdom, however, seems to be belied by the PROSALUD experience in Bolivia. PROSALUD already has a growing system of health facilities in operation that are self-financing through the fees it charges. Clients are predominantly low-income families. Services include free preventative health care and child survival interventions. Curative services are provided free of charge to families that cannot pay (between 8 and 13% of PROSALUD's patients). PROSALUD has conclusively demonstrated the feasibility of self-financing primary health care services, even in a country as poor as Bolivia.

Any NGO seeking to charge fees for a service should recognise the difficulties that poor people have in paying for anything in cash, even when they accept the principle that the service should be paid for. NGOs should be prepared to take payment in kind (chickens, firewood, grain, for example) and turn this into money itself, or use the item for its own purposes (thereby saving itself the cost of having to buy it).

Spin-off activity that exploits skills and expertise

This involves specialist skills and expertise of the NGO being marketed at a profit to others who are not its beneficiaries.

It is quite possible that richer people or other organisations are prepared to pay for the kind of services that the NGO is offering to poorer people. It is also possible that the NGO, by a smart examination of commercial possibilities, can see ways in which its own skills and equipment can be packaged in a different way to provide a product or a service that can generate an income. In some cases, this activity will contribute to the mission of the organisation, but in a different way. In other cases, it will be simply an enterprising way to raise money.

Alternative Tourism

The usual kind of tourist is one who craves basic creature comforts familiar back home, but likes them packaged in an exotic setting. They are often unaware of the actual environment in which they spend their holidays since what they see and experience is decided for them by hotels and tour operators. There is, however, a small but increasing number of tourists for whom a visit to a foreign country is an 'alternative' opportunity to learn more about that country, including the reality of life 'behind the scenes'.

Basically there are two kinds of NGOs who have appreciated that they have special knowledge and experiences which are marketable and can earn money – those who offer tourists an introduction to the realities of life in a particular country – and can organise exposure tours to villages and aspects of rural and urban life that other tourists would miss (these are offered in India and Thailand, for instance): and NGOs who are involved in environmental matters who offer eco-tourism, that is specialised visits to places of particular environmental interest often combined with exposure to particular environmental problems (these are offered in Nepal and Madagascar, for instance). As with much tourism, the ethical problems arise not as a matter of principle, but when the numbers involved escalate. It is difficult for the most sensitive and committed tour guide to bring the 500th tourist to look at the misery of the rubbish mountain pickers of Bangkok, as it is difficult to preserve the wilderness conditions required for the interesting biological diversity in Madagascar under the visits of very many tourists, however pure the motives of the tour organiser.

An NGO which works in agriculture, for instance, and whose usual work is agricultural research and the application of that research to increase the crop yields for landless and marginal farmers, may well find that it is the only organisation in the vicinity which has the knowledge and equipment for soil testing, or that it is the only local organisation with agricultural machinery repair facilities. If the NGO is looking for a way to earn an income for itself, it needs to look at its resource base, and see who might be interested to pay for its services, either as they are, or with some modification. Larger farmers might be prepared to pay for soil testing, for instance, and smaller farmers for machinery repair. It also needs to look at what it charges for its commercial work to ensure that it is generating sufficient funds to make the activity worthwhile. A problem, and this is true for all income generation, is that the income generating activity may start to assume an unbalanced importance in the work of the NGO – to the detriment of the work that it was originally formed to do.

If it works for us, it may well work for you

PACT, a US NGO, has a health insurance plan for its employees, as do many other US NGOs. The particular health plan is a good one and very well run. PACT found that other US NGOs were asking it for advice on running their own health plan, and were very receptive to PACT offering to include their organisation into the PACT health plan. Soon PACT was earning a modest but important income from providing health insurance facilities for a number of other US NGOs. It knew how to do it, it could relatively easily scale up, it had a number of interested potential customers, and it could do the work without undermining its services to its own employees.

Sideline income generation – doing anything to make money

This involves the NGO looking for a money-making enterprise that has no link at all with its own work.

Where an organisation has a pressing need to develop some income of its own, the idea that it might be possible to develop a secure and substantial source of independent income from a business activity seems like a fantasy. But it is possible, and there are some real-life examples of how this might be done. One which is quite common is for the organisation to raise the money to buy a property, which is often used as its office, but also with enough space to rent out office space to other organisations or to provide conference and meeting rooms which can generate an income for the organisation.

Another type of enterprise which an organisation might seek to develop (or to have a share of) will relate to the local economy, local benefactors (who may give goods in kind), and local entrepreneurial flair. An NGO in Bangladesh, BRAC, owns a garment factory making garments for export, a cold storage plant for potatoes, and a printing press. An NGO in Zimbabwe, ORAP, owns part of a factory making batteries. And an NGO in Sri Lanka, Sarvodaya, owns a motor vehicle repair garage.

The whole point of doing this is for the organisation to make money to fund the work it was set up to do. To make a handsome profit (or even any profit at all) requires a person with experience and flair to run the business – and such people are rare in the world of NGOs. A second point is that while the idea is very attractive, and finance for such a venture may be possible (though not always easy), many such ideas founder upon the difficulties of identifying a business enterprise that is likely to continue to make money into the future. Another difficulty comes from the need to separate the management of the enterprise from the management of the NGO. A third problem is the old one that bedevils all enterprise activities of NGOs – the potential clash with the vision and mission of the organisation, and the possibility of the enterprise becoming more important than the NGO which created it.

> **The bus company that failed**
>
> Proshika, a large NGO in Bangladesh, was helped to buy a bus company which it intended to run as an income generating enterprise. No-one in Proshika had ever managed a bus company before, and the inter-city bus business in Bangladesh is not only very competitive, it is also pretty lawless as businesses try and capture passengers from each other. Proshika soon got bogged down in problems of maintenance, ticket collection, cash flow problems, and in the end found that it was taking much too much of the senior management's time – time that should have been spent on the economic and social development work that Proshika was set up to do. Added to which the business itself was not making much money – certainly not enough money to justify the management time that was being spent on it. Proshika very sensibly divested itself of its bus company and stuck to what it was good at. It is now generating income for itself from a service fee on its large credit programme, and by renting out a spare floor in its own office block.

Joint ventures with business

This involves the NGO setting up in partnership with a commercial concern to develop an activity which is beneficial to both parties.

It is quite possible to find a commercially-run business whose business activity has some relevance to development problems, but who have not yet recognised how they might do something. In such contexts, it is possible to suggest ways in which the business can reach a new market for its products, or save costs, or benefit from the NGO's particular experience and expertise – and which at the same time can be beneficial to the NGO, and through the NGO to the poor people it is there to serve.

Such ideas require a difficult balance of idealism and pragmatism, creative vision and practical hard work. A business can be asked to collaborate at many different levels – for example, a book publisher might collaborate on a joint publication right through to working with the NGO on a complete literacy programme. The opportunities for business-NGO partnerships will depend on particular circumstances, but here are some possibilities:

- Publishers of books might to be interested in literacy projects,
- Manufacturers of farming machinery might be interested in agricultural projects,
- Banks might be interested in micro-enterprise or small scale entrepreneurship projects,
- Drug companies might be interested in medical and health projects.

A bit of creative thinking will suggest more possibilities. The well-known firm, Body Shop International, for instance, makes its money from a variety of beauty and skin care preparations made from natural, often exotic plant products. It is definitely interested in environmental projects which are concerned with protecting bio-diversity, and discouraging loss of habitat.

There is another advantage in working with the business world, which is of strategic importance. By collaborating with business, NGOs become better known to other businesses and to government, and their contribution to development then can become better recognised.

Blocked funds and debt swaps

This involves the NGO taking advantage of a country's currency restrictions or debt repayment problems to increase the amount of funds for its development programme.

In many Southern countries there have been restrictions on currency movements. Companies which earn profits in the local currency have found themselves unable to return any or all of that profit to headquarters, or were required to hold some of their funds in a special blocked account. Such a situation can provide an opportunity for an NGO wishing to remit funds raised in hard currency for spending locally. The NGO could, for example, enter into an agreement with a company to purchase the company's local funds with hard currency at a very considerable discount on the official exchange rate, or to persuade the Ministry of Finance to allow blocked funds to be spent on development projects (with the added possibility that the company might be able to obtain a tax credit on this charitable expenditure in its home country). Just as many NGOs were beginning to recognise these possibilities, Structural Adjustment Programmes and trade liberalisation were beginning to create more open economies and convertible local currencies – which will reduce or completely remove these opportunities.

One way of mobilising very large sums of money which might then be used to create an endowment is through a debt swap. Here hard currency can be used to purchase, at a discount, the debt of a country with a large debt problem – and the debt is then cancelled in return for the money being spent in that country for development. This enables the organisation to get funds in local currency worth much more than making a purchase at the official exchange rate. It is a complicated way of generating income, but has been done a number of times now, and there are guidelines and suggestions about how to do it. It has been particularly used by environmental NGOs.

Sustainable attention to the environment – the Philippines Foundation for the Environment

This Foundation, registered in 1991 with the Philippines Securities and Exchange Commission, is intended to be a grant making organisation to provide support to Philippine NGOs and other groups tackling conservation and sustainable development challenges in the Philippines.

It arose from the success of a 'debt for nature' swap between one Philippine NGO – The Haribon Society – and USAID in 1988. USAID agreed with a wide coalition of Philippines NGOs and a US NGO, World Wildlife Fund USA, to fund a further 'debt for nature' swap which eventually led to a fund of approximately US$ 10.2 million worth of Philippines pesos. The Foundation's trustees are from NGO coalitions, NGOs, the Church, the business community, USAID, and the Government of the Philippines.

The Foundation is a tax-exempt institution, and invests its funds by agreement with the Philippines Government in Central Bank Notes with interest similar to Philippines Treasury Bills which provides interest at approximately 15%. Its special fields of work are: conservation of biological diversity, community based resource management, institutional support and training. One problem that it has faced is to develop a consensus for the Foundation amongst NGOs throughout the Philippines.

5.2 Problems and issues

The need for an entrepreneurial approach

The reliance for so long on grants has discouraged an entrepreneurial approach amongst NGOs (except for the honing of skills in how to approach donors and package proposals for them). A very definite change in approach and change in perception is needed by leaders of NGOs if they are going to consider seriously the variety of possible income generating possibilities. In many cases it will involve re-examining prejudices and entrenched beliefs; it will usually mean thinking like a business person looking for investment opportunities – and this is not something which many NGO leaders have experience of. The background of most NGO leaders is politics, social work, academia – very rarely business.

NGOs have usually been run by budgeting their expenditure against available funding – the idea of a revenue budget with targets for income to be generated is often a foreign concept. The idea of using marketing and selling techniques to generate an income (rather than fundraising) and of investment (spending money now to produce a return later on) will need new skills and new approaches. Before an organisation gets serious about generating income, it may need a complete overhaul of attitudes and preconceptions and a new look at its vision, mission, and strategy. This is not without risk. Organisations may find that this entrepreneurial, opportunistic kind of thinking, and the subsequent changes of attitudes that this engenders may drive out some staff who are not prepared to accept it.

A conviction that income generation is important, and better donor packaging is not enough

Donor manipulation, donor packaging, donor managing has become a learned skill with many fundraisers, and a fall off in donor funds is often met by increasingly desperate attempts to discover and exploit previously unexplored donor territory, or to agree to increasingly onerous donor requirements.

It will be a hard step for many organisations to be convinced of the value of moving towards a greater financial self-reliance. The decision to do so must not simply be one of seeking alternative sources of funds, but must be accompanied by an analysis and acceptance of the political and social implications of being dependent versus the implications of being independent.

Looking for and developing alternative sources of financing can be very difficult, and it is easy to slip back into previous attitudes. A decision to travel this road, however, has to be a serious one, arrived at after serious consideration of all the options, and with a clear understanding of the organisational changes that will be required. It is often a good idea to undertake a serious strategic planning exercise before starting into alternative financing.

Losing the vision

NGOs and voluntary organisations are driven by a shared vision of a better society. The work that they do, for the most part, reinforces that vision. The health outreach, the credit scheme, the literacy programme, for example, bring project workers into touch with their client group – the poor – and reinforces their motivation to continue doing the work. When the main purpose becomes making money (albeit that the money made will be used for the work of the organisation), a new set of attitudes starts creeping in; and many organisations become concerned that they will lose their internal cohesion which comes from a shared vision of a better and less exploitative society.

Some organisations become so concerned about this that they would prefer to separate out the income generation from the rest of the work of the organisation, recognising that two different personality types are likely to be attracted, and that one will tend to 'infect' the other to the detriment of the organisation as a whole. This also takes account of the fact that a different kind of staff will need to be hired if the organisation is serious about developing the income generation activity. Reward systems are likely to be different, and salary structure with incentives and benefits are likely to evolve differently.

Tax and law

NGOs work within the legal context of the countries in which they are registered. The laws usually define non-profit agencies differently from for-profit agencies and few countries have clarified the legal position of an entity which makes a profit in order not to enrich its stockholders, but in order to benefit its client group – the poor. The law is for the most part not helpful, and the lack of a clear legal identity and legal guidelines make many NGOs scared of getting into organisational income generation in case they are accused of breaking the law, or in case they are taxed to such an extent that they do not make enough income to warrant the work expended, or in case they lose their tax privileges on donated income.

The legal status of a non-profit company and a charitable foundation exist in most countries of the South – and with this comes the possibility of tax relief on locally donated income and on profits earned from income generation which are applied for a developmental or charitable purpose. But in no country is the path for income generation well used and smooth.

Worries about becoming an exploiter

Many NGOs are chary of getting into business enterprises because the models of business practices that they observe in their own countries have persuaded them that exploitation of the workforce in order to satisfy the greed of the owners is the norm. They are therefore very worried that they will have to behave in a similar way to make the profits that they desire, and that they will become part of society's problems, rather than part of the solutions to those problems. The idea that an NGO can become not only a fair employer, but also a successful and profitable entrepreneur is a mighty challenge, but one that some NGOs are wary of taking up.

Furthermore many NGOs are sensitive to accusations brought against them of being disguised profit making, self-aggrandising organisations, and want to have a clear public relations strategy before walking into what many would see as a minefield.

Politically there is a lot of confused thinking. Governments (even those who like the work of NGOs) recognise the value of decreasing dependence on grant aid, but worry that NGOs which have their own sources of funds will not be controllable in the same way as they are when the receipt of government grants controls what an NGO does or the receipt of foreign funds is subject to a government approval mechanism. Governments who do not like NGOs will find many ways of accusing NGOs who are trying to become financially self-reliant of being a new class of exploiters.

Anti-business feeling

Profit making has been in the past a dirty phrase with many people of a leftist persuasion, and many NGO staffers have come from such an ideological background. Models of fair, honest, and just entrepreneurs who have contributed to society by transforming raw materials into publicly available goods, and in the process have not exploited their workers, damaged the environment, broken or evaded the law, or suborned public officials are few and far between. As a result of this many NGOs have had little contact with business people, and distrust has built up and fed on itself.

The increasingly pervasive ideology of the market place and privatisation has eroded some of these attitudes, but they are still strong with many NGOs. As the useful book *'Filthy Rich – and other non-profit fantasies'* puts it: *"Traditional non-profits are distrustful of money. Many of them disagree with the traditional 'bottom-line' thinking of the for-profit world. They fear that if concerned with money they will lose their social goals. They fear money will pollute their mission. They fear they will lose their non-profit virginity."*

These attitudes apply equally to mounting a fund raising event to coax money from the rich, to running a business venture to create money, to investing endowment funds in a bank which will then on lend to others. Closer acquaintance with well-managed businesses may help dispel these attitudes.

What percentage of financial autonomy?

If and when organisations do some serious research into the income generation strategies that are available to them, they are frequently dismayed by the small quantity of income they are likely to get for the amount of time and effort invested. Complete financial autonomy seems an impossible dream at the levels of expenditure to which they have become accustomed. There are two observations on this:

1. The availability of large amounts of external grant aid has, in many cases, accustomed NGOs to a life style and programme and management practices that are out of keeping with any sort of cost-effectiveness, and completely different from the approaches that comparably sized but locally funded organisations have to adopt. If grant aid became harder to get, and if the available income had to be hard won from local fundraising and income generation ventures, the NGO might be forced to adopt a simpler and less expensive method of operation. One response to worries about how to raise sufficient funds is to reduce the level of expenditure – and, therefore, the quantity of funds that need to be raised.

This has implications for levels of administrative and overhead costs, but also for the way that the organisation designs and carries out its programmes. If funds are relatively freely available, there is tendency to subsidise projects, give away money and avoid the hard logic of sustainability. If funds have to be earned, then there is more attention paid to cost recovery, to sustainable methods of working, and to cost effectiveness. An organisational commitment to financial autonomy (as was mentioned before in connection with 'Losing the Vision') is likely to lead towards a serious reappraisal within the organisation about its work and operating style.

2. Many organisations approach income generation with a desire first and foremost to diminish their dependence on external financing, and to give themselves some more control over their expenditure than is possible in the donor aid and project dominated world of the present. They are happy to apply for and receive external funds provided that they are not dependent for their survival on this method of funding. A good case can be made for saying that an NGO should generate sufficient funds to cover its basic operating costs from indigenous sources, but use donor aid for investment and project development costs.

Funding agencies exist, and look likely to continue to exist, and they have money to spend. Their job is to spend their money to promote the development of the poor. A small organisation may be aware that the amount of funds available may diminish, and that the organisation will function better if it is integrated into the local economy and into civil society, and if it is able to decide on staffing levels and long-term development plans without reference to donor pressures. Such an organisation does not see receipt of funds from external sources as being a problem – providing this is done on acceptable terms.

5.3 Getting started

Sources of capital for the enterprise

The most important step in getting started in income generation is making the decision to do so. Trying to generate your own income for your organisation is likely to be very different from your usual methods of fundraising from donors – either domestic or foreign. It is very important therefore that your organisation has thought the idea through, and has decided that it is going to put its energies and resources into generating its own income. But once this decision has been made, where can you find the money which will help you make the money?

From goods in kind

Do not always think in terms of money – organisations can generate income from goods in kind (land, buildings, equipment), or from financial instruments (shares, deposits, stocks). If you can find someone who is willing to give you some capital in kind, consider what you might be able to do to make use of it so that it can bring a sustainable income into your organisation. Not all of us will be so lucky as the Institute for Cultural Affairs in the USA who were given an empty skyscraper in Chicago by a benefactor, but it is possible that your organisation could be given land or buildings or used equipment which could be put to use to earn income.

From borrowing, renting or use

Do not always think in terms of owning capital in order to make organisational income. It is equally possible to borrow, rent, or get user rights to capital goods. A small primary health care organisation in India applied to the Waste Lands Board for the use of a piece of wasteland to plant with fast growing fuel wood trees. Once the trees were mature, the NGO harvested fuel wood cuttings from the trees, sold the firewood, and paid their health care workers salaries from the proceeds. Other banking institutions in the South are eager to provide credit to the poor – they are often very interested in lending money to NGOs so that the NGO can on-lend the money (with a service fee) to the poor. There are often a number of schemes intended to help small or medium scale industry to start in the South, including soft loan terms – let the NGO apply for these along with the private entrepreneurs.

From savings

If you are thinking in terms of acquiring money in order to make other money, then consider how you can build up your own capital fund from a variety of small enterprises until you have reached a sufficient amount of capital for you to invest in an enterprise. This process is very well explained in IRED's book 'Towards Financial Autonomy – a manual on financing strategies and techniques for Development NGOs and Community Organisations'. They suggest that a capital fund can be built up from:

- Local fundraising (subscriptions, collections, contracts, etc.).
- Self-financing (memberships, sales of products and services, investments, etc.).
- Creative use of external funds (renewal funds, general reserves, exchange rate changes, etc.).

From grants

The thinking of donors, especially external donors, has become astonishingly conditioned to the idea of 'projects' (i.e. time-limited agreements whereby money is given to an organisation to enable that organisation to deliver certain specified goods and/or services to certain specified people). This is based on the concept that the donor is 'contracting' the NGO to do the donor's work for it. If pressed, many donors will proclaim their belief in the validity and value of an NGO sector, and the importance of having citizen's organisations as part of good governance and a civil society – but very few of them have followed the logic through to the extent that they are prepared to 'invest' in a sustainable NGO sector, rather than just covering the costs of discrete time-limited projects delivered by a specific NGO.

The donor's usual expectation is that, once the funding for a particular project is finished, the organisation will find funding from somewhere else for another project. Very few have conceptualised and designed instruments whereby they will fund the institutional self-reliance of the organisation, which includes, most importantly, its financial self-reliance.

Donors need to be educated about the importance of this approach. Here and there one can find examples – at one extreme, CIDA in Bangladesh was prepared to give funds to small organisations so that they could buy small businesses like rickshaws and ferry boats as a way to cover their administrative costs. At the other end of the spectrum, USAID in many countries of Latin America has been prepared to buy a lot of external debt for environmental organisations to be set up in endowments which will allow them to operate from the income on the invested money. Largely, however, donors are driven by a desire to see the greatest possible amount of their funds go to the final beneficiaries, rather than go to build up the organisations which will, in the long run, be a long term source of support to those same beneficiaries.

Organisations need to start educating their donors about the value of capital grants to provide the investment needed to set themselves up with a source of sustainable income.

Kinds of people and skills needed

Very few NGO leaders and fundraisers have the necessary entrepreneurial approach for successful income generation. Even those who may have had it, have possibly lost it through disuse, as it has become so common simply to look for external grants whenever any money is needed. It is possible that NGOs need to extend their recruiting to people who have come from more of an enterprise culture, to people who have come from the trading and manufacturing traditions in their country, rather than just the social work traditions. Not all businessmen and businesswomen are interested in profits and personal income alone, there are many who are interested in working for a good cause and who share the values and goals of many NGO people for a better society. There are also increasing numbers of western educated MBAs in the South who can combine a business mind with an understanding of the principles of development. NGOs in their recruiting need to expand their horizons – which also means extending and developing their networks of contacts, to include more entrepreneurs and business minded people.

Useful Addresses

IRED
3 Rue de Varembe, P.O. Box 116, 1211 Geneva 20, Switzerland.

This organisation has produced the definitive work on organisational income generation, *'Towards Financial Autonomy – a manual on financing strategies and techniques for Development NGOs and Community Organisations'* and *'Workshop Reports on Alternative Financement for NGOs and People's organisations (Sri Lanka, Philippines, Bangladesh)'*, and has experience of applying income generation mechanisms in many countries of the world. It is linked to RAFAD (see below).

PACT Bangladesh/PRIP
House 56, Road 16, Dhanmondi, Dhaka, Bangladesh.

This office of the US NGO, PACT, has pioneered a lot of material on organisational income generation. It has also published: *'Alternatives to External Donor Funds for South Asian NGOs'*; *'Options for Sustainability – endowments as a modality for funding development work'* (2 vols: Seminar Report and Reader); *'Private Sector Funding of Development in Bangladesh – what possibilities are there?'*; and *'Towards Financial Self-Reliance: an Overview for NGOs, Community Groups, and Donors'*.

Prince of Wales Business Leaders Forum
Partnership Unit, 5 Cleveland Place, London SW1Y 6JJ, UK.

This organisation has pioneered and documented business/NGO partnerships around the world. The following publications may be useful: *'Partners in Action – the business and the voluntary sectors working collaboratively towards sustainable development'*; *'Partnerships for Sustainable Development – the role of business and industry'*; *'Tools for Partnership Building'*; and *'What is Partnership – a collection of essays on the theme of cross-sector partnerships for sustainable development'*.

RAFAD
3 Rue de Varembe, 1211 Geneva 20, Switzerland.

This organisation has pioneered a variety of innovative financing tools for NGOs. See the following publication: *'Financial Engineering for the People's Economy'*.

USAID
Centre for Development Information and Evaluation, Program and Policy Evaluation Division, Bureau for Program and Policy Coordination, Agency for International Development, Washington DC 20523-1802, USA.

USAID has pioneered a lot of useful work in financial self-reliance and organisational income generation for NGOs (and this centre is the place to track it down), including: *'Achieving Financial Self-Reliance – a manual for family planning NGOs'*; *'Endowments as a Tool for Financial Sustainability – a manual for NGOs'*; *'Institutional Mechanisms to raise funds for Indonesian Private Voluntary Organisations'*; and *'Profiles of Sustainability – practical applications in Kenya'*.

6. Techniques

6.1 Setting up a local fundraising group

Whether you are an established national organisation or a small group just starting out, raising money locally through events and collections can be an important source of income.

But organising a fundraising event or collecting money locally requires time and effort. There are two main approaches: using staff to do the work or using volunteers. A lot depends on the budget for the event. Using your own staff will cost a lot more, and only really makes sense for very large events. Using a group of volunteers can make a lot of sense, particularly if there are people with the right abilities and enthusiasm prepared to do the fundraising work for you. They will work largely independently, but you will need to provide proper management to ensure that they operate effectively, and some back up in the form of literature, ideas and advice.

There is another benefit in working this way. The more groups you establish, the more money you will raise. You can establish local fundraising groups in different towns and cities, or in different areas of the same city. Each will be responsible for raising money in 'its patch'. And then there is the possibility of getting a returning volunteer or overseas contact to set up a support group in another country to raise money for your work.

Setting up a local fundraising group takes considerable effort and patience. It can take a long time to get the group established and raising money for your work. But the investment can be worth it. The volunteers you recruit, if properly supported (see *Section 7.1*), could well stay involved with your organisation for many years.

Getting started

To establish local fundraising groups, you need to:

- **Find people** who are willing to put in the time to raise money for you, and in particular:
- **Find someone to lead the group** (as the Chair).
- **Establish the group** with a constitution, which defines how it will work and the relationship with the organisation it is raising money for.
- Help the group identify **appropriate fundraising activities**.
- **Supervise** and support the group in its fundraising work.

Forming a fundraising group

The following story illustrates how you might set about forming a local fundraising group. The key is to follow up on every idea or contact, and to ask persuasively.

Getting a local fundraising group going

My brief was to form a fundraising group in a large city. Where should I start?

My usual way of working is to check my address book and contact my friends for their suggestions. I knew one person in the area who was worth approaching. It was a priest I had known for thirty years. I felt sure that he would set me off in the right direction. I made an appointment to see him.

The meeting gave me a detailed insight into the social needs of the town, and was a fascinating morning. But I left realising that anyone that the priest knew who was at a loose end would have already been snapped up for the much needed social work of the parish.

I wrote to a Member of Parliament I had met some 25 years ago, to a business man from my home city who is on various local boards in the town and to other luminaries. All wrote back most helpfully, but only one suggested any specific people to visit. I followed this up and it led me to a wives' group who I don't think wanted me to recruit their people as they met for purely social reasons. However, through this contact I did meet one person who said that she would be free to help in a couple of years. Too long to wait, alas!

In driving around the well-heeled suburbs, I felt that there must be someone in there longing to help the cause. But who? And when would I find them?

Then I was invited to speak at a Rotary luncheon. My hopes were high. Unfortunately the meal was so delicious and the company so convivial that my allocated time to speak about our charity was severely cut, and the one-to-one cultivation didn't happen (no-one 'offers' on these occasions!).

My big break came in a totally unexpected way. I was arranging a visit to see a city child-care project by a group of people from another town. I said that I would send them a map to show the location of the project. *"Don't worry"*, was the reply, *"I was brought up in the city"*. This was my cue to act. *"Do you know anyone who lives here who is at a loose end and could help me form a fundraising group?"*, I inquired. I obtained the name of a relative and another name.

I set off with new enthusiasm having ascertained that the first person would probably be in on a certain morning. I knocked on the door, and although the lady had been rung by her relative to explain who I was and that I would be making contact, I received a strict telling off for calling unannounced. I apologised and, grasping my diary, suggested that we might find half an hour for a chat sometime else. *"Half an hour"* was the horrified reply! *"Where have you come from?"* I explained, and said it was about 45 kilometres away. It must have sounded like the other side of the world, as I was invited into the kitchen for coffee *"as I was here"*. Immediately we got on like a house on fire. We might have known each other all our lives. How easily I could have fled at the first tirade! Names and suggestions flowed and an agreement that she was willing to be part of the new group in spite of her numerous other commitments.

The next visit was also quite alarming. I was invited into the house. *"I was wondering if you know anyone who would be free to join a fundraising group?"*, I asked. *"Are you asking me – or asking me if I know anyone?"* I kept my cool and said, *"I was really asking you if you knew anyone, but if you are able to help as well that would be wonderful!"*. Not only was she willing to help, but she thought deeply, and made suggestions of others who might be interested. She contacted them. She telephoned me. I visited most of the people she suggested. Others I just spoke to on the telephone. All agreed to help.

The most exciting introduction was to a person who had that very month given up her job (although still young and very active!). She was an obvious candidate to take the chair. Soon we had twelve people and were able to have our first meeting over lunch, kindly arranged by one of the group. This is always a highly charged occasion. Are people going to get on well together (they did)? Is anyone going to offer to be Secretary (and be responsible for the dreary organisational work)? But I had already arranged that three of the people take on the posts of Chair, Treasurer and Secretary after some undercover work beforehand. The democratic procedures can follow once the group is established – at future AGMs!

The first fundraising function was fixed for a few months later, and all members worked well together and enjoyed themselves. My initial idea was to hold two functions a year, and also to sell Christmas cards and perhaps to distribute some collecting boxes. The first two events organised within the first 13 months raised £1,200 and £1,400. We were on our way.

Recruitment is the key to success. You may need to find people to serve on committees and fundraising groups or you may be looking for one key person to chair a committee or take the responsibility for a particular area of fundraising. You will want to identify the skills and resources that they will need for the job (time available, use of their homes, contacts, ideas, initiative, enthusiasm, etc.). You should allow yourself plenty of time for this. You can also ask existing contacts to suggest other people (their friends or people who they think will be able to do a good job). As the group begins to organise fundraising events (and to be seen to be successful), you will find that more interest will develop in what you are doing and more people will be prepared to volunteer their time. At any stage good publicity in the local press or radio can bring further support. If you are setting up a local branch of a national organisation or network, ask them for their mailing list for the area. These will be people who are already interested in the cause, so when you approach them you may find them eager to give their support.

What makes a good fundraising leader

1. **Good organisational skills**, so that the work is shared out amongst the team and everything gets done.
2. **Attention to detail**, so that nothing is forgotten, and everything runs smoothly.
3. **Ability to lead**, motivate and manage the team of volunteers who are doing the work.
4. **A good judge of people**, recognising and using the abilities of individual members of the group, understanding people's strengths and weaknesses such that they contribute their best and enjoy being part of the team.

Constituting the local group

You need the people, and you need something for them to do. But you will also need a constitution, which defines how this group of people will operate and clarifies their relationship with the central organisation (that is with you). If you are setting up lots of local groups, then you will probably want to draw up a model constitution.

You will need to decide whether the local committee is:

- Simply a **sub-committee** or branch of the main organisation, with no separate legal identity of its own, or whether it is...
- A **separate organisation** in its own right, but with the purpose of supporting the main charitable organisation.

A separate legal structure will be more expensive to operate, but it will hand over full responsibility and control to the local group – who will be completely

> **Drawing up a constitution**
>
> The following are some of the headings for the constitution of a local fundraising committee:
> - The relationship with the charity.
> - Support to be provided by the charity.
> - Responsibilities of committee members.
> - Name of the committee.
> - Location or geographical area of operation.
> - Objects or purposes of the committee (what it is there to do – to raise money for the parent charity).
> - Any ethical values which will guide the committee in its work.
> - Organisational structure: officers and membership of the committee, how they are elected and their responsibilities, resignation or termination of membership from the committee.
> - Rules for handling money and bank accounts.
> - Meetings and the Annual General Meeting, when they are held and any quorum for decision-taking.
> - Expenses for committee members (normally they will not be remunerated for their work).
> - Powers to alter the constitution or wind up the committee.

accountable for what is raised and how the money is spent. Which is the most appropriate structure depends on a lot of things, including the legal and fiscal requirements for groups raising money that exist in your own country, the length of time the committee has been in operation (how well established it is), the amount of money it raises (how successful it is), and the number of local groups around the country who are raising money for you.

Sometimes you may find that an individual or a group decides to raise money on your behalf without your permission. In certain circumstances you may feel that because of the nature of the particular individual who is doing this or because of the fundraising method adopted, the good name of your charity will be put at risk. There is probably little that you can do to stop them raising money for you, but if you are unhappy about what they are doing, then you should speak to them about your concerns.

Local fundraising activities

There are an enormous range of fundraising activities that local support groups can undertake. Here we list here a few that work well to give you some ideas:

- Coffee mornings and other 'socials'.
- Bridge tournaments and other games (whist, chess, etc.).
- Sponsored walks, jogs, cycle rides, fun runs and anything else that can be sponsored.
- Heritage walks or cultural evenings for tourists.
- Craft fairs and sales of work.
- Fashion shows.
- Film premieres.
- Concerts and other cultural events.
- Dinner dances and balls.
- Discos for young people.
- Picnics and outings for families, if possible at interesting locations.
- Auctions of donated goods and 'promises auctions' (where a promise to do something useful or interesting is auctioned off).
- Raffles, lotteries and sweepstakes.
- Competitions with an entry fee to participants.
- Sports events and tournaments.
- New Years Eve parties, and events on other festive occasions.

- Getting supporters and businesses to advertise in calendars and diaries, brochures and annual reports.
- Sales of greetings cards.
- Public and house-to-house collections.

Organising fundraising events is covered in *Section 6.2*, organising public and house-to-house collections in *Section 6.3*, lotteries and raffles in *Section 6.10*, and getting companies to advertise in *Section 4.5*.

Supporting and managing the local group

The point of having a local group do the fundraising is that the 'hard grind' of doing the fundraising work is farmed out to a group of volunteers, leaving you free to concentrate on other tasks. It often is not cost-effective for a paid member of staff to spare time organising craft fairs or dinner dances or coffee mornings. But you need to make sure that the group you have established to do this actually does the work, does it well, and does not call unreasonably upon your time.

On the other hand, you will need to support and manage the group to get the most out of it. You will need to:

Setting up a local group – some key questions to answer

- **How should a local fundraising group be constituted?** Should it be an independently constituted group with its own separate legal structure and charitable status? Or should it be a branch or committee of the main organisation?
- **Who is legally accountable for the money that is raised** (to see that it is spent for the purpose for which it was given)?
- **What freedom does the local group have** to make statements in public on matters that concern the organisation?
- What role does it have in the **determination of where its money is spent**? Does it decide what to support and any terms or conditions to be attached to the way the money is spent? Or do you (when it is yours without strings attached)?
- **What sanctions do you have** if you feel that they are bringing your organisation into disrepute in any way?

- Provide the group with some form of **induction**, so that they understand the importance of the work being done by the organisation, see the staff at work and meet and talk to staff and beneficiaries. If they can see the work at first hand, it will help fire them with enthusiasm, so that they know what they are raising the money for and can convince those they are asking of its importance.
- Help steer the group towards those **fundraising methods** which are more likely to work. Your experience will help, and you can also research what the local fundraising groups of other organisations are doing.
- Give the group a **budget** (they will need to spend some money to raise money) and fundraising targets to achieve. Don't expect too much too soon. It is best for them to start slowly, and to allow more time than they think will be necessary. If you are too optimistic at the outset, there will be a sense of failure when the targets are not achieved.
- Continue to show your **personal interest** in what they are doing, and acknowledge your appreciation of their hard work at every opportunity.
- Monitor their **progress** and be available to **advise them** if they have difficulties.
- Provide them with appropriate **literature** about the organisation that explains its work clearly and powerfully.

6.2 Organising a fundraising event

All sorts of event can be organised to raise money for charity. But whether you are planning to organise a concert in your home town, arrange a celebrity cricket match or celebrate your organisation's centenary with a firework party in the park, you need to think not just about the fundraising potential of the event, but of the cost and effort involved in putting it on and also about the possible risk of losing money (rather than making money) from the event. For every event that attracts thousands of new supporters and gives everyone a good time, there is another that collapses, is rained off, or fails because sponsorship was withdrawn at the last moment. While there is money to be made from a well run event, many absorb a great deal of energy and deliver only small returns.

An advertisement for an event

☆☆☆☆☆☆☆☆☆☆☆☆☆☆☆☆☆☆☆

DANCE THE NIGHT AWAY

☆

On Saturday September 30th,
9pm to midnight at Founders Hall a
'Dancing Only' get together.

☆

Bring a friend, your best bopping music on tape, snacks, drink and lots of energy!

Donation of £1 at the door.
Proceeds to Waldorf Kindergarten.

☆☆☆☆☆☆☆☆☆☆☆☆☆☆☆☆☆☆☆

Just to show that events do not have to be world class to raise useful amounts.

Objectives of the event

An event may be of almost any size and complexity. But what all events have in common is that you will be asking your members or the general public or a selected audience to participate, and you will be giving them something to enjoy in return for their money. You should not just be creating an opportunity to take as much money as you can from those who attend – you should do this, of course, but you should be aiming to give them a good time as well!

You must be absolutely clear about the purpose of the event from the start. Is it for PR, to get your name known? Or is it to raise as much money as you can? Or is it an opportunity to entertain your volunteers and supporters to thank them? Or is it simply to give an enthusiastic fundraising committee something useful to do for you? Or to bring your work to the attention of an influential audience? The objectives for the event will help mould the exact form of the event itself and how you run it. Whatever the purpose of the event, events always provide an opportunity to get your message across, even if only in a low key way (by handing out leaflets to participants or mounting a small exhibition illustrating your work at the event venue, for example).

The five ingredients

Whatever your event, there are likely to be five principal groups of people involved. Get them working together in harmony and you are well on your way to success. These people are:

1. The performers

The performers are those people upon whose skills and appeal the event is centred: the band that is booked to play at the ball; the auctioneer undertaking the sale for you; or the football teams and 'star' players who will be playing in the charity match. They are critical to its success. It is on their performance that the success of the event depends. But they also have something to gain from participating in the event. It could be a fee (although you should always try to get a reduced fee or a free performance). It will often provide them with good publicity, and an association with a good cause – which is good for their image.

2. The sponsors

Sponsors may be underwriting much of the costs, and this makes it possible for the event to be held without exposing your organisation to unnecessary risk. They also have a good deal to gain from the event. They are often interested in reaching your audience (with information about their product) and in being seen by the general public (and by their employees) to be supporting something worthwhile.

3. The media

The media are in business to report events such as yours, especially if it brings genuine talent to the fore or is of particular local interest. Whether the event is genuinely newsworthy depends on the nature of the event itself and on how creative you are in generating media interest. They may be interested in being given exclusive coverage of the story in return for publishing a major feature or picture. Or they may be interested in becoming a 'media sponsor', offering you not money, but free advertising and press coverage to promote the event in advance, and thus attract an audience.

4. The charity or NGO

The next ingredient is you and your organisation. Your involvement gives the event a focus – the real reason for its happening is to raise money to support your good work. The audience may come because they are your supporters, or because they are interested in your cause. The performers will not come to just any event, because they may have many other commitments. But an event for your organisation could be something that strikes a sympathetic chord with them. The sponsors will decide to back the event because of your reputation and the audience that you can deliver for them. Your contacts with well known patrons can be a further inducement.

5. The audience

Some people go to a charity event simply because they are interested in attending the event. Others consider it an enjoyable way of supporting a cause or a particular organisation that they would like to support. But everyone attending knows that it is a fundraising event, and expects to be asked to contribute in some way whilst they are there (in addition to paying the cost of the ticket). Making sure they enjoy the event is important. But finding ways of raising more money from the people who you have attracted to your event is a critical factor in the financial outcome.

Deciding what to organise

One starting point is to examine your market. Who are the people who will come to the event – the people who are already in touch with you (your donors, your members, your volunteers, the readers of your newsletter) or that you can reach through a particular type of promotion? What are the interests of these people? Are they old or young, active and energetic, particularly interested in your cause?

What are you and your helpers interested in – and what contacts do you have (access to performers, for example)?

Sometimes you will want to start from the sponsorship end, and ask a potential sponsor what sponsorship money is available, what sort of event they might be interested in, and what needs to be done for them to decide to back it.

An alternative starting point might be to think in terms of some of the major types of event and see whether any seems appropriate. A short list might include:

- **Sporting events**.
- **Musical and cultural events**.
- **Balls, dinners, auctions** and other entertainment events.
- **Exhibitions, festivals and fairs**.
- **Events involving schools** and young people.
- **Mass participation events**, with the participants collecting sponsorship money.

Most events are run on a one-off basis – although you will always want to re-run the event next year if it is successful, thereby creating a regular source of income for your charity. Some events take place over a period of time – for example a knockout football competition or a film festival. More complicated (and more risky) events should perhaps be left to when you have more experience.

Depending upon the nature of your plans, you may need some sort of licence (to run the event, to collect money in a public place, or to run a bar). Check the legal requirements with the local administrative authority before you start any detailed planning.

Management

The ability to run the event well is crucial. It will almost certainly take much longer and involve more effort than you think. There seem to be three main approaches to organising the event: do it yourself; get a professional do it; or recruit a group of volunteers. All approaches have their drawbacks and their advantages.

1. Do it yourself. Perhaps the single most important problem of doing it yourself is the opportunity cost that organising it will involve. What else could you be doing with the time? How much money could you be raising if you were not stuck with doing the organising? Almost any event will require constant attention to detail, and checking and double checking at every stage. If you are in the middle of a busy fundraising programme, then organising something that requires so much of your time may simply not be feasible.

2. Engage a professional to do the organising. Very often the event will be run through some sporting organisation or cultural institution, whose job it is to organise this sort of activity. If not, there might be professional event organisers in the musical, sporting and entertainment fields. For a fee or a percentage of ticket income, they can be engaged to take over all the day to day administration from you. Alternatively a suitable public relations or professional fundraising company could be used – again for a fee.

3. Establish a committee of volunteers to take all the responsibility for running the event. The key appointment will be the Chair. This need not be someone who knows how to run an event backwards, but someone with the leadership qualities and the good management sense to link the commercial needs of the event to the requirements of the charity. You will want to select a multi-disciplinary team that incorporates all the skills that you will need to make the event work – people with the sporting or musical background to deal with the programme, the accountant who will advise on the budget and ticket pricing, the people with marketing and PR skills. You need to give yourself plenty of time to find the right people.

There are several important aspects of successfully managing the event:

- **An accurate budget**. It is essential to control costs, if you are to run the event profitably. Your budget will also give you an indication of the size of audience you will need to attract and what price to charge for tickets. At an early stage you will need to make an assessment of all the likely costs and the potential sources of income – and just to be safe you should include something for contingencies. On the income side it is worth making a high and low estimate to illustrate what may happen in different circumstances. This will highlight the risk involved.
- **Plenty of time**. Although it is possible to organise an event in a short space of time, the longer you leave yourself the better. The best is an annual cycle, with the planning of the next year's event starting just after the completion of this year's. Booking a venue or obtaining the services of star performers may take a lot longer and be an important factor in how far ahead you need to plan.
- **Legally binding contracts**. You will also need the arrangements with performers, the venue and any sub-contractors, expressed through some formal written agreement. This sets out precisely what has been agreed and is signed by both parties to confirm the agreement. This avoids disagreement later on. It is especially important that you agree how any money is to be split (both expenditure and income); who has the rights to the recording of the event; and who is responsible for what costs; what the obligations are in the event of cancellation. Where considerable sums are involved, the agreement should be drawn up by a lawyer.
- **Good administration and record keeping**. For your first event, you have to start from scratch. But next time it will be much easier, since you will be building on experience. Keep records of everything, so you will know what to do next time – for example whether insurance is needed, where to go for it and how much to pay. Immediately after the event, have a de-briefing – find out what went really well, what went wrong or could be improved, what suggestions there are for doing better or raising more money next time, and all this can be used to ensure that the event is even more of a success the next time you run it.

FEBA Radio's fundraising dinner

FEBA Radio, a Christian broadcasting organisation in Kenya, decided to raise money to convert an office into a small temporary studio as an alternative to the expense of hiring studio space.

"Since we had not held a fundraising event before, we chose to host a dinner for about 50 people who already knew us and the work we do. We invited members of our Council of Management and their spouses, and asked them to invite one couple each to a dinner in a local hotel. We also invited a guest speaker and a couple to sing at the dinner.

"In our planning we decided not to ask the guests to pay for the dinner, believing that they would be more generous as a result. We prepared a presentation for the dinner, including the history of FEBA Radio, our purpose and work, and something about our future plans. We also provided quotes from FEBA listeners showing how our programmes had affected their lives. At the conclusion of the dinner one of the Council members talked about why we needed the studio, and its estimated cost (about Ksh 60,000 or £750). He then appealed for cash contributions. The total we raised in cash and pledges was Ksh 100,000. The dinner cost just less than Ksh 20,000.

"Because of the small number of invited guests and the fact that most of them are aware of our work, we did not produce any publicity materials specially for the occasion. We made follow up telephone calls after sending out the invitations to confirm attendance. After the dinner, we sent thank-you letters to all those who attended and reminders to all those making a pledge.

"This being our first attempt at fundraising, we felt that it was quite successful in that we raised more than we had planned. One of the contributing factors to the success was that the guests were people who were aware of and sympathised with our work and also personal friends. Also because this was a one-off request, many people would find it easier to make a single gift than a long-term commitment. Finally we were raising money for a specific project, and the amount we needed was not a very large sum."

Contributed by Leah Gachegu, Audience Relations manager, FEBA Radio

Reducing the risk

The best way of reducing risk is to have a well thought out event, and good planning, organisation and marketing. But things have a habit of not going to plan, so you need to think about your exposure to risk and how to reduce it. There are several ways of doing this:

- **Financial sponsorship**. Get all the costs of the event covered by a sponsor, so that there is nothing to lose, and everything to gain. An additional advantage is that you can tell everyone coming that all proceeds will go to the cause (since all the costs have already been covered). This can be a tremendous encouragement for ticket sales.
- **Commitments and guarantees**. One way of running a charity ball is to have a committee of say 20 people, each of whom agrees to get 12 people to come to the ball. They take responsibility for selling the 12 tickets, or for paying for them themselves in the event of being unable to find others to contribute. This means that you have an already guaranteed attendance of 240 people – enough to fill the venue or make sure that the event is a success.
- **Cost cutting**. You might try to get as much as you can lent for the occasion, donated or sponsored, so that you do not have to pay for it. Venue costs, performers costs, and the cost of prizes can all be substantial, and if they are too high can jeopardise the success of the event. Not having to pay or paying less is a simple way both to get more out of the event and to reduce risk at the same time.
- **Insurance.** It may be possible to insure against public liability, theft or damage (in case something goes wrong), and for an outdoor event, even against the possibility of bad weather.

Promotion

Effective promotion will turn an event from being a modest success into being really profitable. First think who is likely to want to come to the event – this is your target market. And then decide how best to reach them – which you can do through getting coverage in the press and on radio, paying for advertising, displaying posters in the street or in public places, mailing your supporters and other lists of people. All this can be extremely hard work, and some of the things will cost money. But it is through having a full house that the event will be successful.

For an important event, try to get **media sponsorship** – the backing of one of the main newspapers or radio stations. They may preview the event or interview those involved. Radio may be prepared to broadcast the event live and give frequent mentions in the run up to the event, giving the date and how to get tickets. A media link can create its own promotional momentum. Another possibility is to give away free tickets as prizes to be offered to readers or listeners. You could devise a competition of some sort or offer two free tickets to the first 25 people who write or call in.

One way of generating publicity is to use **celebrities** who may be attending the event or performing in it. This will be especially true of sporting or cultural events where the performers will be the main attraction. Or you may be inviting a celebrity to act as compere, to open the event or to present awards. Involving famous people adds credibility to the event and will attract people to it.

How to attract people to your event

- Have a really **attractive event** that people will want to come to. And make the event fun for everyone who participates in it.
- Find plenty of **ticket sellers** who between them will take responsibility for selling all the tickets.
- Target the event at a readily **identifiable and reachable audience** – your supporter, the business community, local politicians, etc.
- Everyone should be encouraged to **ask people in person or by telephone**... and not just rely on sending out printed invitations.
- Get coverage of your plans in the **local press** – so that people hear about what you are planning. Media sponsorship, posters and leaflets distributed widely will also help promote the event.
- Use **celebrities** to get publicity. And if you can get them to help you (see Section 7.2), their presence will encourage people to come to the event.

You also need a strategy for getting people to come if ticket sales are slow, but not so disappointing as to have to cancel the event. Once you are sure the event will happen, it is important for everyone (those who have bought tickets, the performers and the organisers) that the event is well attended. At that stage it is more important to see that people are there than that all the tickets are sold. This means that you should be prepared to give tickets away free to groups who might be interested in coming – through schools and student unions for young people's events, through hospitals and other institutions for other events, or via a media promotion. The people who come will contribute to the success of the event just by being there, but they might also spend money whilst they are there.

The ActionAid Kenya Gala Night

There were three objectives for organising the gala: raising public awareness of the work of ActionAid in Kenya, raising funds to alleviate the water problems of the people of Malka Galla by sinking a borehole, and strengthening relationships with the local corporate sector.

A gala night committee was set up to organise the event, with sub-committees for catering, entertainment, invitations and ticket sales. The ten members of the organising committee were, in addition, each given particular responsibilities, including public relations, NGO support, corporate fundraising, getting raffle items, VIP guests, invitation sales, venue and security, etc.

The gala night organising committee compiled a list that was used as a basis for approaching supporters and sponsors. This included:

- Friends of the organisation, whose moral and material support could be counted on.
- Suppliers of services and materials to ActionAid Kenya, who had a customer-supplier relationship.
- A 'shot in the dark' category, which included all those bodies and individuals who had been approached by ActionAid in the past for support, but where there was (as yet) no established relationship.
- Personal contacts of members of staff, who contacted those people and organisations they were in touch with who might be helpful.

The targeted number of guests was 400, but more than 400 invitation cards were printed to allow for loss or damage during handling. The cards were priced at Ksh 2,000 each (£25), and members of staff were able to get a discount of Ksh 500, which was not extended to spouses. The Country Director received 27 complementary cards to invite VIPs from government and the diplomatic corps, and major sponsors.

Letters highlighting the aims and objectives of the gala were sent to prospective donors with a request that they help underwrite the costs of the gala night, such that all the proceeds could then go to the well sinking project, or that they support other specified projects being run by ActionAid Kenya, or that they donate something that could be used in the raffle or auction to raise money on the night.

The raffle offered various attractive items. Most prizes had been donated by companies, friends and members of staff. Tickets were priced at Ksh 100 each and Ksh 500 for 6. Raffle prizes included dinners for two at restaurants, week-end breaks for two at hotels and a night for two at the Mount Kenya Safari Club, two first class return tickets Mombasa-Nairobi, a complete beauty treatment, clothing and handicrafts and much more. Some items were held back for sale at an auction, including a coffee table, a self-drive car hire for one week, a designer suede jacket, two sets of car tyres, a car respray. Entertainment on the evening included a traditional dance troupe, a live music band, a fashion show, and an 'a cappella' group.

"A total of Ksh 1.2 million (£15,000) was raised from the gala, which indicates that with proper planning over a period of time any organisation can raise money locally. ActionAid enjoys a lot of goodwill in Kenya, and this already gives it a head start in fundraising. Much of the potential for raising funds locally and building a core group of business and individual supporters remains largely untapped."

Contributed by Janet Mawiyoo, Programme Manager, ActionAid Kenya

Getting sponsorship

Events are ideal vehicles to attract business sponsorship – because they offer a possibility of getting their message to your audience and an opportunity of entertaining staff or customers, and for you because sponsorship brings in money and can help reduce your risk.

Sponsors will need to know a great deal about the event and its expected audience. How many people will come? What sort of people will they be? How will they be exposed to any advertising messages? By having their name and logo printed in the poster and in the programme, and included in any publicity before the event and in the media coverage of the event, by having free samples of their product distributed, through a prize in a competition, by having a 'name link' with their product – there are all sorts of ways, and it is up to you to devise something that will be attractive to them.

You should have a clear idea of how much money you are asking the sponsor to contribute and what you are offering in return. Besides the good publicity, you might be offering special hospitality facilities for their senior staff, or for more junior employees, or for clients and customers, with opportunity to meet the celebrities.

For more advice on getting business sponsorship, see *Section 4.6*.

Developing extra income

For many events, such as a dinner dance or a ball, the ticket price may cover the cost of organising the event and not much more. If you want to generate money for your work, then you will have to devise ways of getting those who are attending the event to give or spend more. It is by generating this extra money that your event becomes a real success. There are all sorts of ways of doing this. Here are a few ideas:

- Getting local businesses to take **advertising in the programme**. This is called 'goodwill advertising', and is sold on the basis that they are helping a good cause and being associated with a successful event.
- Having **an auction**, where interesting items are auctioned during the course of the evening. A holiday donated by a travel company is often the 'star item'. Alternatively, the items can be prizes in a raffle or prize draw.
- Having **a tombola or a raffle**, where small gifts donated by local shops and by supporters are the prizes. Each prize is numbered, and each ticket purchased has a number which corresponds with a prize or does not win. To be a success there should be lots of prizes and a good chance of winning something.
- Having **pledge forms** for each person to fill in, and making an appeal during the evening. Or collecting money from those present in a bucket. To make sure that people respond generously, you should say what the money is for and perhaps suggest a level of donation. You might get the performers to say something during the evening.
- **Advertising the appeal** in the event programme. Not everyone there will be an existing supporter or know about what you are doing and why the work is important.

Spin off for future fundraising

A great advantage of a successful event is that you can build up a clientele for future occasions. By keeping the names and addresses of those who have attended, you can invite them to participate next time you run the event – perhaps next year.

You will also want to capture the interest of the people who attend the event so that they learn about your cause and understand the importance of your work. This can be done by trying to raise money from them in one of the ways already suggested. But you can also add the participants' names to your mailing list and

The experience of organising events

Intervention (India) is a fundraising and marketing consultancy operating in Bangalore, South India. It has organised many fundraising initiatives for local charities in Bangalore, including:

- **Pub night** at the Black Cadillac Pub, with the hire of premises, the refreshments and the band sponsored by local companies. Entry fees for this 'evening of fun' raised Rs50,000 (£1,000 approx).
- **Red Rose Week**, an event organised to coincide with Valentine's Day, which celebrates true love. Roses were sold to individuals and companies, raising Rs50,000 for a Street Children's charity.
- **Film Premiere** of a hit Hindi film, which raised Rs110,225 for a charity working in leprosy rehabilitation. The principal sponsor organised an intensive product promotion for a shampoo as a result of the sponsorship.
- **Charity Art Show**. The paintings of two contemporary artists were exhibited at a top 5-star hotel. Rs300,000 was raised for Street Children, with over half coming in the first two hours. The main sponsor used the occasion to launch Smirnoff Vodka to an elite target group.
- **Painting Competition** for Children at the Governor's Palace organised for SAVE, an environmental charity. The children painted their concept of environmental harmony on the lawns of the palace of the Governor of Karnataka, with the Governor giving the prizes. Rs70,500 was raised, with wide media coverage and a happy paint company sponsor.

"An important lesson learned was that sponsors are not very choosy about the NGO or the cause, provided the event gives them a lot of publicity, for which they have budgets and which they can directly correlate to sales of their products or services."

Contributed by Ajit Mani, Intervention, Bangalore

---

make sure that they receive any appeal literature you are sending out. You might even make them an 'honorary member' for three months to get them used to the idea of being a supporter. You could think about organising an 'open day' where they could come and see your work, meet your staff and talk to your beneficiaries.

Organising a particular type of event can help you reach new audiences. For example, if you want to appeal to the middle class cultural elite, you might consider running a concert or art exhibition. If you are interested in the educational establishment, you might think about an exhibition of children's paintings. Or if you want to appeal to the business elite or top politicians, an event involving leading TV or cinema or sporting stars might be worth considering.

Sponsored participation events

Organising a 'sponsored event' is not the same as getting business 'sponsorship' for your event. In a sponsored event, which might be a walk or a swim or a cycle ride, the participants who are involved get their family, their friends and their colleagues at work to 'sponsor' them by contributing a certain amount for each kilometre or each lap they complete. Lots of small sums pledged by lots of sponsors, multiplied by lots of laps or kilometres, and multiplied again by lots of participants can generate really substantial amounts of money for your organisation.

Remember though that the people are supporting their friends to participate (perhaps to do something interesting or unusual) because they are asked. The participants may become involved because it is a fun thing to do or a challenge.

Sponsored events are one of the most commonly used ways of raising money for charity. You can sponsor just about anything! Ideas that have been used include:

- Giving up smoking (sponsoring the number of days without a cigarette up to a specified limit).
- Slimming (the number of kilos lost during a set time).

- Knitting (how many centimetres knitted during an afternoon).
- A litter pick (how many kilos of litter cleared from a river bank).
- Marathon runs (number of miles raced plus a bonus for completing the course).
- Penalty shoot outs (number of goals scored if you are the penalty taker, or goals saved if the goalkeeper).

In deciding the event, find something that will be sufficiently popular to attract lots of participants (the more participants you attract, the more money you will raise) and that is trouble-free to organise. Also you want something that you can repeat year by year, building on your experience and success to achieve greater returns the next time you run it. A sponsored event can also be used to get across an important message about your cause (an environmental charity could organise a sponsored clean up, alcoholics anonymous a sponsored give-up-alcohol, for example).

You need to take into account what will be attractive to your target audience. Younger people may be interested in disco marathons, but will not be interested in a sponsored knit. For older people, it would be the other way round. If your target audience is young families, can you think of something that will involve them all during the weekend? Family strolls (a strollathon), fun runs and swimming are all popular – your imagination is the limit to what is possible.

You can expect three types of person to join in:

- Those **people who have participated before** and who know it will be a lot of fun; so it is important to keep a record of who has participated in previous years.
- **Supporters** and sympathisers of your cause. So mail your members and donors; they may be interested in doing something to help raise money.
- Those **people who just enjoy the particular activity** you have chosen (cycling, walking, etc.) who may not be interested in your work – although their participation gives you the opportunity to interest them.

A fourth group are those involved in your organisation:

- Members of your **Management Board** (it is a good opportunity to get them doing something useful!).
- Your **staff** (involvement in a sponsored event can improve morale).
- Your **beneficiaries** (a cycle ride for an organisation which assists the mentally handicapped that includes mentally handicapped people as riders can show that they are 'people just like us' and make the cause seem more relevant to participants).

Sponsored event checklist

1. Choose the right activity: something that people will want to do and is novel enough to warrant others sponsoring them. But also something that is relatively easy and inexpensive to organise.

2. Set a date and venue: make sure you plan well ahead to allow time for preparation and for participants to get their sponsorship.

3 Get any permissions you need, for example to use a public place – from the police or from the local authority or from the owner of the property.

4. Produce sponsorship forms: give examples of what amounts you expect and set each participant a target for the number of sponsors and the amount to raise.

5. Involve other organisations, as they can be a good source of participants. You might even think of doing a joint event with another organisation. The more people who participate the better.

6. Organise local publicity: get celebrities to sign up as participants, and use this to publicise the event. Get media sponsorship – which can be another way of getting participants.

7. Get local business sponsorship: to cover costs and pay for any prizes being offered. This will reduce your risk, but will also ensure that as much of the money as possible that participants raise goes to the cause.

8. Prepare for the day: ensure you have all the stewards, equipment and information for the event, that the route is well marked, that everyone is well briefed.

9. Tidy up afterwards.

10. Thank all the participants – both for their participation and the amount that they raised. Tell them what you plan to do with the money.

11. Chase up all uncollected pledges. This is most important. People are not being asked to participate in the event for fun, but to help you raise money.

12. Add the names on your sponsorship forms to your mailing list if the forms include details of the each sponsor's name and address. You will then be able to send them an appeal letter in due course suggesting that they continue supporting your work.

Walks for Millions

The Community Chest in Hong Kong raises money to distribute as grants for community betterment and welfare purposes. The total funds raised by the Community Chest in 1994-95 was HK$181 million. Of this total, HK$26 million, representing 14.4% of the Community Chest's income for the year, was raised through three walks which involved 46,000 walkers. The following are some of the tips for planning the walk based on the experience of the Community Chest:

- **Best time for the walk**: a Sunday morning or a Saturday afternoon.
- **Route**: three routes – easy, tough and a family walk – to encourage maximum participation. The assembly point should be easily accessible and spacious enough to accommodate all the walkers. The routes should be wide and flat wherever possible. The finishing point should be accessible to transport so that walkers who have completed the course can disperse. Route reconnaissance should be conducted before a firm decision on the route is made.
- **The walk can celebrate**: the opening of a new road or bridge, and this could bring additional sponsorship and publicity.
- **Facilities:** first aid, toilet facilities and communications with marshals all need to be in place.
- **Target for fundraising**: this should be set according to the size of the event. The budgeted expenditure should be kept below 15% of the expected income. Expense items include: media, print and production, awards and souvenirs for the walkers, a reception, photography, temporary staffing, transportation, direct mail to get participants, site expenses, drinks and refreshment, and sundry. Some if not all the expenses can be met through sponsorship.
- **Supporting organisations**: the police for crowd control and safety along the

route; the urban or regional council for the use of public amenities; the transport department for agreeing and announcing road closures; St John's Ambulance Brigade for first aid services; Boy Scouts and Girl Guides to help with registration of the walkers on the day; Civil Aid Services for crowd control and radio communications on the day.
- **Printed material required**: route map; poster; sponsor forms; appeal letters; certificate of appreciation for completion of the walk; souvenir material; reply form for participants to register.
- **Problems**: the event requires a lot of manpower and detailed organisation; effort must be put into collecting donations and sponsorship from participants; special arrangements for road closure need to be made, unless the event is performed in a park; the event could be ruined by bad weather.
- **Ideas learned from experience**: set up a prize or awards system; plan the walk for walkers of all ages and to include people with physical disabilities; entertainments and music can be arranged at the start and finish and along the route to make the walk more interesting; encourage each walker to have their own fundraising target.

The start of the "Walk for Millions"

Contributed by Winnie Sek, Deputy Director, Campaigns and Donations, The Community Chest

Organising the event

Organisation takes place in three stages:

Stage One: Before the event

Before the event, you will need to:

- **Decide the event** and agree the route or the venue; get any permission or insurance necessary.
- **Plan the promotion**.
- **Prepare the sponsorship forms** and **explanatory materials** about the work of your organisation.
- **Provide advice and support to participants** to help them collect pledges.
- **Organise volunteers** to help on the day.
- **Mark out the route**.
- **Welcome participants** on their arrival and certify their completion.

Preparation of the sponsorship forms requires thought. The form must describe exactly what is being done, but should also say why the money is needed. Then it should list the names and addresses of the sponsors (the participant will need the address to collect the sponsorship that has been pledged afterwards; you will want the addresses so that you can mail your appeal literature and try to get further support afterwards) and the amount pledged. You want to encourage sponsors to commit themselves to a generous amount of sponsorship. They need to know how many miles (or things) they are likely to be paying for. Is there a maximum number of miles for example? And remember that you are likely to get more if your sponsorship is per kilometre than per mile. Most sponsors do not know what level of sponsorship is expected, and are guided by what others have written before. Thus you might indicate some preferred amounts in the form of one cent, two cents, five cents or ten cents per kilometre, or encourage participants to approach their more generous supporters first. Some people may prefer to give a fixed sum. The form should allow for this too.

Since the ultimate success of the event depends on the amount raised, it is important to have lots of participants raising lots of money. Once you have got the participants, you can encourage them to raise more money by:

- Setting **a minimum sponsorship** requirement which they guarantee to pay.
- Giving them **a target**, both in terms of the number of sponsors they should aim to get and how much to ask for.
- Having **an entrance fee** for participating in the event.

You will be surprised by the range of sums people raise. And this depends as much on the effort put in by the participant (this can be encouraged by you) as on their financial circumstances.

Stage Two: On the day

On the day, you need to make sure that everything runs smoothly, that there are sufficient helpers, and that they are properly briefed. You also need to ensure that participants are welcomed (and especially any celebrities), that newspaper and radio reporters are welcomed and briefed about anything unusual (including anyone participating in fancy dress, any stunts, anything unusual about what the money will be used for), that there is information at the start of the event to advise performers and public what the route is, and where the refreshment and toilet facilities are, and for events that involve physical exertion where medical help can be obtained. At the start point you may want to set up an exhibition about your work – which provides a further opportunity to 'sell' your cause. You will need to have sufficient helpers to staff the various check-in procedures and to mark the route.

Stage Three: After the event

After the event, the key activity is to collect the money from participants and to thank those who actually took part. Collecting the money can be difficult. This must be the prime responsibility of

---

Ideas for a sponsored event

"As well as the more usual sponsored swims, walks and runs, I have heard of sponsored beard shaves, bungee jumping, chess marathons, and group silences. A group of local churches organise a sponsored cycle ride visiting 60+ local churches each summer. Children attempt hopscotch marathons or carol singing. Knitting groups organise sponsored patches – as well as each knitter being sponsored for the number of patches knitted, you get the most wonderful patchwork blanket to donate to a raffle for further funds. I've even heard of a sponsored vasectomy! And I know one brave leukaemia patient who had a sponsored head shave in public just before he went into hospital to undergo a gruelling period of chemotherapy, when he was told to expect considerable hair loss anyway. But don't stop here. Use the basic outline to work out your own ideas. You are only restricted by the limits of your imagination!"

Sarah Passingham, writing in 'Tried and Tested Ideas for Raising Money Locally' (published by Directory of Social Change)

the participants in the event who got sponsored in the first place. Keep a register of all participants. Stress the importance of collecting the money. Give a deadline date. Follow up in person if you can or by phone, or if all this fails by letter. Follow up letters may be needed too. Offer prizes for the largest amount actually raised – which can provide an incentive for people to collect their sponsorship money.

6.3 Collections

Public collections can be a successful way of raising money – if you have enough people prepared to do the collecting. This can take several forms:

- **House-to-house collections**, where you knock on doors and ask for support. Or leave an envelope and information about your work, and call back next day.
- **Street collections** and **collections in public places** (such as shopping centres or cinemas). Typically here a collector will have a collecting box, and may give some token in return for the donation (such as a sticker).
- **Collecting boxes placed at shop counters** for people to leave their small change, or larger collecting devices outside the shop.
- **Collecting boxes in supporters' homes**, where they can leave their small change or ask their friends to contribute.

The great strength of local collection schemes is that over time they can reach very large sections of the public. Not only does this have advantages in fundraising terms (you will be asking lots of people), it can also have a great educational or publicity impact. Imagine the impact of a national AIDS campaign that contacted every household in your town, not just to raise money but also to provide information. You could provide information on the disease, gain publicity for the organisation concerned and of course raise funds at the same time. Equally important is the reverse, where sloppy volunteer work will quickly bring an organisation into disrepute.

Because there is always the possibility of theft or fraud from collections, it is important to ensure that the conduct of the collection is undertaken in a way which minimises the chance that the money might not reach the benefiting organisation. Points to watch out for, in particular, are proper authorisation of collectors, proper procedures for remitting the money to the organisation and accounting for it, and procedures for returning all unused materials and authorisations at the end of the collection. Codes of practice on the conduct of house-to-house collections and use of static collection devices are given in *Appendix 4* at the end of the book. These codes of practice have been developed by the Institute of Charity Fundraising Managers in the UK, and adapted for this book.

House-to-house collections

House-to-house collections are very popular with both national and local charities as a way of asking everyone in a particular area to help. Remember that the main reason why people say that they don't give is because nobody asks them. A house-to-house collection provides the opportunity to ask people on a one-to-one basis with sufficient time to explain the work of the charity and why the money is needed.

Right at the start you need to plan how you will run the collection. Local knowledge will help you decide which neighbourhoods are likely to be most responsive. Consideration should be given to the affluence of the people who live there, but also to the ease of access to each house (apartment blocks are easier than suburban houses with large gardens, where security guards may also present an obstacle).

Another factor is the group of volunteers who will be doing the collecting. Typically you may want one volunteer to take responsibility for one street, either their own street or one nearby. If you have a local fundraising group, then plan the collection with them; if you don't, you will need to recruit collectors either from amongst your supporters or from the general public. The collectors should be given some training. They can be told when to call, what to say (explaining the importance of the work of the charity, what the money will be spent on, how much to give), what difficult questions to expect, and so on. You might do this by arranging a meeting for all the collectors, or by briefing people individually.

The collector's main function will be to deliver an envelope on which there is some message, with an accompanying brochure or letter from the charity. People might want to give there and then, or the collector can return after a short interval (of days) to collect the envelopes. The collector will encounter all sorts of responses. There will be those who decline to help you, and those who choose to be abusive. Most people will be polite. Some will be interested or even enthusiastic in what you are doing, some may have heard of you already, and some may even have supported you before. This is an ideal opportunity to recruit a new member or volunteer, and the collectors should be briefed to supply you with the names of people who seem particularly enthusiastic. For those who just return their envelope, make sure that their name and address is noted. You will want to say thank you. You also have a new donor and will want to keep in touch.

Another option is to take a collecting box with you, and ask for money there and then. This can also be effective. However you ask, some people will offer an excuse for not giving. They do not want to be seen to be mean, so want to justify their not giving. You can try to persuade them to change their mind. But often they will just make another excuse. In the meantime, you may be missing the opportunity to recruit other supporters elsewhere in the street.

The returned envelopes should be handed in at one central point and opened under the supervision of two people. The money received should be noted. This will help avoid fraud. A local bank may agree to help you with this. Make a note of how much money is coming from each area for future reference – so you know which streets and which areas are more generous and which collectors are the most successful.

There is always the possibility of fraud being perpetrated on your charity by someone carrying out an unauthorised collection in your name. All collectors should be given a permit from you authorising them to collect on your behalf. If you receive any reports of unauthorised collecting, you should investigate this as fast as you can. Any bad publicity will damage your organisation.

Checklist for organising a collection

1. Check the date. Avoid holiday periods or times of the year when there are other collections going on.

2. Seek any authorisation that you will require: from the police or local authority, and from the landlord (for cinemas and shopping centres).

3. Identify the areas and locations for collecting. Go for middle class housing and busy shopping streets. And think about the best time of day to call (during the daytime, if they're not working; or in the evenings or at the week end, if they are).

4. Recruit your team of volunteers; the more you have, the more you will collect. Get those who have agreed to suggest their friends.

5. Prepare any materials you will need, including: collecting boxes or envelopes, leaflets about the work of the organisation and details of any membership scheme, and stickers.

6. Brief the volunteers about the work of the charity, and provide some basic training in effective asking.

7. Organise how the money will be received and accounted for. Bank all proceeds immediately upon receipt.

8. Thank the volunteers, telling them how much they raised and how important this will be to your work.

9. Thank all the donors, by sending them a letter (with a further appeal). Follow up on those who have been noted as being particularly interested.

10. Debrief with your volunteers. Find out what went well, and what not so well. Suggest ways of doing better next time. Keep a record of which locations or neighbourhoods did best.

Street collections

Running a street collection is more difficult that a house-to-house collection. Volunteers find it less agreeable standing on the street with a collecting box, and you, the organiser, have to provide enough collectors on the same day or during the week, scheduled so that there are people there all the time and so that everyone is approached.

The choice of location is extremely important, and you should aim to give your collectors access to the maximum number of people. The main shopping street in the city centre is usually best, though collecting at supermarkets or at out-of-town shopping centres or at well attended events (such as at sports events or cinemas) may also work well. You will want several collection points (both sides of the street, outside the busiest stores, at all exit points of a stadium). Draw up a rota for each collection point. See that volunteers stay for an hour or two and are then relieved by a replacement. They can also be asked to visit restaurants and bars in the area (asking for the manager's permission before they start asking customers).

To make the most of the collection, you need to train your collectors. Collectors should not shrink back from passers-by. The collector who is prepared to vigorously rattle the box or tin, who is prepared to look people

What you need for a successful street collection

- **Lots of enthusiastic volunteers** prepared to stand in the street and ask passers by to contribute.
- **Good organisation** to ensure that everyone turns up when and where they are required.
- **Printed information** about your organisation, to brief the volunteers and hand out to passers by.
- **Stickers** (or flags or tokens) to offer people in return for their donation.
- **Collecting boxes**, suitably labelled to advertise your organisation.
- **Good local publicity** in advance, so that people hear about the collection and know what it is for.
- **A proper accounting system** for receiving and banking all the cash that is collected.

in the eye, who is prepared to station themselves in the middle of the pavement, and who is prepared to engage people in conversation will do very much better. Street collection requires a positive attitude. Collectors will need a sealed collecting device which is convenient to carry, convenient for the public to put money into, and easy to get the money out of again after the collection. They will also need a 'flag' or a 'sticker' to give to everyone who puts something in the collecting box.

Collecting boxes should be opened in the presence of two people, and the money should be immediately banked. Make a note of those locations which have produced the most money, and those collectors who have done best. All this can be used to make the next collection work even better. Thank all your collectors.

The Paraguayan Red Cross Society Flag Day: thirteen steps to a successful fundraising event

1. Establish an organising committee. This is composed of the Event Coordinator, the Head of Public Relations, the wife of the President of the Paraguayan Red Cross Society and volunteers.

2. Determine the number of fundraising stands and find suitable locations. In 1991, 68 stands were put up in Asuncion, the capital city, and the surrounding area. This represents 1 stand per 14,700 inhabitants.

3. Determine the most suitable date. The most suitable date is when most money will be raised, and when the volunteers are available. School holidays and long week-ends are not suitable, and it should not coincide with other organisations' fundraising campaigns. In Asuncion, the Flag day is held in the first week of May during the morning (from 7.30am to 12.30pm).

4. Mobilise collectors
- Cards are sent to various State bodies, clubs, banks, diplomats inviting the wives of important public figures and officials to take the responsibility for a particular fundraising stand.
- Letters are sent to the Heads of secondary schools inviting groups of students to assist at each stand. Each school is assigned up to 4 stands, and the young people pick up the collecting boxes from the stand to which they have been assigned and cover the area in the vicinity. The young people have to be at least 13 years old, and are properly briefed through an explanatory circular letter sent some days prior to the Flag Day.

5. Hold a briefing session. Once sufficient stand officials have volunteered, these are brought together for a briefing session, and are given a detailed instruction sheet covering: location, number of collecting boxes, which students will be assisting. They are given Red Cross flags to decorate the stand with, and invitation cards so that they can invite their friends and colleagues to visit the stand.

6. Set a budget. It is important to set a target for the fundraising drive, which should also relate to the needs that the Society is trying to meet. Costs should be kept as low as possible. In 1991, just over $100,000 was collected in Asuncion, of which 5-6% represented organising costs (obviously these will be higher the first time the event is held). As the Red Cross is well established, publicity costs are practically nil.

7. Launch the event to create public awareness. Once the organisation has been set up, it is important to launch the event to create interest in the media and amongst the public. This will include articles based on interviews with staff and volunteers.

8. Order the materials. Flags, collecting boxes, explanatory leaflets and display materials will be required. These have to be ordered in sufficient time to be distributed to the stands.

9. Publicise the Flag Day. The Flag Day is publicised for 15 to 18 days prior to the date of the event via television, radio and newspapers. In 1991, 3131 column-centimetres of space was taken in newspapers, and just under 120 minutes of advertising time taken on two TV channels. A recorded message was also sent to the radio networks. Posters were put up on poster sites donated by a soft drinks company with the slogan "Service in Action".

10. Inform the media of the results. Once the total amount collected has been counted, the press should be informed. The Central Bank of Paraguay helps with the collection, where cashiers count and bank the proceeds, which are handed over to them by stand officials.

11. Recovery of material. All unused material should be returned and inventoried. This provides useful guidance (on the best stands and the best collectors) for next year.

12. Send out letters of thanks. To everyone who helped, including a report on the final results at the stand they were responsible for. Suggestions and comments are also asked for.

13. Hold a debriefing meeting. To know in detail what worked, what didn't go well, to draw conclusions so as to be able to correct mistakes and improve performance next time.

Source: Paraguayan Red Cross Society

Collecting boxes in public places

Locations for collecting boxes can range from bars and shop counters to cinema foyers – anywhere where people are paying for things. They will usually be on private property or on the street immediately outside a shop. Most airports now have collecting boxes for travellers to place unwanted foreign currency (and some airlines circulate an envelope for the same purpose).

There are two types of collection device. First, those that appeal to children; these need to be visually appealing and have some sort of moving part that is operated when the money is inserted. Adult boxes on the other hand need to be functional and have a good design or label, which clearly expresses the cause for which the money is being given.

Finding good locations for collecting boxes can be a job for a persuasive volunteer – who has to persuade the owner or manager of the premises. Once the device has been placed, it still needs to be looked after. You need to see that it is not vandalised or stolen, that it is well displayed, that it is not so full that people can no longer put their money into it, and so that you receive the proceeds regularly. One approach is to suggest that the box become the responsibility of the proprietors of the establishment. But it is far better if one of your volunteers has the overall responsibility, as this will ensure that the scheme runs smoothly and that the money is regularly emptied, banked and accounted for.

Collecting boxes in supporters' homes: small amounts multiplying to large sums

In India

The Association for the Welfare of the handicapped, a Muslim organisation in Calicut, South India, placed 32,000 plastic collecting boxes in the homes of families in and around Calicut. This supporter base was built up over 4 years. The average take per collecting box per annum is only the equivalent of 40 UK pence, yielding the organisation a total of just under £13,000 per annum. The challenge for the organisation now is to try and find a way of getting each supporter to give or raise more money.

In South Korea

Collecting boxes for supporters to have at home have been a tremendous success for World Vision in South Korea. The boxes are made of plastic and in the shape of a loaf of bread. Each box is 10 cms long and weighs 5 grams. The boxes were originally introduced from World Vision in North America, and are known as *"Love Loaves"*. 4.5 million boxes have been distributed to households all over South Korea since 1991 – reaching families through schools, churches, banks and other commercial concerns, and to a lesser extent by house-to-house and street distribution. A third of those distributed are returned, and the average collected per box is around $5 or £3. So far $13 million has been raised in 5 years for World Vision in South Korea, and at the same time World Vision has been able to build a wide awareness of its work.

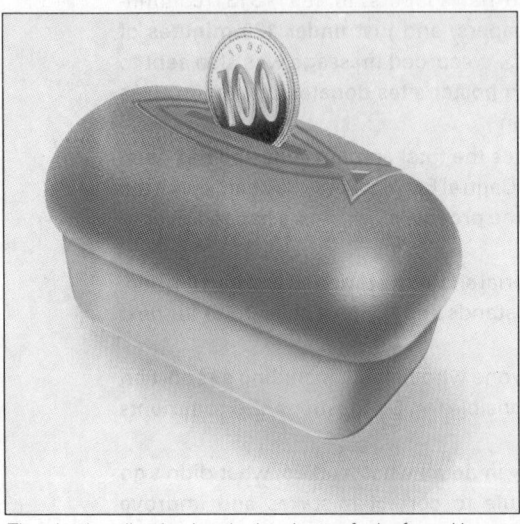

The plastic collecting box in the shape of a loaf used by World Vision, Korea.

6.4 Direct mail

Ken Burnett, author of *'Relationship Fundraising'*, describes direct mail fundraising as:

"One person writing to another person about something they both care about. It is an opportunity for both the writer and the potential donor, for it allows both the chance to do something personally to help."

Sending letters to people provides one of the most flexible and powerful tools in fundraising. Direct mail is just one of a number of direct marketing techniques which are used commercially and have been adapted for fundraising. At a price, and it can be expensive, you can reach out to large numbers of people and try to gain their support. Once you have got their support, you can then encourage them to give at higher levels and on a regular basis.

A direct mail fundraising programme can provide an assured source of income for your organisation, and one that will grow over time if it is managed well. Unless you already have an active and enthusiastic list of existing supporters, you will have to spend time, effort and money to build this up. Direct mail should not be seen as a source of quick income.

The essential feature of this medium is the ability to direct a personalised message of the length that you choose to a target audience at a time of your choosing. It requires the use of:
- A **list of addresses** to send the letters to.
- A **'communication package'** – usually a brochure with a covering letter and some mechanism for replying.
- A system for **dealing with the response**.

The principle is to get the following three elements right:
- **The audience**. There can be an enormous variation in the sort of response rate you achieve. Sending the letter to people who are more likely to respond will reduce the costs of acquiring a new donor considerably.
- **The message**. Likewise what you tell them and what you ask for is extremely important. A powerful message that will move them to give will be much more effective, than a 'downbeat' message. The creative approach, that is the way you angle the story you are telling them, and the 'offer', what you are asking them to do, are the two important components of the message.
- **The timing**. When to send the letter. Some times of the year may be better than others. In Christian countries, the period leading up to Christmas works best, as it is a time when people feel predisposed to give. If there is a good reason for the appeal, for example as a response to a natural disaster, then the immediacy of the need and demonstrating that you are responding efficiently and effectively means that you should get your appeal out as quickly as you can.

There are three types of mailing:
- **'Cold' mailings** to people with whom you have had no previous contact.
- **'Warm' mailings** to your existing members and supporters, where you already know that they are interested in your work and are likely to get a far higher response.
- **'Reciprocal' mailings**, where you swap your membership list with that of another organisation and use their list to recruit new members for your organisation (they will use your list to recruit for their organisation).

The power of the medium comes not only from the ability to target your message precisely, but also from the possibility to send the same message to very large numbers of people, which provides an economy of scale. You also have the possibility of sending slightly different messages to different groups of people. This is called 'segmentation'. You will certainly want to say something different to your existing donors to what you will be saying to those you are trying to recruit who have not yet given to you. And you may want to subdivide further, treating larger donors differently from smaller donors, those who have supported you consistently over a number of years differently from recent recruits, etc.

But as a mass communication medium, there are some dangers. The whole idea is to make the medium seem personal; the most effective letter is one written by hand to a friend. As the number of people you are writing to gets larger, then the opportunity for making it personal gets smaller. There is a cost, for example, of producing a handwritten salutation on 5,000 letters, and it is much easier to print "Dear friend" on every one. This depersonalisation will usually have an impact on the level of your returns.

Ten ways to personalise your mailing

A personal letter works far better than a circular letter. However, if you are writing to thousands of people, you will have to send a circular letter. But you can personalise it to make it appear to the recipient that it is a personal letter written specially to them. Here are some ways:

1. Handwrite the donor's name in the salutation at the start of the letter (Dear...") and handwrite the signature at the end of the letter. With large mailings this can be done by a volunteer. Or **use a word processor** to incorporate the donor's name in the salutation ("Dear Mrs Khan" rather than "Dear Supporter") and where appropriate also in the body of the letter.

2. Personalisation is not just a matter of name and address. It is also any **personal detail** which might be incorporated into the body of the letter – such as the amount of the last gift and the purpose for which it was given. Such details can often be incorporated using a word processor.

3. Type or handwrite the address on the envelope.

4. Use an **ordinary postage stamp** rather than put it through a franking machine.

5. Make **handwritten notes** or **underline parts** of the text of the letter even if this is then going to be printed!

6. Have a **handwritten PS** (a postscript) at the end of the letter which reinforces the message. Again this can be printed.

7. Ensure that the **response form** has the donor's name on it.

8. Use a **reply envelope** that is handwritten with the sender's name, as well as the organisation and reply address, on it (so that the reply letter is addressed to someone and not to an anonymous organisation).

9. Stamp the reply letter. Although this will double the postage bill, it should generate much better returns. But keep track of the response to ensure that it is worth doing this.

10. Even think of **handwriting the whole of the appeal letter** – which can be short, with the work of the organisation and the purpose of the appeal being explained in an accompanying leaflet.

Components of a mailing

Typical components of a mailing can vary widely. A well used model consists of five parts:

- **An outer envelope**: with a window so that a name and address can be printed on the reply device included in the envelope. The envelope can be overprinted with some 'teaser copy' to encourage recipients at least to open the letter.
- **A letter**: this is the main communication, and should be written as interestingly and personally as possible. Advice on writing appeal letters is given in *Section 8.3*.
- **A reply device**: this is what the donor returns with his or her contribution. It summarises what the appeal is for, and suggests donation levels. It is printed with the donor's name and address (which appears in the window envelope). And it may carry a code, so that you can track the response from the different lists you are using (to see which work well and which don't).
- **A pre-printed reply envelope**: making it simple for the donor to reply will increase your response considerably. The reply envelope could be

stamped or pre-paid. This adds to the expense, but again will improve response rates.
- **A brochure or leaflet**: which reinforces the text of the letter, and illustrates the need and the work of the organisation. If the donor is interested, he or she may want to find out more – and you can suggest ways of doing this.

Another advantage of this form of fundraising is that you can include as much information as you feel you need – in the brochure and in the letter. There are several views about how long the letter ought to be – from a single page, to several. It depends how much you have to say, and whether you can capture the reader's interest. Even the simplest mailing package can include a lot of information. But beware of producing letters and brochures that are too full of words – there is a great danger that they will go unread. Use pictures to tell the story, case studies and quotes to illustrate that you can make a difference, and all sorts of graphic devices to break up the text.

Getting the message right

Getting the message right is at least half the challenge (the other half being sending it to the right people and at the right time). For a mailing, there are two key components:

1. The proposition

Each mailing should have a central proposition. This might be *"50 rupees can help a child in distress"* or *"Urgent action is needed to save the rainforests of Brazil"*. This proposition should become the visual and verbal theme used throughout the mailing. This ensures the recipient receives a clear and strong message.

2. Making the request

The essential purpose of the letter is to get someone to support you. It is often assumed that the recipient will know what you want from them. But they don't. You have to ask. You want money, not their sympathy. A good letter will repeat the request for support several times. It will also show how the money will be used to benefit your work – and how many people it will help. It may also suggest various levels of giving for the donor to choose from. Then there can be no mistaking what you are really wanting from the reader.

Improving your appeal response

Here are six ways in which you could increase your response rates or average donation values. Before committing yourself to any of these you should attempt to test the idea first.

1. Wherever possible, **personalise your communication**.

2. Mail a different appeal to your **large and regular supporters** which refers to their past giving, recognises its value to the organisation and asking for a generous response to this new request.

3. Read through your letter and **rewrite** it to **improve its impact**, and introduce case studies of how people are being helped.

4. Try including a **leaflet with pictures** of your work.

5. Ask for **specific amounts** to achieve particular things. *"50 Rupees will buy a new syringe"*, for example, and mention this in both the letter and in the response device.

6. Put a **stamp** on return envelopes. No one likes to see a stamp wasted, and the only way to avoid this is to reply to the appeal!

Warm mailings

Sending letters to those people who have already given to you is the most cost-effective way of raising money by direct mail. They have already demonstrated an interest in your work and should be predisposed to support you if you **ask again**.

The high response that you can get from warm mailings to people who have previously supported you is the real reason for recruiting new donors by direct mail in the first place. Response rates will vary enormously – typically they can range from 7% to more than 30%. You can expect to raise up to £10 for each £1 spent in fundraising costs. Writing to your own supporters demands a number of special requirements. Get the message right and you will succeed in raising a lot of money.

There are varying views about how often you should write to your donors. Some feel that more than once a year is an invasion of their privacy, while others want to keep in touch at least once a quarter (and some even on a monthly basis). A test is sometimes the best way to see whether more frequent mailings will be worth your while. If you find it cost-effective to mail more frequently, then do so. Another possibility is to ask your donors how often they would like to receive information from you, and if your list of donors is large enough, you can then divide this into different groups who wish to be mailed at different frequencies

Whatever the frequency you decide, you need to develop a planned programme for the dates when you will mail and the sort of appeal that you will make with each different mailing.

Cold mailings

It's all very well to dream about the returns you could get if only you had 10,000 supporters on a computer mailing list. Somehow these people need to be identified and won over to your cause. One of the main ways voluntary organisations do this is through the use of cold mailings. 'Cold' because the person in receipt of your letter has not demonstrated any warmth for your cause before.

The practice then, is to create a mailing list from directories or to rent lists from another organisation (such as a bank or an insurance company) or from a list broker who specialises in doing this. And then to combine these lists with any other promising names you can find to send the appeal package to.

The difference between warm and cold mailing lies in the cost and also in the message. Because the people you are contacting are not your existing supporters, you can expect a much poorer response rate. Thus to raise the same amount of money, you may need to mail up to ten times as many people – at ten times the expense. And there will also be the cost of renting the list.

Because most of the recipients of a cold mailing will not know much about your work, your message will need to have a slightly different approach – a rather more simplistic approach to describing your cause and some reassurance about the value of your work. This might take the form of providing endorsements from well-known people; or you might present the answers to frequently asked questions, like how little is spent on administration; or you might highlight your achievements and successes.

Not all of the people on the list will be new. Some may be duplicates of people who are already your supporters. Wherever possible you should try to find some way of removing these duplicates – sending two letters to the same person, or an inappropriate message to long-standing supporters can have a negative impact. There are extremely sophisticated computer programmes that do this. If this approach is not possible, you can try to remove duplicates by looking through the list, trying to identify duplicates (which are not always that easy to detect – as names may be mis-spelt or the surname and first name reversed, etc.).

Though cold mailing response rates may be as high as 4% or even 5% in special situations, for example, an emergency appeal following a natural disaster, usually 0.5% to 2% is the likely range. Since you have to pay the printing and postage costs, cold mailings rarely pay for themselves – even with the benefit of a few high value responses. Why do it then? There are several reasons:

- To get new supporters in order to replace lapsed donors (just to stand still).
- To increase your supporters list (to develop your fundraising base).
- To obtain a source of future income. You are balancing the cost of acquisition against the likely lifetime value to you of those who respond – this is the total support they will give you over the years minus the costs of continuing to mail them. Once a donor has given, you will get much higher response rates from future mailings to them, and these should more than pay for themselves. If half the donors continue to support you for five years, your list of new recruits is a valuable asset. And some may even go on to leave a legacy. You have to calculate the cost of donor acquisition with the 'expected lifetime value' of the supporter that an average donor will give you in order to determine what is a reasonable donor acquisition cost.

> **Issues in cold mailings**
>
> **1. Whether to buy other people's lists.** There is a vocal group of the public which regards selling lists as an invasion of their privacy when they receive unsolicited mail. These people will contact you from time to time and complain in the most vocal way. Be prepared with your response.
>
> **2. It can appear a waste of money.** If only 3% of people respond, then 97% will be throwing all that paper away – which is why it is sometimes referred to as 'junk mail'. It is those who reply, not those who don't, which makes direct mail an effective fundraising method. But you do have to watch the response rates and mail out costs to ensure that you are being effective. But even if you are, those that are not responding will think you are wasting both your money and the world's resources. Using recycled paper can give the right signals, despite its greater cost; and suggesting the letter is handed on to a friend may also help.
>
> **3. It can be expensive.** You must ensure that you have the capacity to invest in this form of fundraising which requires a large expenditure commitment, a significant degree of risk and a payback period of several years. If you can't do it properly, then don't do it.

If you are just starting in direct mail, you may find that the programme only begins to generate any surplus after two or three years. However, at that point, the returns can rapidly build up. The question then is how to get started.

Finding the right lists

Your success in cold mailing will depend very substantially on the list you are mailing. Some lists will work extremely well for you, whilst others will achieve much worse results. There are several places to look:

1. Publicly available information, such as electoral registers and telephone directories. The electoral register (if published) can give you names and addresses in particular areas, and you can then select those areas which you feel are more likely to give – because of the affluence of the neighbourhood. The telephone directory at least gives you access to everyone who is able to afford a telephone. But not everyone is predisposed to respond to a request sent by post, and these lists compiled from public information do not always work that well.

2. Lists compiled from directories. Typically these could include lists of leading business people or the largest companies, which should be treated with care, as you may find that such people are the target of many appeals. But there may be directories available which provide you with just the right list of names to send your appeal to.

3. Lists that you obtain from other sources. These may be lists of people who have purchased something by post, lists of account holders at a bank or with a credit card company, lists of subscribers to a magazine or information service, lists of graduates from a university. It depends what is available. Questions you will want to ask include:

- **Does the list have any affinity with your cause?** If the list is of people with an interest in gardening, then an environmental cause may be particularly relevant, for example.
- **How old is the list?** If it is several years old, many people will have moved, so the returns you will get will decrease accordingly.
- **How frequently is it mailed?** Some lists are used regularly for mailings, and recipients may come to expect 'junk mail' which they throw straight into the bin.
- **How is it held?** Will it be supplied as labels or on disk? If it is supplied on disk, do you have the capacity to merge it with other lists, including your own supporters, in order to remove duplicate addresses (people do not like being mailed twice with the same appeal, as they will feel that you are wasting money – even where it is cheaper to mail them twice than remove duplicates).
- **How much does it cost?** There is usually a charge made for supplying the list, which will cover the cost of printing out the addresses, but which also reflects the value of the list. You will usually only be given permission to use the list once (which is why the process is known as list rental), and the list will often contain one or two addresses inserted into the list specifically so as to identify any mailings that are made using the list. The cost of list rental will usually be only a small part of the total cost of doing the mailing, so it can be worth paying more for a list that works really well than using a list which is available free of charge, which might generate only a very poor response.

Experience will tell you which sorts of list tend to work better for you. It is important to code your mailings so that you can identify which list the response has originated from. And for large mailings, there is always the possibility of testing a sample of the names on the list first (see *Appendix 1*).

Reciprocal mailings

One answer to the low response rates to cold mailings is to undertake reciprocal mailings. The idea is that your best potential donors are those people who have recently given to you (warm mailings); but the next best are those who are giving to similar organisations. These people are likely to be socially concerned and are known to respond to direct mail appeals. They may also be happy to support two similar causes. So that if you mail your supporters with an appeal from a similar charity and they mail your supporters, you will both gain. And that's how it usually turns out in practice. Typically, response rates can range from 2.5% to 10%.

The best results will be obtained by choosing to swap lists with organisations that are closest to your own, even though they may be your competitors. Before you do make sure that your organisation backs you in doing this. Most organisations will want to devise a simple policy to safeguard the interests of themselves and their donors. A 'code of practice' on reciprocal mailings is printed in *Appendix 4* at the end of the book.

Getting started in direct mail

The real difficulty in direct mail is getting started. Once you have a large donor base and an active mailing programme, it is a question of good management. But before you get there, there are considerable sums of money which will need to be spent; and this means considerable risk. Here are a few tips:

- Find as many ways as possible of **capturing the names of supporters**. People who write to you or visit you. People who have participated in a fundraising event. Volunteers who are giving their time. Keep their names and addresses on a database.
- Get these existing **supporters to suggest friends** who might like to be written to.
- Try to get a **sympathetic organisation** to agree to let you mail their list for free. This is a reciprocal mailing without giving something back in return.
- Acquire **other lists**, but test them first. It is a good strategy to send a small test mailing to several lists in order to see the response, then if they do respond well, you can mail the rest of the list later on. Dip your toe in the water first; do not dive in!
- Use **directories**. This does not always work. For example, if you were to use a telephone directory and target people who lived in a certain area, you will be writing both to responders and to non-responders – some people never respond to direct mail. If you wrote to someone else's mailing list, they would all be known responders. This is why people prefer to rent other people's lists rather than compile them from public information.
- **Hand deliver** where this is possible to save costs, and start with a simpler mailing package – though the message must be powerful for it to work at all.
- **Start slowly**, and build up.

Getting started: a case study

The Association for the Physically Handicapped, Bangalore, dredged about 300 names and addresses from its files (including past donors, visitors to the project and other contacts) and sent a simple letter which was personalised and signed by the President of the Association. Within 6 weeks they had received $2,000 in response to the mailing, including a first donation of $65 and individual donations of $300 and $150, which was more than double the target set for the fundraising.

Management

Because a lot of money is involved, direct mail needs good management. Here are some factors to consider:

Costs and budgets. You need to invest money to make money. But you also need to budget for response rates and average levels of donation. In this way you can control your costs, but also set targets for your income. On the cost side, be as cost conscious as you can. Find a cheap format of your printed material, and get competitive quotes from printers.

Testing. Before you mail a large list, test it by mailing a section of it. This will give you a good idea of the response to expect from the rest, and will prevent you from wasting your money on mailings that do not work. There are mathematical formulae which tell you what sample size will give a significant result. But if you are small and not using advanced techniques, a rough guide is to mail 10% of the total – that is one from every ten names, to ensure a random selection. In order to do a test, you need to code the response – which is easily done by having a code number on the reply coupon, which tells you which mailing list it has come from.

And more testing. You can test all sorts of other things. The approach, the headline, the amount you are asking for. But never test more than one factor at a time. Otherwise you will not know which is producing the result you are getting.

Segmentation. Perhaps the most important advantage of direct mail as a medium is its ability to target particular groups of supporters with a different message. Depending on the sophistication of your mailing list software and the information you are recording, you can subdivide your list into different segments – for example: long-standing members (perhaps those that have been members for at least 3 years); the rest of the membership; people who have recently made a substantial donation; people who live locally, and those that live outside the area; people who have participated in a particular fundraising event; people with a known interest in, say, conservation. Segmentation gives you the power to address a slightly different message to each group, which reflects their particular relationship with you.

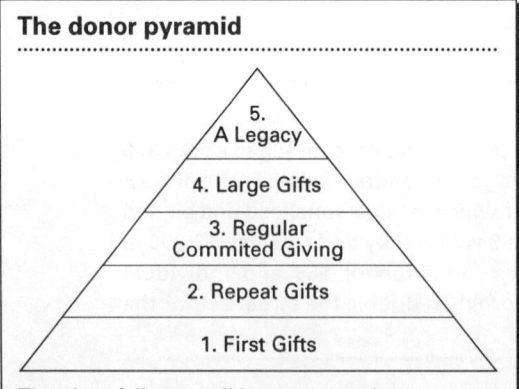

The donor pyramid

5. A Legacy
4. Large Gifts
3. Regular Commited Giving
2. Repeat Gifts
1. First Gifts

The aim of direct mail is to get people on to your donor base (which is expensive), and then move them up to become regular, committed and substantial givers. And possibly to consider leaving you a legacy when they die.

Increasing the average donation. If you can find ways of getting donors to give more and to give more frequently, then you have one of the keys to success. Just because a donor has given, does not mean that they will not want to give again. On the contrary, they have demonstrated their support for you. So if there is a reason to ask them again – for example you are launching an appeal to purchase a new piece of equipment – then ask your existing supporters, even if they have recently made a donation. Try to get them to give to you quarterly or even monthly – they will give much more if they give frequently than if they make an annual contribution. Try to get them to commit in some way to supporting you for a long period of time. ActionAid asks it supporters to give a monthly contribution for ten years – on the basis that if the donor is serious about helping, then it needs a lot of money over a long period of time to have any impact.

List management

The most valuable resource you have is your own list of donors or members. Guard it carefully. If your list is held on a computer, how safe is it? Have you got a security copy of your file held somewhere else for safety's sake? You should produce regular back up copies of your files. If you lose it, you may never be able to recreate it without a massive investment of time and money.

You also need to manage your list in a number of different ways. You need to keep it up to date by removing all inactive or deceased supporters. Periodically you should review whether you are holding the names of people who are no longer active donors (say, those people who have not given for two or three years). One way of determining this is to segment this part of your list and look at the response you get from it. Where the yield is below that of a cold mailing you should consider removing their names. You can also ask them if they want to continue receiving information from you. If some reply, then at least they are interested and you should keep their names on file.

You need to make sure that there are no duplicates. If you are mailing the same person twice or three times each mail out, then this is a waste of money and can cause aggravation. Automatic de-duplication can be a complicated business which requires a sophisticated computer programme. If you are small, you will have to do it by eye. Remember that a person's name may be misspelt, or their address wrongly typed in, which can easily create a duplicate record.

Lastly, add all new names immediately. The sooner you can do this, the sooner these people will be able to receive further appeals.

Advice and consultancy

Direct mail is a highly technical fundraising method. The skills which are required include:

- Writing effective copy.
- Producing a cost-effective mailing package.
- Knowing how much to ask for.
- Planning a mailing programme.
- Selecting the best lists to rent.
- Testing (and coding) of the response. Testing is dealt with in more detail in A*ppendix 1*.
- Knowing what response rates to expect.
- Evaluation of your performance.

'The Good Mailing Guide'

1. Use **emotion** in your writing.
2. Include **stories** about individuals.
3. **Ask** for money, directly.
4. Use **simple language**, avoid jargon.
5. Make all written material **visually attractive**.
6. Portray **your beneficiaries** as 'doers' rather than as 'victims', not as helpless, but needing your help.
7. Catch the **reader's attention** immediately, perhaps with a snappy headline.
8. Use someone specific as the **signatory** – this could be someone well known, your director or chairman, or a frontline worker.
9. Get the **timing right**.
10. **Make the reader give**.
11. Appeal to the **reader's conscience**.
12. **Read what you are sending** before sending it – would you give in response to your own appeal letter?

This is a list of success factors developed by Oxfam after studying ten years of appeals to supporters.

You may not have all (or indeed any) of these skills. But it is possible to get advice from others, including:

- Other organisations with direct mail programmes, who might be prepared to share their knowledge and experience with you.
- Professional consultants, who specialise in this medium. But you will have to pay for their expertise. So it is as well to know what you want, to brief them well, and to have a contract that sets out precisely what they are expected to do and for how much. Consultants divide into two: charity fundraising consultants, and advertising or promotion consultants specialising in direct mail (which is a technique that is used for business promotion as well as for charity fundraising).
- The International Fund Raising Group's network of fundraisers and training courses.

6.5 Committed giving and membership

Committed giving

Committed giving is what really makes sense of your direct mail (and other donor acquisition activities). The donor acquisition process is expensive, and unlikely to cover its costs through the immediate income it produces. But it is the first step in building up a supporter base. The follow up mailings are what generates the real revenue – for as we have seen, the people who have given already respond much better to any appeal. Your aim is to:

- Get your first time donors to **continue to give**, by sending them further appeals, only removing them from your donor list when you are convinced by their non-response that they are no longer interested.
- **Stimulate their concern** for the cause and interest in your work, and this should then lead to an increase in the level of support they are prepared to give.
- Help them recognise the **importance of giving long-term support** to the work that you are doing (your work may take time to yield results, and you need their continuing support to help you do this). And then get them to commit themselves to supporting you on a long-term basis.
- **Make it easy** for them to give on a regular basis. Set up a simple payment mechanism to enable donations to be paid regularly (see below), which offers convenience to the donor and a continuing stream of income for you. You might also want to use some form of 'membership' or 'friends' scheme to suggest levels of giving.
- Encourage donations to be paid in a **tax-effective way** (if there are tax incentives for charitable giving available in your country). Explain the tax benefits that are available, and help the donor take advantage of them.
- Ask them to think about **legacy giving** as 'the ultimate gift'. Legacy fundraising is covered in *Section 6.7*.

This list of tasks sets an agenda for you to develop your direct mail and donor acquisition programme, and to turn your first-time giver into a committed and enthusiastic long-term supporter.

Standing orders

Having an automatic system for donations to be paid to you regularly (annually, quarterly or even monthly) by transfer from the donor's bank account will ensure that the support continues until the donor cancels the arrangement, and it will make the process of collecting the money far simpler for you to administer (the money appears in your account on the due dates, and you do not need to send subscription reminders) and far simpler for the donor (who does not have to write a cheque and send off the payment each time).

There are a number of mechanisms that can be used for this, including a standing order, direct debit, autogiro, pre-authorised checking and EFT. What system you use will depend on what banking facilities are available in your country, and the cost of using such facilities.

Promotion

Not every donor will agree to enter into a long-term commitment, but it is important to give every donor the opportunity to do so. For this reason, a clear promotion strategy is needed. This should include answers to these questions:

- What are the **interests and motivations** of your supporters?
- What are your **financial requirements** – how much income do you need to raise, and how much do you think your donors will be prepared to give?
- How will you **promote a scheme to your existing supporters**, to encourage them to make a commitment?
- Are there any **other prospective committed supporters** that you can identify?
- How should you **report back** to your committed givers, so as to maintain their continued enthusiasm and support?
- **What else can you do** to get them to feel more involved in the work of the organisation and the cause it is addressing?

Committed giving: two examples

Greenpeace (in the UK)
Name of scheme: Greenpeace Frontline
Type of scheme: a club offering closer involvement, at a price
Set up: 1991
Price: £20 minimum per month
Incentives: visits, videos, publications, briefings, etc.
Number of monthly givers: approximately 2,000
Main target audience: existing supporters
Method of promotion: direct mail
Support publications: no special newsletter is produced; access to existing but previously unavailable reports, research documents, internal memos, etc.
Annual income from scheme: about £500,000
Additional appeals: yes, made regularly to members
Administrative staff: 1 person full-time, 2 people part-time
Key points: a dramatic increase in subscription level but in return for a level of donor service that has significant organisational implications; too early to judge its success in relationship building, but results so far look encouraging

Community Aid Abroad/Freedom from Hunger (Australia)
Name of scheme: AWARE
Type of scheme: project linked (women's projects)
When set up: 1982
Price: $10 per month minimum, average $25
Incentives: yes
Number of monthly givers: 12,500 (as at September 1993)
Main target audience: 'thinking' donors
Methods of promotion: press advertising, inserts, direct mail
Support publications: a short monthly bulletin
Annual income from scheme: $3,750,000
Additional appeals: emergency appeals, or appeals made in the bulletin only
Key points: builds awareness with committed supporters; the programme is about communicating more with these supporters rather than giving them a way to 'buy themselves out' from hearing from the organisation
Source: Ken Burnett, presentation at the First Paris Fund Raising Workshop, 1994

The following are some of the promotional techniques you can use.

1. Approaching active givers. If you analyse the response to your appeals, you will see that a number of your donors will have given more than once. They may give each year in response to an annual appeal. They may give more than once during the year. They may respond very promptly to the appeal. These are your priority targets for committed giving. They should be contacted, pointing out the advantages of giving regularly and offered all the appropriate forms that are needed. If there are only a few 'prospective targets', then you can do this contacting in person or by telephone.

2. Member-Get-Member or Supporter-Get-Supporter. This is simply an invitation to an existing member or supporter to nominate or recruit another. Various incentives (such as a free entry prize draw or some form of gift) can be used which are offered either to the original member or to the new one. This relies on the personal enthusiasm of existing members and their ability to persuade their friends and colleagues. It is a system of membership promotion which works extremely well.

3. Promoting committed giving more widely to your donor base. One strategy is to undertake one appeal per year which promotes regular giving and encourages payment by standing order or some other regular payment system. This will involve a loss of response from those not in a position to give regularly, but who might otherwise have made a one-off cash donation. Another approach is to mention the value of committed giving in each mailing, but by way of an afterthought or postscript, and to give people the opportunity to give in this way.

4. Child sponsorship and similar techniques, where the donor is linked to a specific project, community or family. This works best where the link is to a particular child, as it commits the donor to continuing to give support whilst the child is growing up, perhaps for 10 to 15 years. In return the donor receives news of the project and the sponsored family, and even letters written by the sponsored child. Such an approach works extremely well in fundraising terms, but has to be handled with care. Problems can arise where the donor really wants to help just one individual child, although most schemes provide support for the whole community, to improve livelihoods, education and health, but show the benefits to the life of one family or child. Or where the donor builds up an expectation of a relationship with the sponsored child, which may not be what the family wants.

Keeping in touch, maintaining enthusiasm

A common problem is that once you have obtained their committed support, you then begin to take your supporters for granted. You know that their contribution is going to arrive, so you don't bother much to keep in touch with them or to tell them what you are achieving. You must avoid neglecting them at all costs. They are your most important givers. You need to do everything you can to maintain their enthusiasm and support.

You should take every opportunity to keep them in touch with what you are doing – and with any further developments and need for support. You might feel that once a donor has made a commitment it is an indication that they do not want to be asked for further support. A better approach is to view their commitment as being affirmation of the value and importance of your cause. When you approach them, always recognise their commitment, so that they understand you are approaching them precisely because of their commitment. Using this approach, you can appeal to them on a regular basis and ask them to give additional support. This will especially make sense when there is an obviously good reason for the appeal, such as an emergency. Or if your supporter list is big enough, you can develop special appeals which you are asking members to support. You want your friends to help you equip an operating theatre or sponsor the new theatrical production, and you need to raise £10,000 from them just to do this.

You will need to report back to your committed givers on what you have achieved with their money. You might ask them to visit you to see your work. You might organise talks and discussions about your work with an expert. These ways of getting the donor to understand the value of what you are doing and to see your work at first hand can only increase their commitment. They are used successfully by many organisations – including overseas development agencies such as Oxfam who now organise trips for their donors to see projects at work. The payback of this is the increased support you will receive as a result.

You might produce a newsletter or a magazine or send a specially personalised letter from the Chief Executive. This 'special treatment' can make them feel

> **Your invitation to join the Hospital Well Wishers**
>
> *"'Well Wishers' is a special group of caring people. People who care enough to lend their support to our critically ill children. As a member of this group, you will receive our free regular newsletter. Each issue will bring you news of the latest research, treatment, breakthrough and real life stories of outstanding courage, determination, hope and success. It will give you an insight into the day-to-day running of the hospital. It will also keep you in touch with other Well Wishers."*
>
> After the huge success of the hospital building Appeal, this idea for a membership scheme was created to maintain funds flowing into the hospital.

important. Committed donors are likely to want to see a minimum of expenditure on 'unnecessary' items, and so they should not be approached too frequently or too lavishly.

Membership

A membership subscription scheme is the method many organisations use to encourage supporters to get more involved with their cause. But the aims of a membership scheme are not necessarily to raise money. There are several different types of membership scheme:

- Schemes that **confer benefits of a constitutional nature** (such as the right to attend and vote at Annual General Meetings, and the right to receive an Annual Report). The rights attached to membership will normally be spelt out in the organisation's constitution.
- Schemes that provide more **tangible benefits**, such as free or reduced price entry to museums or wildlife facilities.
- Schemes that give the donor a **'sense of belonging'**, for example as a 'friend' of an organisation committed to helping it raise money, or as a member of a campaigning group such as Amnesty International (human rights) or Greenpeace (the environment) supporting the aims of the campaign.
- Schemes that are used as **a mailing list** – typically a theatre or cultural centre will offer to circulate information on forthcoming productions to this mailing list, and there may be benefits such as preferential booking and discounts on tickets available to subscribers.
- Schemes that are designed to **encourage committed giving**, where donors are made to feel more a part of the organisation. Besides encouraging supporters to give long-term (see *Committed Giving*), it is also possible to develop a scheme where large numbers of supporters each pledge regular support as part of some sort of friends' group. Although individually small, these donations can amount to a useful source of income if the scheme is developed on a wide enough basis.

Some membership schemes are aimed primarily at people who are interested in doing something – helping the organisation campaign, attending cultural events, volunteering their time. The aim of these is not to generate an income, although members may be happy to give when asked. Membership schemes of these types may have their annual subscription levels set deliberately low to encourage as many people as possible to join. Then there are those schemes that have a fundraising purpose – their primary aim is to generate an income for the organisation.

There are three main benefits which you can derive from having a membership scheme:

1. Commitment. A membership scheme offers a convenient peg upon which to obtain committed long-term support for your organisation.

2. Involvement. Membership opens up and provides a mechanism for democratic control through the right to vote at annual meetings (if this is included in the constitution of the organisation), thereby giving the members some influence over the direction of the organisation.

3. Money. The annual membership fee provides an income, and the membership list is an ideal hunting ground for further donations. Members have demonstrated their interest in the organisation, so become likely prospects for obtaining further financial support.

Another important purpose of having a membership base is the indirect benefit it can bring to your organisation. If you wish to mount a campaign, your members are the first who can be called on to participate in it. And your membership numbers indicate the degree of the public support for your campaign or issue. A high membership level can increase your influence and impact.

Membership lists are usually held on computer, but when you are just starting out, your addresses can equally well be held on a card index system. Members will be mailed regularly with newsletters and annual reports to be kept in touch. Appeals to members will be carried out using standard direct mail methods – the membership list should generate extremely good returns. Members may be asked to make contributions for special projects or in an emergency. Since they are already contributing their membership subscription on a regular basis, the appeal should be seen as additional to the subscription that member is making, a completely separate contribution for a specific purpose.

Standing orders and other systems to facilitate payment of the subscription when it becomes due can be used. But if membership subscription rates rise, then some system for alerting the donor and increasing the amount paid on the due date needs to be put in place.

Frequent giving

The value of committed giving or membership subscription income depends on:

- **The number of donors or members**. The more you have, the better. Once you have established a scheme, your aim should be to find ways of recruiting new donors or members economically.
- **The annual subscription level**. With a membership scheme, this will depend on your objectives – to make money or to involve as many people as possible. Some organisations give the donor or member different levels of annual subscription to select from, each with a different name and possibly different benefits or levels of involvement in the organisation. A supporter scheme might have three categories: a 'friend', a 'good friend', a 'best friend'; or a 'supporter', a 'sponsor', a 'patron'.
- **The cost of running the scheme**. This includes the cost of member acquisition, and the annual administration cost including the cost of communicating with the member and sending information such as newsletters and annual reports. This should be calculated and budgeted for, so that an organisation has a clear idea of the surplus income that will be generated by each member after the costs of running the membership scheme.
- **The value of any additional income** that is generated from further appeals to members.

You will also find that the frequency of giving is important. If you ask for a smaller sum on a more frequent basis, you will find that you can get people to contribute much larger annual sums. For example, ActionAid in one of its most successful promotions asked, *"Does this child need 50 pence more than you?"*. They were inviting supporters to give 50 pence per day, which seemed a trivial sum. In fact, they were asking donors to enter into a monthly commitment of £15 (which again did not seem that much in terms of what their money would be achieving for the charity). But if they had been asked to give £180 a year, people would almost certainly have refused to do so, as it would seem to be far too large a commitment.

There is enormous value in seeking frequent payments as they build up to large annual sums but still sound reasonable to the donor. You can ask people to give once every three months (quarterly) or once a term (three times a year, which might be appropriate for a school project), or monthly (which is the frequency of many people's pay) or even weekly (for the real enthusiast!). You might even suggest a certain level of donation, and ask the donor to select the frequency (which is a variation on the usual practice of asking the donor to suggest the amount from a list of suggested levels of giving). The value of encouraging frequent giving is something that can be tested quite easily in one of your mailings. The usual outcome is that requests for monthly or quarterly giving will be no less effective, and will produce dramatically higher average annual donation levels for you.

> **The WWF membership scheme**
>
> Become an associate of the World Wide Fund for Nature today!
> *"Yes, I want to support the worldwide campaign to protect wildlife, by becoming an associate of WWF now. Please send me quarterly issues of Wildlife Magazine and WWF News. I wish to pay my subscription of £20 by direct debit, and have completed the instruction to my bank below."*
>
> This is a part of a WWF mailing. Though they are not inviting you to become a formal member with constitutional voting rights, it is styled as a membership with an annual 'subscription' and newsletters. A cold mailing using this approach achieved a response rate of 2.35% and was considered a great success.
> Source: Chapter One Direct (fundraising consultants)

Administration

The administration of membership demands a high degree of organisation, especially if you wish to maximise the benefits of your fundraising effort. There are two key issues:

Membership renewal

How should you organise the task of inviting members to renew their subscriptions. When any fixed term commitment comes to an end, there is both an opportunity and a need to ensure that as many people as possible renew. The usual way to do this is through sending reminder letters:

- A few months before the expiry, giving them time to renew.
- Coinciding with the expiry if they haven't yet renewed to remind them that renewal is due.
- A follow up reminder some months after expiry, telling them that they haven't yet renewed and that their membership will lapse if they don't.
- A further follow up some months later – which is the final reminder.

The telephone is also a valuable tool. It can be used to ask donors why they have not yet renewed. This reminds those who have just not got round to dealing with their membership renewal, and it also gathers useful market research information about why members are not renewing.

Membership renewal can be done on a fixed date each year (with annual membership running from the 1st January to the 31st December, for example).

This means that all renewals are handled on one date. But you have the problem of what to do with members who join during the year, and especially with those who join in the later part of the year – when they will feel that they have already paid their subscription. So an alternative mechanism is that each member's membership expires exactly twelve months after the annual subscription was paid. But this requires more efficient organisation, as you will be dealing with membership matters throughout the year.

Any substantial membership scheme is likely to require a reliable computer system to make it work well. A key point is the ability of the system to identify renewal points so that you can mail not only on the point of renewal but also both before and after to stimulate the highest possible renewal rate.

Maintaining donor records

With your committed givers and members, you have a group of people who will be giving money to you regularly and possibly also supporting you in a number of different ways. You need to keep track of their support, so that you are able to identify people who might be able to give you special help when you need it, or to invite to special events such as receptions, or simply to personalise the appeals you write to them as much as possible. This means that you need to keep all the information on one record, and that you should avoid at all costs the mistake of sending them duplicate mailings. You need to merge donor information, which is collected when members make additional donations, with their membership record.

It is essential not to keep two separate sets of information – so that you are able to look up one person in one place to find out how and when they have supported you with how much.

6.6 Personal solicitation

Meeting and speaking to potential donors in person provides good opportunities for fundraising. As a technique, it has many similarities with direct mail fundraising. You have to identify people to approach, communicate with them effectively, and motivate them to give. The medium is different. You will be meeting them and asking face-to-face, or by using the telephone.

But there are significant differences. With direct mail, you are approaching thousands or even tens of thousands of people with the same message, which you try to 'personalise' through clever copy writing and by segmenting your mailing list into different categories of donor. With personal solicitation you are approaching one (or a few) individuals in person to put over a message that is personal to them. It is obviously much more effective to persuade people this way, but it is not very efficient – you just don't have the time to approach the same quantity of people that direct mail can reach. So it is important to recognise when and how personal solicitation can be used to best effect.

Under the heading of personal solicitation we are including:

- **Face-to-face meetings** with existing donors in their homes (warm visiting); but face-to-face meetings with people you have never met before to recruit new support (cold calling) is covered in house-to-house collections (see *Section 6.3*).

- **Making presentations** at meetings; both meetings with outside people you are asked to speak at and meetings with your own supporters to keep them in touch.
- **Telephone solicitation**; although not as powerful as face-to-face meetings, it is a useful fundraising technique.

Warm visiting

Warm visiting involves face-to-face meetings with people who have already supported you or with whom you already have some form of contact. There are two reasons for doing this:

- A 'soft sell' approach where you visit to talk about your work, to find out more about their interests, and to try to develop a warmer relationship with them, rather than to ask for money. This is an investment in the relationship which you hope might lead to more committed giving (or even a legacy) later on.
- A harder sell as part of a major appeal, when you really do need their support. And having got the support of your committed donors, you are then in a better position to go public on your appeal.

Some larger charities employ individuals whose job it is to visit all their more substantial donors. Though the visit is ostensibly being made to thank them for their past support, in practice substantial sums can be collected and other ways for them to support the organisation can be discussed.

Since you are dealing with people who already have some relationship with you, you must make sure you:

- Have **precise information** on the support they have given in the past, so that you can thank them and tell them what you have been able to do with their money.
- Are **well briefed** about the work of the organisation, so that you can talk about current work and future plans in an informed and interesting way.
- Have some idea of **the sort of support you need**, and the sorts of ways in which they might be able to help you – so that if the opportunity arises, you can introduce the idea of some further support.
- Know about **tax-effective giving**, as that can be one excuse for being there in the first place – to tell them how their money can be used even more effectively, by donating it tax-efficiently.

Meeting potential new supporters

Where someone has indicated an interest in giving to you, you may want to meet them personally to 'seal the deal'. At this meeting, you will be able to answer all their questions, and suggest ideas for the sorts of things that they might like to support. Such a meeting should be held in an appropriate venue; the charity's offices are not always the best place to meet potential supporters – a site visit where the beneficiaries are around, or a meeting at the offices of an important existing supporter may be better. But if it is at your office, make sure that everything looks well run and busy – as this gives a positive image about your organisation and its importance. Alternatively, some people might feel more comfortable meeting you in their own homes. For such a meeting you need to:

- **Research the donor** and their capacity to give, so that you know their interests and understand the scale of giving that may be possible.

- **Have a 'shopping list'** of projects which they might like to support, so that you can discuss with them what will most interest them.
- **Have good clear information** available about the organisation and its work, including photographs of the organisation at work and endorsements from prominent people.

Don't be in too much of a hurry. The skilled fundraiser knows when to ask – and it may not be immediately, but later, the person's interest has been stimulated and they have had time to think about it.

Presentations at events

Many organisations have the opportunity to provide speakers at other people's meetings or conferences. This is an opportunity to speak directly to the people present about the work of your organisation. This can also be a good opportunity for talking about the fundraising needs and getting people interested in the idea of supporting you.

The presentation has to be carefully thought out. It needs to be tailored to the needs of the particular audience. A presentation to young farmers will be very different from one to a group of doctors. The main problem is to work out how your audience can respond to any appeal you make, as it is someone else's event and organisational matters are not under your direct control. After you have spoken, will the audience be leaving quickly after the meeting to move onto something else? Will the audience be circulated with information about your organisation or appeal literature? Will you be able to take names and addresses of people who are interested? Or will you be able to circulate everyone who was there subsequently? Will there be time for questions and discussion – and if there is, will it be friendly or hostile? Can you actually raise money at the event by organising a bucket or plate collection (where volunteer collectors are placed at the door or at the end of each row)?

The good public speaking guide

- Find out how long you are expected to speak for
- Plan your talk. But remember that it is more spontaneous to speak 'off the cuff' than to read out a written speech.
- Start with a joke or a story, to enliven the proceedings.
- Explain your involvement in the organisation, and inject a sense of personal commitment to the cause.
- Use case studies and personal stories to explain the work. This is far better than a stream of statistics about the problem.
- Do not use jargon.
- Appeal to your audience's emotions – their hearts not their heads.
- Ask for support if you need it.
- Have business cards, explanatory leaflets and even pledge forms to hand out to those who are interested.
- Tell people to telephone you if they are interested, and say that you would be delighted for them to visit you to see your work at first hand.

Your own events

Other people's events offer you new audiences. But you can also organise your own events for existing and potential supporters. These can be visits or study tours or open days to see your organisation at work, small discussions with an expert speaker so that they can see the problems you are addressing in greater depth, or receptions of some sort (drinks receptions, dinners, etc.), perhaps at the home of a well respected donor and possibly with a guest speaker or some sort of presentation afterwards.

Such events can be an excellent fundraising investment. You will make your existing donors feel important, and give them a better understanding of the issues. This may lead to them giving more substantial support or committing some time to your organisation as a volunteer.

Think carefully about your objectives for such an event, and about your audience and the sort of event that will most appeal to them. It is not just organising the event, but having the right event for them that is important. One idea is to mix existing supporters and people who have expressed an interest at such an event. If you do this, all the new people attending should be told to expect a follow up visit from you afterwards.

Telephone solicitation

Asking on the telephone has many of the same characteristics as personal solicitation. But it is much more efficient – in that you can contact many more people in a given space of time. It is even possible to organise mass telephoning campaigns (either warm or cold calling) using your own volunteers, or even a specialist telephone selling agency.

The telephone can be used successfully for:

- **Emergency appeals**, where there is a particular urgency. This could be some disaster, or because you have the opportunity to purchase a property if you can raise the money by a deadline.
- **Large appeals**, where you are trying to get lots of your supporters to give something. The telephone will be more effective than direct mail. But asking people to attend meetings will be even more effective. But the telephone could be used here as a follow up reminder to the written invitation. Or to contact those who could not attend the meeting or who did not reply to the invitation. They may still be persuadable. Remember the biggest reason for not giving is that people are not asked.
- **Discussing tax-effective giving** with people who have given. Here there is a particular reason for telephoning – you have some important information which could save them money!
- **Cold calling** – but remember that the telephone is intrusive, and people being disturbed by an unsolicited call can be hostile or even abusive.

To succeed with the telephone, you need a confident sounding voice, a good start to your conversation (practising to increase your confidence, and preparing a script help here) and enough knowledge about the work of the organisation to respond positively to any questions that come up. If you are using agents or volunteers to do the calling, you must make sure that they are well briefed, that they understand the organisation and its values, so that they can present it properly, and that they know why they are making the call and what they want as the outcome. Using the telephone is discussed in more detail in *Section 8.5*.

What you will need to succeed

Here are some of the things that you will need to succeed in personal solicitation.

- People who are really **good speakers and presenters**. You may wish to provide some form of training for them in presentation skills and asking skills. You might even try to develop a 'speakers panel' of people interested in speaking about your organisation at meetings who are also good at it.

- **Donors who have already given**, who are prepared to speak at meetings which potential donors are attending. There is nothing like being able to say "The organisation is great, and I've given to it" to get others to give.
- **Volunteers** with similar skills for warm visits.
- **Good pictorial and other visual material** that can be used to illustrate a presentation. It is important that these show people (people helping, and people being helped).
- For meetings you may want **visual aids** (for use with an overhead projector or a flipchart) or even a short video (no more than 5 minutes long).

Any visit should be prepared with care. Although it may seem to be overdoing it to rehearse a presentation which is going to be made to just one person, this can pay off. You should try to predict what questions will come up. Use a colleague or friend to help. You will need to be well armed with written information and visual material. You should leave some prepared material behind when you leave. Most people will not make up their minds immediately, and will be guided or reminded by the material you have left with them – and you can telephone them a few days later to get their response to the meeting.

Throughout the meeting, you should give people the opportunity to put questions. If you are not getting much feel for how the meeting is going, ask them some simple questions. Do they feel it is an important issue? Do they think the project will achieve what it is setting out to do?

At some point in the conversation, you will need to ask for money. There are several different approaches to this. One is to say that you want them to consider helping in one of several ways, which you then set out (having researched their interests and potential level of giving as well as you can). A more direct approach dispenses with such niceties, explains the urgency of the need, and simply asks for the money – but always try to ask for a specific amount. Probably the most effective way, is when someone who has already given support is making the ask, and is able to mention what their own donation has been.

And finally remember that the best person to do the asking may not be you. Someone who has already given, someone known to the donor (peer group giving) may be more appropriate. The skilled fundraiser will organise the right person to ask that particular donor.

6.7 Legacies and memorials

By the time most people die, they will have decided how their assets (their money, their property, their investments, their belongings) should be distributed. Different societies have different traditions on how wealth is distributed amongst family members after death. But if someone wants to leave specific instructions on the distribution of their assets, this is done by writing a 'Will', which sets out who should benefit. On their death, their property is then distributed according to their wishes as set out in their Will. The people responsible for distributing the proceeds of the Will are called the 'Executors'.

Normally people leave the greater part of their assets to their immediate family (a surviving spouse, children, close relatives). But many people also take the opportunity to leave something to charity. Some have no family, and then leaving their money to charity becomes an obvious option. There are several reasons why people might like to support a charity with a legacy:

- **Their immediate family is already well provided for** and does not need all their money.
- They would like to 'do good' on their death, as this seems an **appropriate gesture**, or possibly a passport to heaven!
- They can help **create a better world** for the next generation.
- The gift can be coupled with some sort of **memorial** to them.
- **It costs them nothing**! They are not there when the money is paid over.

Legacies are often large amounts – and sometimes huge, where there is no surviving family to leave the money to. Legacy fundraising can generate quite large sums of money. You should remember that you will not get the money immediately. Only when the donor dies; and by that time, the donor may have written a new Will, and changed his or her mind about your legacy. And even then it may take some time before you receive the money.

You need to think carefully about the appropriateness of asking for legacies or proposing this as a method of giving. Attitudes towards death, expectations regarding the passing down of wealth from one generation to another, the support needs of the surviving spouse, and the legal background to inheritance vary so much from country to country and culture to culture.

If you do decide that it is an appropriate fundraising technique for you to use, then how do you invite people to give you a legacy? Like other forms of fundraising, what you get out depends on what you put in. You need to think about who to ask, the best way of asking them and what to ask for – and preferably prepare a plan. There will usually be a time-lag of between three and four years before you begin to see any return for your effort. But after that a steady stream of income should develop. It is a matter of investing time and effort now in the expectation of a future return.

Target audience

There are three groups to consider:

1. Your existing supporters. Your Management Board, your volunteers and your existing supporter base is a good place to start. They already have a good understanding of your work and have made some commitment to you. If getting them to give regularly is a natural progression from occasional giving, then a legacy is a natural next step up from regular giving. What is more appropriate than to make their last gift to the charity their biggest and best? This is something you need to suggest to your supporters and encourage them to do.

2. The general public. Approaching the general public has the benefit of increasing public awareness of your work, but it is expensive unless it is clearly targeted. You should try to target elderly people who you think might be interested in your cause. You can use cold mailing, advertising or posters.

3. Intermediaries and advisers. Yet another strategy is to concentrate on people who advise on legal and financial matters: a lawyer, a bank manager or an accountant. When Wills are written, so the argument goes, these professionals are the ones who advise. They may be a source of information about charities, and certainly have their own preferences or prejudices. You can reach them by direct mail or by advertising in professional journals and tell them about your work and the opportunities for their clients to leave you a legacy. At a local level for a local cause, you can communicate directly through personal contact or by talking at meetings.

Memorial giving

Another funding source is memorial giving. This is particularly appropriate for charities with a medical or health slant or where the deceased is known to have had a strong interest in the cause. Memorial giving is actually giving by the friends and family of the deceased in memory of him or her. Pieces of equipment, rooms in buildings, or bursary funds, lectures, planting a garden are all possible items of expenditure which could be funded through a memorial fund.

Memorial trusts: two examples

The Willie Musarurwa Memorial Trust

When national hero, Willie Musarurwa died suddenly in April 1991 at the age of 63, a group of his friends got together and decided that the best way to honour his gallant service in the cause of Zimbabwe's liberation struggle was to establish a Memorial Fund in his name. They decided to raise funds to continue an ongoing struggle for which Willie had made real, personal sacrifices – freedom of expression and journalistic excellence through a responsible press. The Memorial Fund provides bursaries for the further education of journalists and awards a 'Best Editor' prize at the annual Media Awards. The initial funds were raised from friends and large local firms (mostly banks, insurance companies and travel companies), and from two German and one Norwegian donor organisations. Subsequently, funds have been added to through two fundraising banquets (with Archbishop Desmond Tutu and a Deputy Governor of the Bank of England as speakers).

The Herbert Chitepo Library Trust

The late Herbert Chitepo was a prominent nationalist and leading architect of the struggle for liberation in Zimbabwe. He was assassinated in Lusaka in 1975. In his memory, the Chitepo family made a notable contribution towards the Herbert Chitepo Library at St Augustine's School, Penhalonga, where Herbert Chitepo studied and taught. In addition, the Herbert Chitepo Library Trust has been established to promote the development of literacy in Zimbabwe. The trust funds the supply of books to needy school libraries and other educational institutions in remote and rural areas of Zimbabwe.

Getting started

The first thing you will need to do is to understand how legacies work, and the legal and tax background – there are often estate duty benefits in leaving money to charity.

Next you will need to produce some literature which gives a background to your work, outlines your needs, suggests a legacy and tells the readers how they can set about leaving you a legacy. Important points to make are:

- Any tax exemptions that exist for legacies made to a charity.
- The importance by the charity placed on legacies as a source of income and some idea of how legacy income will be spent.

- The sorts of legacy that are possible (and the legally correct forms of words for a Codicil if there is room to include this on the reply form).
- A pledge form, so that they can tell you what they plan to do – and if they decide to give you a legacy, you can then continue to keep in touch with them through putting them on your mailing list (a special segment for legacy donors).

You may also want to produce explanatory material on legacies. This is something that only very large charities with large supporter lists can afford to do. If you can produce your own material, then you might think about getting together a few simple practical books on Will making.

Next you will need a promotion plan. Who will you approach? And how? This should be linked to a budget – as it will cost money to produce the material and for the promotion, as well as your time – which is also a cost.

The value of the legacy income you receive will depend on a large number of factors. The most important is the age profile of your supporters. If they are young, then on average a considerable time will elapse before they die – which means that however successful you are in getting people to agree to leave you a legacy, the prospects of your getting any income in the near future is much reduced.

How do you decide how much to invest in legacy fundraising? If you are starting out, you will have no immediate legacy income against which to calculate a fundraising cost. You could set a target for the number of pledges that you will receive each year. As time goes on you will find out both how many turn into legacies and how much it costs to get a pledge. If you are already receiving legacy income, you might set aside a percentage (say 10%) of your current legacy income for legacy promotion.

6.8 Capital appeals and big gift campaigns

Charities are able to attract big gifts from time to time, but this is a particularly important component of a major building or endowment appeal, or any other sort of capital fundraising campaign. In many ways, large-scale fundraising is just the same as any other fundraising – you have to ask effectively. But because you are asking for a lot of money, it is important to plan your campaign and to put sufficient resources behind it to be successful.

A major appeal will be run very infrequently, so you will need to create the structure specially. But if you run it successfully, there are a number of spin offs which can significantly enhance your organisation's fundraising capability:

- You may have developed a **large donor list** (of people who contributed to the appeal) and the systems to deal with this. You can continue to raise money from this list towards subsequent projects or running costs.
- The **public image** of the organisation should have been significantly enhanced as a result of all the publicity obtained during the appeal.
- The confidence of the management and fundraising staff will have increased as a result of the success of the appeal. And in fundraising, confidence creates success.
- You will have attracted **important people** to the organisation to serve on committees and to lead the appeal. These can be asked to continue their involvement with the organisation.

And because you will not be running another major appeal for some years (if ever again), try to incorporate all your capital needs into the appeal budget.

Planning an appeal

The planning stage will involve a number of separate activities. These include:

1. Planning the development, with drawings and costings. you need to be able to justify the development as being important to your work and the future of your organisation. If you can't make the purpose of the appeal sound really important, you are unlikely to be able to persuade others. You will need to do a business plan for the development, to assure yourself that there will be enough money to keep going once the development has been completed. Too often a new building has to close or a new piece of equipment lies idle, because there are not sufficient running costs to pay for its use. You will also need to consider the costings and how much you will need to raise to undertake the proposed development.

2. Establishing the feasibility of the running the appeal. Many organisations will decide to take on a consultant to offer advice on how to conduct the appeal. One of the first steps a consultant will take is to conduct a feasibility study which will, apart from anything else, advise on whether the appeal is likely to be successful. This is an important process, as it will serve to highlight any inconsistencies or ill-conceived ideas.

The stages of an appeal

There are likely to be several clearly defined phases in a properly planned appeal:

The planning phase which will include the preparation of:
- A case document, which sets out and justifies the purpose of the fundraising.
- A business plan or feasibility study, which sets out the plan and time scale for the fundraising.
- Research, into likely sources and givers.

The recruitment of an appeal committee, and in particular of the appeal Chair, who will lead the appeal.

The private giving phase, in which major gifts are sought and obtained.

The appeal launch, when enough major gifts have been obtained to ensure that the appeal will be a success and the charity is happy to go public.

The public giving phase, when contributions are sought from a wider range of people and through public fundraising activity and events.

The consolidation phase when all contacts who have not given are followed up in a final push.

The appeal closes – hopefully when the budgeted sum has been raised.

Completion of the project, which might be accompanied by a 'thank you' and dedication ceremony.

The importance of going through this process is not only to ensure that the appeal is properly organised, but also to allow a feasible time scale for the appeal. It may take at least two years (and sometimes as long as five years for a major appeal) from start to finish. During the initial stages of the appeal, you will be spending money without seeing any return. The whole organisation needs to understand the appeal process and have confidence in the outcome, and the nerve not to panic before the income begins to flow.

---

3. Planning the structure of the appeal. This is likely to involve an appeal committee to lead and oversee the appeal. The key appointment is the Chair of this committee. The function of this committee is to raise big gifts, and people should be appointed for their asking capacity, rather than for any other quality. You may also want to establish sub-committees to oversee the running of events and for publicity and media in order to harness volunteer help. These committees will be supported by a professionally staffed office to provide the back up that is needed.

Table of gifts needed

Number of gifts	Value of gifts required	Total to be obtained
1	25,000	25,000
2	10,000	20,000
5	5,000	25,000
5	3,000	15,000
10	1,000	10,000
25	500	12,500
200	100	20,000
500	50	25,000
748 donors		152,500

This typical table of donations gives a clue as to the number of donors and amount of fundraising and research that you will need. You might expect a success rate of one in ten, meaning that you will need to approach 230 people who could give 1,000 or more. In the example given, you will see that the top three gifts account for 30% of the income and the top eight for nearly half. This is typical of these sorts of appeals and illustrates the importance of planning the leading gifts at the right level, and then going out and getting them.

4. Reviewing the likely funding sources. A vital planning tool is a table setting out the number and size of donations needed. This lists the gifts that you plan to get, and helps you identify possible donors and gives guidance on the level of support to ask for. You will need to develop a plan for how you are going to raise the money you need: through soliciting major gifts, via a mailed appeal, or through fundraising events and activities are the main ways.

5. Documentation and research to back up the above. For the major gifts, you should undertake some preliminary research at this stage into possibilities, and you should certainly explore possible government and aid grants.

6. Preparing the case statement. This is a vital document, which will be the strategic plan for the appeal. It will include sections covering the following:

- A **background to the charity** and its history.
- A description and justification of **the project**.
- The **costs** of the project.
- The individual **components of the project**, costed.
- The **gifts needed** to achieve this target.
- The **plan** to meet the needs and raise the money.
- The **sources of money** expected.

This should be nicely produced as a report, and you may wish to produce some Overhead Projector slides as visual aids for presentations.

7. Identifying those people who will lead the appeal, and approaching them to ask them if they would be prepared to help. This is usually done by drawing up lists of leading businessmen and other influential people gleaned from a wide range of sources, including personal knowledge and contact. They will meet infrequently, but are there to help solicit the largest gifts through their contacts and credibility. The Chair will also be the public figure leading the appeal, so this is a critical appointment which can determine the success or failure of the appeal.

Leadership

The leadership of the appeal campaign is enormously important. There are two important principles to bear in mind:

- People respond better when asked by people who are at or above their own level in society – this is called peer group giving,

- People respond better if the person who is asking has already given and given generously. One question they will ask is *"Have you given?"*. If the answer is *"No"*, then it is far easier for them to refuse.

The qualifications to look for in the Chair and in Appeal Committee members are that they have the resources to give major gifts on the scale you need (either personally or through the company or foundation they are associated with); that they have important contacts; and that they are able and willing to ask others to support the appeal both in person and by letter.

The first stage is to identify people to help you plan the appeal. Since you are asking for advice, it is easier for them to say "Yes". Later on you will be asking them for money! A group of two or three senior people with an interest in your work can be invited to act as a planning group. Their role is either to act as the formal leadership of the appeal or to select that leadership. They should be people who are well respected in the community and who may have not been associated with a similar appeal in the recent past – if they have, their asking capacity will have been diminished. They should have plenty of contacts. One of their tasks will be to select other people to form the nucleus of the Appeal Committee.

You need to understand the motivation that will make important people want to work for your cause. Research seems to suggest that almost every motive under the sun will be present. Some people find themselves genuinely supporting the cause; others find the approach from a senior person in the community difficult to resist; others find the link with other business people attractive for their own purposes; some are motivated by the notion of some sort of recognition for what they have done at the end of the day; and some just like the challenge of achieving something rather unusual and worthwhile. All those involved at this level are likely to appreciate (and be used to) efficient administration and being provided with the back up they need. This will ensure that they spend the minimum of time in committee and that their time is effectively used.

Many people don't know how to ask effectively, and you may wish to provide some induction into the work of your organisation and its importance, and some training in the principles of effective asking.

The private phase

With all the building blocks in place, you should be ready to begin the slow yet vital task of soliciting the bigger gifts.

The first task is to get the members of your Appeals Committee to agree to give. It is important that your early gifts are of a sufficient size to give a lead to those that follow (who will probably be giving smaller amounts). Most committee members should be aware of the scale of the donations needed. They will have been engaged in discussions about what is expected of other prospective donors, and will be familiar with what might be expected of them. If they find it difficult to give the amount suggested, then why not suggest that they give a smaller sum regularly over a number of years – and you can accumulate their total contribution as being the value of their gift.

Once they have made their own commitment, they should move on to the task of approaching others. For this purpose you will have already drawn up lists of prospective donors. They will be able to help by adding new names and deciding how an approach can best be made. The role of the fundraiser is to provide smooth administration; the task of asking for big gifts is best done by the committee member. Once you have identified who is the best person to approach a prospective donor (and this is one of the prime functions of the Committee), a wide variety of ways can be used. The one that will be used is likely to be the one that the person feels most comfortable with.

Often, big donations take time to be decided (and this is particularly true when approaching public sector sources). A decision should not be expected within the course of a single meeting. What might happen is that there will be a series of meetings – possibly including a reception, followed by an informal chat, even a visit to see the organisation at work and meet some of the beneficiaries. This will culminate in the prospective donor being asked to support the appeal, and offering a range of possible ways of doing this (but attempting to get their support at the level of giving you have decided for them). They can also be asked to give support in kind and suggest other people who might be approached.

The objective of the private stage of the appeal will be to collect promises of between 25% and 50% of the appeal target. This will give a tremendous boost to the public phase of the appeal when it is launched. Indeed, you should not actually launch an appeal to the public until you are confident of its ultimate success.

The public phase

The public phase commences with the launch. This can be done in any number of ways. It should certainly involve a press conference and might also involve an event, such as a reception, to which you invite prospective donors who have not yet committed themselves.

In the public phase of the appeal, much of the money will be raised from large numbers of people in smaller donations. This might be through personal solicitation. But you could also develop a direct mail campaign both to existing supporters on your mailing list and 'cold' to people you have targeted as being likely to be interested in the appeal. It is important though that direct mail be left towards the end of the process, so that nobody gives a small donation in response to a letter who might have given a bigger one if approached earlier in person. This is in fact the biggest danger in running an appeal – that you get a tiny donation from someone who, if approached properly, would have given you very much more.

A press and public relations campaign is important to give your appeal a continuing profile. Some of the bigger appeals recruit PR committees and involve a range of PR and media professionals on a voluntary basis. You should certainly have someone working hard on public and media relations, as this will underpin your other fundraising activities.

Events are an important component of an appeal, so long as the organisation of the event is carried out by a group of volunteers (perhaps an Events Committee). This will ensure that your time is used effectively – as it is easy to get swallowed up in event administration, when the real money is coming through personal solicitation. Events can attract good media coverage, and can reach a large audience who will become aware of the appeal in this way.

At this stage, you are well on the way to success. There may be a consolidation phase, when you are close to your appeal target, and you can go back to people who turned you down and to those who have already given (particularly the smaller donors) and suggest that just one small effort will see the appeal through to success. And finally there is the business of ensuring that everyone is properly thanked – the volunteers as well as the donors, who together have made the appeal a success.

6.9 Raising money from young people and in schools

Fundraising from children and in schools is virtually synonymous, since schools are by far the easiest place to approach children. If you want to reach large numbers of young people and harness their enthusiasm, then schools are the best place to start.

But there is a word of warning. If you are planning to raise money from young people and in schools, you should remember that you are dealing with a vulnerable and impressionable group. You need to approach them with care and be sensitive of their needs. You should not put undue pressure on them to support you or to get their parents and family to support. You should try to get them to understand your work, the reasons for it and why it is important. A code of practice on fundraising in schools, produced for fundraisers in the UK, sets out the main factors to consider. This is printed in *Appendix 4*.

What children are likely to have is time rather than money, and access to the support of their families and friends. There is also the link between the nature of your work and their educational interests to consider – as the relationship will work very much better if you can build their understanding of the cause or need you are addressing, rather than simply ask them to raise money for you.

To obtain access, and you will usually need the permission of the headteacher (or the support of a committed class teacher, who will persuade the headteacher). You can make the approach directly; or there might be a committed supporter or volunteer who is also a parent or a teacher, who could do this for you. In targeting young people, will:

- **Help you generate money for your cause**. This will not always be a huge sum.
- **Involve young people in your cause**, giving them a better understanding of the issues involved and the work you are doing.
- **Lay an important base for future support**. If people get involved in supporting charity when they are young, this can influence what they do and choose to support in later life.

Some fundraising ideas for schools and young people

- Contests and competitions.
- Discos, and end-of-year and graduation parties.
- Quiz evenings, dinners and dances aimed at parents.
- Litter picking and clean up campaigns.
- Picnics and outings.
- Raffles and auctions aimed at parents, with prizes donated by local firms.
- Carnivals and 'rag days' where the whole school is doing something silly to raise money.
- Collecting and recycling waste materials.
- Sponsored walks, runs and swims, etc.
- A school summer fete with: face painting, name the teddy, high jumping, puppet making, treasure map, book stalls, a tea bar, treasure hunt, tug of war and other exciting events.
- A sale of crafts and produce (such as cakes and jams) made by parents.
- Involving tourists: asking them to become supporters or to collect and send educational equipment and books on their return home.

The Pune Blind Men's Association 'Blind March'

Every year the Pune Blind Men's Association organises a 'Blind March' in which about 3,500 students from about 30 colleges and schools participate. The event is led by famous persons. Participants are given receipt books of Rs2 and Rs5 in advance, and on the day of the march, money is collected from students.

Alongside whatever you do to raise money with young people through schools, the school itself will be raising money through fundraising activities with its pupils and their parents. This can either be to find the money it needs for its own work (for example to create a scholarship fund, pay for books, pay for equipment, or improve facilities). Or it could be to support a local good cause.

Making the approach

If you are a local or city-wide charity (such as a night shelter for the homeless, a training centre for the disabled, or a family planning clinic), then you will want to approach the schools in your area. You will probably be approaching the headteacher in the first instance. A personal visit is the ideal approach. If this is not practical, a telephone call will be better than a circular letter which is likely to find its way into the wastepaper basket.

When you are thinking about what to involve the young people in, a useful guide is to make your activities:

- First **fun** – so that they enjoy what you are asking them to do.
- Then **educational** – so that they learn about the issues (e.g. poverty, disability, health care, family planning).
- And only then **about fundraising**.

Everyday choices

You don't have to join a voluntary agency to begin making a difference to children's lives. Almost anyone can make a difference by being sensitive, aware and persuading others that it is important to get involved. Given below are simple, easy-to-do suggestions you can undertake starting from today at school or college.

Students:
- Place donation boxes in the canteen.
- Write and circulate research papers on child-related topics.
- Adopt a slum.
- Organise street theatre on child-related issues.
- Organise debates on various issues.
- Get involved in voluntary groups doing child-related work.
- Motivate others to get involved in similar ways.

Teachers:
- Influence and motivate students by organising events and helping them understand issues.
- Involve students in collecting materials like clothes, toys and books for deprived children.

From a promotional leaflet produced by CRY – Child Relief and You, Bombay

The usual starting point is to offer to give a talk about your organisation. You will need to make your presentation as attractive and interesting to the children as possible because this introduces the next step – the invitation to do something to help by fundraising. This will either be taken up by the school as a whole or by a particular class if the activity fits somehow into their educational programme.

For junior schools you will need to develop a simple and very clearly set out activity for the young people to use in their fundraising. Quizzes for different age groups designed to fit the curriculum is one idea. Competitions are popular as they give the child the opportunity to learn, and they may be invited to obtain sponsorship from their family and friends for the number of questions they are able to answer correctly.

For secondary schools, the children themselves are in a better position to decide how funds should be raised.

Publications for schools

A number of the larger charities produce publications for children. These fall into two categories:

School packs of teaching materials specially designed for use in the classroom (where they must be linked somehow to the curriculum). With many schools chronically short of books, producing good educational material (either for sale or for free circulation) can get your cause into the school. You also have the opportunity to get the costs of doing this paid through sponsorship.

Simple information aimed at young people. This could include books, pamphlets, newsletters and information sheets. You could send the information to young people in response to enquiries or as a thank you for a donation. You might even consider setting up a junior supporters 'club' to nurture the interests of young people – e.g. a junior environmentalists club. These undoubtedly build a strong loyalty to the organisations concerned and are an important ingredient of school fundraising.

National competitions

National and the larger city-wide charities have another opportunity – to design and develop a national award scheme for young people. An essay competition or an art competition, for example.

You will need to offer prizes, which can be to the young people, or to the school – or perhaps to both. The prizes might be in cash. Alternatives are books, bursaries or travel opportunities. You will need to reach schools with information about the award scheme – which may require a media sponsor, such as a newspaper. And you will need to have the money to do this. The prizes will usually represent 25% or even as little as 10% of the total cost of running the award scheme – since you have to pay for publicity, printed material, the judging, the awards ceremony, and all the administration involved. But this can be a suitable vehicle for sponsorship, as it will appeal to sponsors who are looking for avenues of reaching young people and for obtaining the credit and good publicity from having supported an exciting award scheme.

6.10 Gambling activities that generate money

The big issue: to gamble or not

Organisations with a religious tradition may find the use of gambling as a method of fundraising ethically difficult. For example, Muslims, Methodists and Quakers all actively discourage gambling and would not like their denominational charities to raise money in this way or to accept grants from foundations which generate their income through some form of lottery or gambling activity.

To them, gambling is the issue. It is not really important whether there is any actual link between addictive gambling and buying a lottery or raffle ticket. It is the principle. Does your organisation have any problems with raising money in this way? You need to be clear about the attitude of your trustees before starting to organise any game of skill or chance. Get your Management Committee to agree a policy on this to ensure that there is no disagreement or argument later on.

Types of gambling activity used to raise money

There are three main types of gambling activity which charities use to raise money.

1. The lottery: this is a sale of tickets, each giving an equal chance of success, and where no skill is involved. A sweepstake on the outcome of a horse race or a football competition rates as a lottery. A money game (sometimes known as an instant lottery) is usually run with scratch cards, which the entrant scratches to reveal whether the card has the right combination of symbols to win a prize. These all normally offer cash prizes. A tombola or a raffle, where numbered tickets win, usually offers 'things' such as television sets, video recorders or holidays as the main prizes (which charities usually obtain as donations). The running of a lottery may be governed by lottery laws. You should check out any legal requirements in your country.

2. The game of skill: this is a true competition based on skill or knowledge, where there are prizes for the winners. Competitions with an entry fee can be an extremely successful way of raising money for a charity. There may also be laws on how you can run skill competitions.

3. The free entry draw (where there is no charge for entering): this may be part of a sales promotion (often used for consumer products), or offered as an incentive to members. Here anyone can enter for the prize draw simply by replying to you. This is often a good inducement to membership recruitment. Because no stake money is involved, this will almost certainly fall outside any lottery or gambling laws.

Prizes

Clearly the attraction to many in entering a raffle or competition is the chance to win a prize. The prizes on offer should be things that the audience (who you hope will buy the tickets) will really want.

For most small scale competitions, the audience is relatively easy to assess. In the school fete you can be fairly sure that parents and their children will predominate. In which case toys, food and drinks are safe prizes. It is in these sort of events that the prize is least important. People will often buy a ticket for the fun of it (because they are there), because they wish to support the cause, and because there is someone there persuading them to buy a ticket.

For a larger event with a higher ticket price and which aims to raise a larger amount of money, the choice of prizes is more important. In a recent Save the Rainforests raffle, the first prize was an Amazon adventure for two donated by a travel company, with a second prize of an expedition to Mount Everest. These were targeted to appeal to an audience interested in the rainforest and in the environment generally. Prizes like this are often easy to get donated – because the travel company is donating an empty place on a tour that is being run anyway, or a hotel company a room that would otherwise be unoccupied. New technology prizes are always extremely attractive – computers, televisions, video recorders, music centres, etc.

An unusual and imaginative prize will almost always be more attractive than a money prize. And sometimes will not cost a lot to organise. For example, a museum supporters group might arrange a personal tour with the Director followed by a smart dinner. An arts organisation might persuade leading painters to paint a portrait of the winner (free of charge).

Try to get all the prizes donated – both goods and services – or bought using money donated by a sponsor. This reduces the risk of the venture and increases the amount you raise from the lottery. There is a temptation to go out and buy the best prizes, then find that nobody buys the tickets.

If you are trying to get the event sponsored, identify what you can offer a sponsor. Can you put their name and phone number on the raffle tickets? Can you describe the prize they have donated in glowing terms in any posters you produce? Can you mention their generosity in your newsletter? Link this to the number of tickets you expect to sell and this should make an attractive proposition to any sponsor.

Promotion

Everything hinges on selling the tickets. The more you sell, the more money you will raise. If you sell only a few, you may end up losing money. Whether you have a captive audience at an event or are involving a dispersed membership by direct mail, selling those few extra tickets will make all the difference. If you are able to get the prizes donated, then most of the costs of a raffle are in the organisation and the printing of the tickets.

If the prize is right and if the price of each ticket is not set too high, then raffle tickets are best sold on a personal basis. First approach you own constituency – your existing supporters, your Management Board members, your volunteers, your staff. Ask them to buy tickets for themselves; ask them to sell tickets to their family and friends. Give them a date to sell the tickets by and to return any unsold tickets to you. Then there is your supporter list, where you could try to arrange that a team of volunteers goes round door-to-door to try to sell them tickets (for their own use and for resale to their friends). Unlike cold calling, you are dealing here with people who already support you.

Your supporters may have access to other networks. Groups of medical workers could sell in hospitals; trade union members could sell to other members; and employees to colleagues at the workplace. This can be very cost effective. Similarly, if you are organising a large public event, you can sell books of tickets at the event by personal solicitation. A small team of volunteers can go around a show ground or a conference hall, and ask everyone they meet to buy a ticket or a book of tickets.

Some organisations are now offering incentives for the sale of lottery tickets. Since it is likely to be your own supporters who will sell the tickets, you need to find a prize that will appeal to them and offer it to the person who sells most tickets. The use of the telephone can be a powerful way to find people to sell tickets.

You can also try to sell the tickets by direct mail, sending a book of tickets, a covering letter and some information about your organisation and why you need to raise money to your supporters list. Though many people dislike inertia selling, mailing raffle tickets to supporters or distributing them door-to-door is just about acceptable and can work financially (although the cost of mailing will be higher than for a regular appeal). On receipt, your supporters will either go out and sell the tickets to their friends, buy the tickets themselves, send them back to you, or do nothing. Very few will return them – usually only around 1%. Most will do nothing or throw them away. In one large raffle run in the UK, 20,000 members of a charity were each send 2 books containing 10 tickets each. This resulted in around 100 being returned and a total sale of 96,000 tickets. The result was expenses of £12,000, yielding total receipts of £60,000.

The draw

At any fundraising event, the prize draw for the raffle is a key moment of drama – especially where there are glamorous prizes. The recruitment of a celebrity presenter to make the draw and distribute the prizes can add to the success of the raffle and the event.

It is important to build the timing of the draw into your plans. At the event, it should be announced that the draw will take place at a certain time. This time is critical, because after it people will begin to drift away. It is a fixed point in the programme that most people will stay for it. Indeed it can be a time of great excitement: the opportunity to collect a prize from a celebrity. As the time of the draw approaches, announcements should be made to encourage last minute sales.

Running a 500 Club

A 500 Club is a mini-lottery run by the Fiji Red Cross Society selling 500 tickets at Fiji $10. The lottery is run 4 times a year. Each lottery is launched 6 to 8 weeks before the draw date, and tickets are distributed by the organiser to ticket sellers and distributors, who have to sell them, or if this is not proving possible, to return them to the organiser in time for them to be redistributed to other sellers and sold before the draw. It is important that all the tickets are sold. If half the tickets remain unsold, the proceeds will not cover the amount that has to be distributed as prizes. Another variation of a 500 Club (or a 100 Club, 200 Club, etc.) has supporters who agree to buy a ticket each lottery, so guaranteeing that all the tickets are sold. For the Fiji Red Cross Society, the budget is as follows:

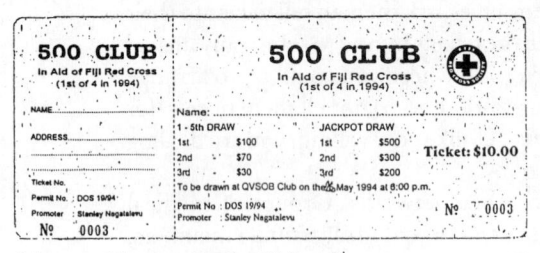

A Lottery ticket used by the Fiji Red Cross.

Expenses:	cost of permit	$22
	ticket printing	$100
	advertising	$100
	Prizes	$2,000 ($500, $300, $200, and 5 prizes each of $100, $70, $30)
	Total costs:	$2,222
Income:	ticket sales	$5,000 (500 @ $10)
	Net income after costs:	$2,778 per lottery ($11,112 per annum for 4 lotteries)

Source: Fiji Red Cross Society

6.11 Advertising for support

Paying for an advertisement in a newspaper or magazine can be a powerful way of promoting your cause or raising money – but it can be expensive. You can raise money 'off the page' directly through making an appeal for money, or indirectly by recruiting members, volunteers or those seeking further information (who you will later persuade to give to you).

Advertising can be extremely successful in raising money at the time of a disaster or when an issue has hit the headlines. Your advertisement will reach people at a time when they know that something needs to be done – and you are offering them a way of helping.

You can also use advertising to build awareness of your charity through a promotional campaign on what you are doing. You can sell greetings cards and other products which you are using to raise money for your work. A further use is to invite people to support you with a legacy.

Advertising can take the form of:

- **Press advertising**: taking space in national or local newspapers, through display advertising or small ads.
- **Advertising in magazines and journals** (general interest or specialist).
- **Inserts**: a leaflet inserted in a magazine and circulated with it to its readers.
- **Posters** (both billboard advertising and smaller posters displayed on noticeboards or flyposted in the street).

Press advertising

There are several key factors about the use of the press as a medium for advertising. The cost is high, even for a limited space. As a result, the messages you can afford will be relatively short, and so must be more striking if they are to be noticed. Press advertising has an advantage over other fundraising methods in that you can select your audience by reference to the known readership of the newspaper or magazine. You can also predict with some degree of certainty whether your issues are likely to be given editorial coverage – and if so, whether or not the coverage will be sympathetic. You can link your advertising with the press coverage of the issue – for example when there is a disaster. And you can design and place the advertisement much more quickly than it would take to organise a direct mail fundraising campaign.

Advertising for money is expensive and it is easy to lose substantial sums. It

---

Smaller spaces tend to work best

How big should your advertisement be? This table illustrates what research and practical experience shows about the disproportionate impact of using only small spaces for your advertising. You should bear in mind that you may be able to get a larger space for a greater discount on the posted rates, and this would improve the performance of larger spaces as compared with taking a smaller space.

Space size	Response
Quarter page (25%)	48% of that achieved for a full page
Half page (50%)	71% of that achieved for a full page
Three-quarter page (75%)	87% of that achieved for a full page
Full page (100%)	100% of that achieved for a full page
Double page (200%)	141% of that achieved for a full page

Taken from 'Commonsense Direct Marketing', by Drayton Bird, The Printed Shop.

is likely that whatever response you can achieve with advertising, you can achieve similar results much more cheaply through an effective and well-targeted public relations campaign.

If you do decide to advertise, you should always try to evaluate the cost-effectiveness of the advertising. If you do, you will learn more about which media work well and which don't. And if you don't, you may be pouring lots of money into an ineffective promotional device without knowing it (many charities advertise because they see other charities taking advertising space, and assume that it works). The way of doing this is by using a coded coupon, a coded reply address or a special phone number on the advertisement. You will then be able to link every response to a particular advertisement. The coding should be done for the campaign as a whole and also for each separate promotion in the campaign. This is the only way you can find out which medium works best for you. Results can then be measured in terms of:

- **Income raised** in relation to cost.
- **Cost per new donor** recruited.

Disaster advertising

Possibly the most exciting aspect of using advertising to fundraise is its flexibility. You can place an advertisement extremely quickly. Thus if a disaster happens one day, you could be appealing for help the next day at the breakfast table.

What is a disaster? It is not what you think is serious, it is what the public is being told is serious by the newspaper itself and by the other news media. Timing here is all. One estimate is that 30% of your response is likely to come from getting in with your appeal immediately. The problem here is getting enough information soon enough to be able to create a truthful advertisement. A famine or man-made disaster are obvious instances where disaster advertising can be used successfully. SightSavers (the Royal Commonwealth Society for the Blind) used this approach with the Union Carbide chemical spill in Bhopal.

Acquisition advertising

This is all about finding new supporters who can then be put on your mailing list. The acquisition cost, as with direct mail, is likely to be high, but it is the opportunity to capture them on your list and then profitably appeal to them over the years which makes financial sense of doing this. Except in exceptional circumstances, most organisations will not break even on the initial proceeds of their advertising. They regard it as an investment in developing their mailing list. As an example, the Woodland Trust in the UK takes small spaces in the papers to invite you to send £1 to plant a tree. Many of those responding go on to give more substantial sums on a regular basis. You should decide before you start how much you can afford to pay to find a new supporter. The precise sum for your organisation will depend on how much you can expect to raise on average subsequently from each supporter.

Awareness advertising

If no one knows about you or if you want to launch a new campaign, then your objective may be to build awareness rather than just raise money or find new supporters. This form of advertising is expensive, and demands that you continue the advertising campaign over a period of time if you are to have any real and lasting impact. It is also difficult to measure. So if you want to know whether there has been any impact, and whether it has been cost effective, you may need to carry out market research into public awareness.

Although awareness advertising is much used by large companies and successful consumer brands, is it the best way of using very limited charitable funds? Many would say that the use of public relations (if done well) will buy a good deal more awareness than any amount of advertising. The advantage of paying for the space is that what appears on the page is exactly the message you want – at the time and frequency you have decided. With public relations, on the other hand, you are in the hands of reporters and editors.

A good example of awareness advertising was the 'Hungry for Change' campaign mounted by Oxfam in 1983, where the stated purpose was NOT to raise money, but to create awareness with the public of the reasons for inequality and the need for change. A consequence of such an awareness campaign is that people will send in unsolicited gifts, and they are likely to respond more positively when you do appeal for funds – as they already know about the issues and have heard of you.

Legacy advertising

This is more difficult and demands some careful thought. On the one hand, the likely value of a legacy is very high, if you can persuade people to support you in this way. Whilst on the other hand, you can rarely determine whether the advertising has succeeded – partly due to the length of time that will elapse before you receive the legacy (usually several years) and partly due to the difficulty of linking any legacy you do receive with a particular promotion.

Loose inserts

One of the main problems with buying space in newspapers is the size constraint; the space very limited, and the cost escalates as you take more space. The use of loose inserts gets over half of this problem. Depending on the publication, anything from a small leaflet to a catalogue can be inserted loose or stapled into the publication. There are four important differences between an insert and an advertisement:

1. There is much **more space** available to you – and you can even include an envelope with the insert. There may be restrictions on the weight of the insert imposed by the publisher, and the print cost will vary with the size of the insert. This makes inserts an ideal medium to describe your work and set out the different ways of supporting your organisation. Inserts can work extremely well for membership drives, campaigns for committed giving such as child and community sponsorship schemes, and those appeals that demand space if they are to be promoted effectively.

2. The cost per recipient is much higher, But inserts can often be extremely **cost-effective**. The effectiveness of inserts is a combination of the space available to you, cost and value for money factors, and the ability to design a powerful response mechanism as part of the printed insert.

3. Inserts take **time to arrange and produce**. Thus they cannot easily be produced to take advantage of topical events in the same way that an advertisement can.

4. They can be **easily detached** from the publication, and without damaging it. On the other hand, they can fall out and get lost, or thrown away.

Inserts can provide excellent opportunities for testing the message or format of the appeal.

Door drops

Delivering leaflets through people's letterboxes, or using the postal service to distribute leaflets to every household in the neighbourhood will cost considerably less than doing a cold mailing (see *Section 6.4*). And you may find that you can obtain a good response by doing this. Try it out and see what happens. Some organisations have been able to recruit new donors using this technique with a reasonable degree of success.

Posters

Posters fit least well into the fundraising area, as it is difficult to get a response to your message, but are nonetheless a useful promotional medium. Posters can range from the huge 96 sheet billboard hoardings that you see on main roads, right down to small handbills produced on a photocopier for use in windows and noticeboards.

The impact of a poster depends on the size of the image and the extent of the coverage. Naturally it requires a great deal of both to get a message across (a large image displayed all over the place). And this is expensive. What charities can do is to use the medium in small bursts to highlight a week or the launch of a campaign, either nationally or in a chosen area. Or they could rent a site for just one day to put up a poster which will generate controversy and media coverage (this is similar to a stunt used to generate publicity).

It is also significant what posters cannot do. By the large posters cannot be used in rural areas – most sites being in towns and cities, or along the highways linking them. Perhaps more significantly, posters do not allow for any direct response, except via a phone number. You can't print a tear off coupon! The time in which people see a poster and read its message is extremely short, whether they are travelling in a car or walking around the town. So the message has to be short, powerful and extremely simple if it is to work. Thus, at best, posters can only act as an awareness medium to support other promotional and fundraising activities.

You might try to ask an outdoor advertising company to give you a free poster site – if they have one available. If the site is available, then it would cost them nothing to donate it to you. The things to consider with free sites include:

- **Are sites available** when you want them?
- **Where are the sites** themselves? Are they in the right place?
- Is the **cost of printing posters** (which you will have to do and pay for) too high to make it worthwhile?
- If you do decide that it is worthwhile, would it be useful to produce **cheap run-on posters** in addition to those required for the free sites? The run on cost is likely to be low, but what would you do with the extra posters?
- Can you **get the posters sponsored**? You can acknowledge the sponsorship very publicly. But will this get in the way of the message?

Handbills

In a different league from the billboard posters are the small posters which can be used to publicise almost anything. These are especially attractive for fundraising, since they can be printed cheaply and posted with your mailings to supporters.

These handbills can be targeted at whoever you want. They can be put in the windows of local shops, on library noticeboards and in community centres to publicise a local fundraising event. They can be flyposted on walls or pinned to trees. Distribution can be done by volunteers – distributing thousands of your leaflets and creating highly visible campaigns at little cost.

Two issues in advertising

How does advertising affect public perception of your cause?

Advertising requires headlines, images and few words. This means you have to simplify what is often an extremely complicated problem. If you are trying to attract funds, you will want to illustrate the cause in a way that makes the reader want to do something – then and there. This means appealing strongly to the donor's emotions. The question then arises as to the effect all of this might have on public attitudes towards the problem and on the beneficiaries themselves. And whether in an attempt to improve fundraising effectiveness, the basic aims and values of the organisation get forgotten.

Free or fee?

Advertising is expensive, and it is not always possible to measure the response that you get from it (although you should always try to do so). Is it a worthwhile use of your funds to pay for advertising? You will have to decide what you want out of it beforehand, in terms of publicity for your cause which will support other fundraising activity, as well as the direct support you obtain in response to the advertisement. If it still seems too expensive, there remains the option of trying to obtain the advertising free. A number of campaigns have been developed using free space as it is available. The disadvantage here is that you have no control over the intensity or timing of your campaign. The same approach can be applied to getting the services of an advertising agency. Some will be prepared not to make a profit on charity accounts; some may be prevailed upon to take on your account free.

6.12 Trading

Completely separate from the income generation activities discussed in *Chapter 5*, one of the most visible aspects of charity fundraising is the trading activity they engage in which is targeted largely at members and supporters. This can include:

- **Sales to supporters through gift catalogues** – especially the sale of greetings cards and promotional materials such as posters and tee-shirts.
- **Charity shops** selling donated goods from shops in the town centre.
- **Sales of publications** and other activities directly concerned with the charity's work.

Trading may seem an attractive fundraising option, but in fact represents a long hard slog at relatively low margins, a high input of capital and a considerable drain on management time. Many charities lose (rather than make) money from their trading. Although some, like Oxfam in the UK and CRY in India, find this an extremely successful fundraising method, generating half or more of their annual income from this source. The first issue is whether to do it at all. Can you actually make a profit out of the trading? Is it is the most effective way of using your resources – your time, the money you need to invest and your volunteers – or are there more effective ways of using the same resources to generate much more money? Too many charities get involved in trading over-optimistically, and end up losing money.

Beyond large-scale trading, there are a range of much smaller-scale trading activities undertaken usually by volunteer supporters that any organisation might consider, from running stalls selling old clothing and 'jumble' to making and selling jams and cakes, which can add useful income to an organisation. The same principles apply to these as to the running of any small-scale fundraising event.

Charity shops

Most charity shops are simply a retail outlet, selling merchandise to generate a profit for the charity. Some aspire to do more than this by being an information point, promoting the cause and the work of the charity, and perhaps recruiting new supporters.

To run a shop, whatever the purpose, requires a considerable management effort. The following are some of the key factors in doing it successfully:

- **Location**. Finding the right location is essential. The shop must be sited in a place that can attract passing trade. It must be near enough for the voluntary helpers who will staff it. And you have to balance these needs with the rent.
- **Staffing**. Most charity shops depend extensively on volunteers for their staffing. The usual pattern is to employ one professional manager for a shop of any size, who will co-ordinate a team of 20-40 volunteers. Some shops have a separate volunteers committee which takes responsibility for running the shop. Training, recruitment, supervision and management of this whole group of people is a key determinant of success.
- **The merchandise**. Charity shops tend to sell three types of merchandise. Goods donated to the charity by well-wishers in order to raise money (such as second hand clothing, household items and jewellery); goods produced by the beneficiaries of the charity (for example in workshops for the handicapped and rural development projects); and goods produced by the charity (such as greetings cards). The quality of the merchandise is an important factor, and this is particularly true where the shop is selling donated goods which should be cleaned, repaired or checked, sorted and priced before they are sold.

Selling promotional items

Promotional items that can be sold to raise money with the charity's name, logo and message:

- Greetings cards.
- Calendars.
- Diaries.
- Address books.
- Pens and pencils.
- Tee-shirts.
- Wallets.
- Mugs.
- Posters.

Catalogues

In catalogue trading, new goods are offered to supporters usually by mail order or, as in the case of Traidcraft (which sells products from Southern rural development projects to Northern customers), through local agents. Successful charities may earn as little as a 10% profit from trading in this way, since the cost of the merchandise, marketing and management have to be taken into account. It is often the associated donations that purchasers add to the purchase price that brings any profit at all. The following are some key points:

The merchandise. When selling goods in this way, high standards are needed. The goods are described in print and have to live up to their description when received by the purchaser. If they don't, there will be disappointment, and it will reflect badly on your charity. The goods should also in some way aim to reflect the values of the organisation – either in the use of materials (recycled paper, for example) or through the design. The items in the catalogue should be conceived as a range, rather than be a collection of unrelated products, and the range must appeal to the target market. The goods must be available in sufficient quantity to meet likely demand, or a serious loss of confidence will arise. And the cost must be low enough in relation to the selling price to give the possibility of a profit.

Promotion. Unlike a charity shop where customers can walk in off the street, a catalogue needs vigorous promotion. The mechanism normally used is direct mail, the aim being eventually to build up a list of regular purchasers which will create an assured market for the merchandise. Although some sales will be made through word of mouth and personal contact, most will be made as a result of sending the catalogue to previous purchasers, to your supporters and to other likely mailing lists.

Control and administration. The management of catalogue trading involves a major buying operation, with all the control and cash flow worries that are associated with that. Then there are the warehousing and order processing systems required which for catalogues of any size can be a major logistic operation. There are the questions of proper pricing, cost control and good management of what is a business activity, very different from the normal work of the charity and perhaps requiring quite different skills. And finally, there is the question of how to finance such a fluctuating business, where the purchases may need to be paid for well in advance of the revenue actually being received.

Other trading activities

Items such as posters, tee-shirts, bumper stickers and other promotional items, are often a profitable source of income. Organisations such as Greenpeace find that they can make money and get their message across in this way. The key here is to recognise that it is the design as much as the message that will create success. The ideal approach is to have all the production costs underwritten by a sponsor, so that all the sales proceeds are clear profit. Every effort should be made to encourage sales, whether the merchandise is sponsored or paid for. Losses are often made in this area because of goods failing to sell or overoptimistic production runs.

Generating revenue: a case study

Baphalali, the Swaziland Red Cross Society raises money from the sale of Industrial First Aid Training, including the sale of First Aid Kits. This not only raises income, but promotes the aims of the society through reducing accidents. A donor provided sufficient funds to launch the programme, which cost E40,000 to train the trainer. In the first 10 months E80,000 was raised, and the programme is being expanded to meet demand.
Source: Swaziland Red Cross Society

7. Working with people

7.1 Working with volunteers

The role of the volunteer is important for many charities. Volunteers can be very largely or even totally responsible for the organisation's work. The Samaritans, which is a telephone help-line for people who are despairing or suicidal being a good example; and many environmental campaigns rely substantially on the efforts of volunteers. Volunteers bring extra expertise to the organisation, but also save money, which might otherwise have to pay a member of staff to do the same thing.

Volunteers can also be used to raise money for the organisation, and are especially useful in a range of fundraising tasks, many of which could not be carried out without them – either because the organisation would not have sufficient time or the capacity to do the fundraising in the first place, or because if volunteers were not being used, the money could not be raised cost effectively. Volunteers can also assist the fundraiser by providing all sorts of administrative support and back up.

Volunteers are important in fundraising in all sorts of ways. And it requires more than just finding the people to do the work for you. In order to get the best out of your volunteers, they need to be chosen well, placed with imagination, given satisfying work to do which matches their skills and interests, and managed with skill. They are not simply there to be deployed as 'cheap labour' in all the worst jobs. Rather, they can add hugely to the resources available to you, enabling you to do more with less and to do it better.

Types of work that volunteers can do

Committees

Most voluntary organisations are controlled by a Management Committee, who decide policy for the organisation, oversee its work and ensure that it meets its charitable objectives. This Committee normally consists of volunteers, many of whom also get involved (again as volunteers) in other aspects of the organisation's work.

Committees may also be set up to supervise and develop particular areas of the organisation's work – such as a 'Development Committee' to plan a major appeal or a 'Business Committee' to develop links and partnerships with local businesses or an 'Event Committee' to plan and run an important fundraising event.

The Committees of new organisations usually consist of the founders and perhaps a few friends to assist them. As the organisation develops, there is the opportunity to set out precisely what skills and experience you are looking for in your committee members, and then to go out and find the people that meet your requirements.

Administrative tasks

The administrative office of most organisations is usually an extremely busy place, where there is more work to be done than people can cope with. There are all sorts of ways in which volunteers can help:

- Addressing and stuffing the envelopes for the 1,000 addresses you are sending your appeal to.
- And dealing with the response – banking the proceeds, sending thank you letters, and putting the names of those who responded on to the database.
- Reminding members whose subscriptions are about to lapse that they should renew their membership, either in writing or on the telephone.
- Answering the telephone or acting as receptionist or being in charge of the library.
- Editing the newsletter.
- All sorts of research.
- Organising a public meeting.

Volunteer jobs should match the skills of the volunteers you are using, and the volunteers will need supervision and support if you are to get the most out of them. And you will find, if you ask, that there are a great many people who are prepared to help.

Volunteers who raise money

One of the most important ways in which volunteers can help in fundraising is by helping raise money for the organisation. Again, there are all sorts of ways in which they can help:

- House-to-house and street collections, where success depends on the numbers of collectors that you can produce.
- Organising a fundraising event, such as a sponsored walk or a fair or a dinner dance, where a team of volunteers can be entirely responsible for running the event.
- Contacting local companies and shops to get prizes donated for a raffle.
- Selling raffle tickets or Christmas cards.

Much of this fundraising work can be done by fundraising groups. Many people really enjoy this sort of local fundraising work, doing something useful in their spare time, and working with a group of like-minded people. Inevitably, they will be representing the charity and people will ask them about what the organisation is doing. It is important that they understand what the organisation is doing and share its values, as in a sense they are acting as your ambassadors. Some induction training is quite helpful, so that they can be briefed about the organisation's work and meet some of the staff and beneficiaries.

Peripatetic volunteers

Another sort of volunteer is someone with time to give, but who wants to help at times more suitable to themselves. It is possible to design volunteer jobs for such people:

- Visiting donors to offer thanks and explain the organisation's work in more detail.
- Speaking at Rotary Lunches and other similar events, or in schools.

You will need people for these jobs who are highly motivated and articulate, and who are happy to be given a large degree of responsibility.

Volunteer recruitment and selection

The recruitment and selection of your volunteers is an important task. Exactly as for the recruitment of a new member of staff, there should be a proper job description for the volunteer job, and the volunteers should be selected according to their ability to do that job. You can also be opportunist. If a person arrives on your doorstep and offers to volunteer, you can try to design a suitable job for them to do which matches their particular skills and experience. Recruiting volunteers can be done in one of two ways:

Recruiting people locally

Where you need a number of volunteers in one place – perhaps to help in the office or help out on a fundraising event, a range of recruitment opportunities exist. People occasionally turn up at your office or telephone you for information. If they seem interested, then you could ask them directly if they would like to help as a volunteer.

Your publicity leaflets which ask for support, may offer the option of giving support in time as well as in cash.

Speaking tours, an article in the local newspaper or in your own newsletter, an interview on the radio can all be used to make known your need for volunteers.

You might even take paid advertising space in the local newspaper, just as you would for a paid job.

Who volunteers?

- You may find that the people who are prepared to volunteer are the people with least time on their hands. **Busy people** like to keep busy.
- **Middle class women** whose children are growing up or **recently retired people** may be willing to do something useful and challenging.
- People who have a **particular connection with the cause** may be willing to volunteer out of a sense of commitment. For example, someone whose child has recently died of AIDS might be willing to volunteer for an AIDS charity.
- **Unemployed young people** such as recent graduates yet to get their first job might be persuaded to volunteer just to keep active. You can tell them that they will develop new skills and this can improve their job prospects. The same is the case for people between jobs.
- If you need something done and it sounds interesting, then **just ask**. If you ask enthusiastically, then you may find that people are prepared to help out. It is just as with fundraising, where the main reason people give for not volunteering is that they were never asked!

Recruiting people with specific skills

This needs a rather more directed approach, as you need not just a person but a person with particular skills – such as someone who knows how to write effective promotional literature or a financial adviser or an investment adviser. Each will have its own particular opportunities:

- To find an accountant you might well seek the help of the local bank manager or accountancy firm; or for a lawyer, contact a local law firm.
- Professional bodies and associations are a good hunting ground for recently retired people with time on their hands. You could offer to give a talk, or suggest an article or a free advertisement in their newsletter.

If you know exactly what you want, then by asking people if they know anyone who could do the job, you may eventually find someone prepared to do it.

Working With People

Unsuitable as well as suitable people will volunteer. So the next step is selecting from the people you have identified – which you will do through an interview and taking up references, just as for a paid job. Don't lower your standards simply because someone offers to help you. You need to take particular care where people are expected to represent your organisation in public or where they will be involved in handling money.

You will need to agree terms and conditions, and set these out in some form of 'contract':

- The **nature of the job** to be done.
- The **hours expected**.
- The **supervision and support offered**, and any training that will be given.
- **Grievance procedures**.
- What **expenses** are paid.
- Any notice to be given on **termination of the arrangement** (by either side).

All these need to be discussed and agreed.

> **Before you volunteer...**
>
> Being a volunteer can be demanding and frustrating. The deeper you get involved, the more the organisation will depend on your contribution. A strong sense of commitment and patience will help ensure that you do not tire too soon and drop out, or grow cynical.
>
> Most issues pertaining to children are complex and must be understood thoroughly by those wishing to help. Plan to spend time talking and reading to understand the issues involved. Also be ready to get involved in whatever needs to be done, rather than going with preconceptions of what you will do. Here are some suggestions that will make you a better volunteer:
>
> - **Make a list of your skills** and resources before approaching a voluntary organisation.
> - **Be clear about how much time you can spare**. This will help the organisation guide you.
> - **Don't expect to be paid**. Voluntary organisations usually do not pay volunteers. Check if they will pay for work-related phone calls, travel and so on.
> - **Be prepared to work as part of a team**. Voluntarism usually means teamwork.
>
> *Adapted from advice by CRY – Child Relief and You, Bombay*

Management of volunteers

Volunteers work for charities for a wide range of reasons. Some do it because they believe in the cause and want to do something, while others do it because they want to get something out of it. Some will be there because they have nothing better to do or because they desperately crave human company after the death of a husband or wife or on retirement from a job. All can be useful members of your team. But just like the paid members of staff, they will need managing.

- A volunteer should have a clear **job description**.
- You should set them **objectives**.
- There should be an **induction** process, so that they see and understand the work of the organisation, meet members of staff (who will also need to appreciate the role and contribution of the volunteer).
- You should **train** them in what they have to do, so that they can do the job effectively, and continue to provide on-the-job training as necessary.
- You should ensure that they have enough **information** to do their job, and that they are **briefed** about recent changes and developments in the work you are doing.
- You should **supervise their work**, give them **feedback** on how well they are doing, and congratulate them when they have made a positive contribution. They are just like any other human striving to do a good job. They need to

> **People volunteer when asked**
>
> - 55% of people said that they had volunteered in the last 3 months.
> - 55% of people said they would be prepared to be involved in further volunteering activity.
> - 1% of people said they would not like to volunteer.
>
> These figures were taken from the *Charity Household Survey* in Britain.

know what the job is, how to do it and whether they are going it right. But because they are not being paid, they need other forms of **reward** – and recognising and appreciating their contribution is extremely important.

Overseas volunteers

There are basically three types of overseas volunteer:

- Those who apply to and are selected by **overseas volunteer-sending agencies**. These may be young people with energy and enthusiasm, either in a 'gap year' between school and university or after they have graduated or between jobs. They may be mid-career people with specialist skills. They may be older people who have retired but who have both skills and maturity.
- Those who have **an urge to 'do something useful'** and apply to organisations they have heard about or have some existing contact with.
- **Tourists and travellers** who arrive on your doorstep wanting to spend a few hours seeing your work... and then want to stay on for six months or come back in a year's time.

Each type of volunteer needs to be handled differently.

Volunteers from specialist agencies

A number of countries have a range of agencies specialising in recruiting and placing volunteers abroad. The best known are the Peace Corps (USA), Voluntary Service Overseas (UK), CUSO (Canada) and the UN Volunteer Programme. These and many more specialist agencies are always looking out for volunteer placements. So if you are interested in having someone with a specialist skill, then make contact with this type of agency.

Most of these agencies are supported by governments. So choose your country, and then write to the Embassy, who will know if the agency operates a volunteer programme in your country. People coming through such agencies have (usually) been well screened, and so will be professionally competent and sometimes very good. There is the advantage that the sending agency provides a number of support services – such as cultural orientation and language training before they start, visits and meetings during their term of service, assistance with medical problems, and good de-briefing at the end of their stay. If something goes wrong, then the sending agency can help sort matters out with you. If you know the skill you need, these agencies can usually find someone. The right person can be invaluable, the wrong person a disaster!

Each sending agency has its own expectation of the support which you will be required to provide. This could include accommodation for the volunteer and perhaps pocket money. Contracts are rarely for less than six months, and may well be for two or even three years.

A separate category are young people who have just left school. They will have enthusiasm, but perhaps little in the way of practical skills and experience. The purpose of their visit is to do something useful, but also to gain valuable insights into life in other countries as part of their own personal development. They (or their parents) will usually be paying for their visit, possibly raising the cost through some sort of fundraising or sponsorship, and they will usually be working alongside other young volunteers, and helping out on more basic work.

People wanting to do something useful

All development organisations based in the North and doing work in the South receive a steady stream of 'offers' from people wanting to do voluntary work in a Southern country. Most are put off with a courteous reply. But there are still 1% who persist or who themselves have direct contact with an organisation or who have heard about its work.

If you are approached in this way, one response might be that persons from the North are not needed to do something useful. If you need something done, then why not find someone from your own country to do it. But you might like to be more flexible, feeling that the interchange of ideas between countries can be productive, and that the volunteer will be able to learn about your country and culture whilst working as a useful member of your project team.

First ask for details of such things as: age, health and mental health, dietary considerations, religious beliefs, interests, skills and experience, hobbies, reasons for wanting to volunteer, timing and length of the visit, financial capacity of the individual to sustain him or herself, etc. Do not hesitate to point out that the volunteer should provide his or her own health insurance, and if you are not in a position to provide accommodation or pay pocket money, then say so. Depending on the response you receive to these questions, you can then make a decision as to whether or not to proceed.

People arriving on your doorstep

With the growth of tourism, more and more people with some experience of voluntary work in Northern countries are travelling in Southern countries. When they arrive to see the Taj Mahal in India or the game parks of Kenya, a few wonder to themselves about whether it is possible to 'see the real country' or 'meet the real people'. And what better way of doing this than contacting the office of a voluntary organisation they have heard of. And so they turn up on the doorstep of an office whose address they have got from a directory, or from a friend of a friend.

If you can spare the time, such people are often genuinely thrilled to see something of development work and very appreciative of the time you give them to explain and show something of the work being done by your organisation. Many will want to make a donation there and then – which of course you should encourage and accept! Some will suggest that when they return to their homes they will raise money for your work from their friends. Encourage them to do this. A very few may want to come back for a longer visit, when they can help out as a volunteer. If you feel that they can be useful to you, then say "Yes".

7.2 Working with patrons and celebrities

Associating your organisation with a well-known personality, could lift you from obscurity into the limelight.

Celebrities can help in many ways. Their presence at any function will draw others. For example, the fundraising dinner, which supporters are paying premium prices to attend, will become very much more attractive if there is a smattering of film stars and media people in attendance. They can inspire members and donors, and can turn your fundraising event into a roaring success.

Probably most important though, is the advantages they confer in attracting media coverage. If, for example, a well-known broadcaster is prepared to lead a press conference announcing a new campaign, the press is going to be much more interested than when an unknown charity executive says the same thing. Similarly photo editors of national newspapers are more likely to publish a photo of a well-known and attractive actress opening some new facility, than when a local councillor is doing the same thing.

Many organisations ask well-known people to help them for these reasons, and celebrities are prepared to give their time to the organisation for precisely the same reasons that anyone else wants to support it – they think it is worthwhile and that their contribution can make a difference. However, it is not just having celebrities associated with your organisation, but the way you use your celebrities that will have an impact.

Finding a celebrity

Celebrities who can attract to your cause include:
- Sports personalities.
- TV and radio stars.
- Film stars.
- Pop stars and musicians.
- Business leaders
- Prominent philan-thropists.
- Politicians and retired politicians.
- Journalists.
- Writers.
- Academics and experts.

The list can include anyone who has a high public profile and is well liked by those parts of the public you hope to draw support from. Here is an example of how a celebrity can get involved in a cause:

Shabana Azmi is an Indian actress of international repute, having starred in over 100 mainstream, alternative and international films. Apart from her acting, Shabana Azmi is also a committed social activist. She has undertaken a 5-day hunger strike for the slum dwellers of Bombay and has opposed slum clearance and negotiated alternative land on behalf of Nivara Hakk, the Bombay housing rights organisation of which she is a Board Member.

Using celebrities effectively

You should try wherever possible to find a relevant celebrity. People who have had some direct experience of the problem (if you are working with handicapped children, for example, someone who has a handicapped child) will be a much more powerful advocate for the organisation and the cause. Celebrities should be matched to your target donor audience.

Well-known people can be used in a wide variety of ways – from becoming a patron or joining your board of trustees to appearing in photo calls, launching publications, giving out prizes or participating in fundraising events.

When asking a celebrity to help, you need to think carefully and discuss with them how best they might be used. They want their association with you to be a success, but the time they can offer might be quite limited.

You also have responsibilities to them. Celebrities have their own reputations to consider, so they do not want to become associated with bad publicity or with controversy. And they may be used to a level of personal support and attention that is difficult for small organisations to sustain – everything from being given detailed instructions for what they are expected to do, to having speeches written for them, being collected by taxi or car and driven back after the event, and being accompanied and looked after whilst they are there.

Managing Celebrities

It is often said the celebrities are the most difficult of people to work with and that their presence can result in major culture clashes. This is undoubtedly true for some organisations, but couldn't be less true for others. Some well-known people demand to be treated as celebrities in all aspects of their lives; others can be deeply appreciative of the opportunity to be involved at all. It is important to build your relationship with such people carefully, as indeed you should do with anyone who contributes to your organisation in any significant way.

Because celebrities can bring you great benefits, you should treat them professionally and politely and try to make sure that their contribution is meaningful for you and satisfying for them. In an organisation of any size, it is important to control access to your celebrities tightly. This is to help prevent them being asked to do too many things too frequently, or indeed being asked to do things that they have specifically declined to do.

For performers, the question of whether to pay them for appearing at an event may arise. If you want to avoid having to pay large fees in future, then it is wise not to start doing so now. Most performers do not expect or want to take fees from charity events, and certainly should not be encouraged to do so. As a general rule, you should be prepared to pay reasonable expenses (but not for a convoy of air conditioned limos for them and their friends) and only consider paying the most nominal amounts as a fee, and then only in exceptional circumstances and possibly as a donation to a charity of their choice. The possible exception to this rule is in the use of musicians at entertainment events.

If you are recruiting someone for an event, they will need to have a very clear idea of what is going to happen and precisely what is expected of them. Is a speech going to be necessary? And who is going to write it for them? Will a car be provided? At what time must they arrive? And when can they discreetly slip away? Who will greet them and look after them whilst they are with you? Will there be a presentation of flowers or a public thank you? Who will be responsible for formally thanking them afterwards on behalf of the organisation? And so on. They will also want to be told how much their presence has helped. How many extra people have come this year, how much extra money was raised, how many reporters covered the story. Any professional will want to know that they have really been able to help and that you have got the most out of their presence.

Sometimes it is not possible to deal directly with the celebrity. You have to get to them via an agent or personal assistant. Working with an agent can be both a help and a hindrance. They will be more concerned with fees and payments, and may not want their client to do something for nothing. On the other hand, being associated with you can bring the celebrity a lot of good publicity and help create an image of a caring person. So there is some benefit to their client. Attempt to get a direct line to your celebrity supporter as soon as you can. But the agent can be helpful in identifying long-range opportunities and availability (diaries are quickly filled up); they can also help you get an idea of what the person concerned is looking for, as well as their likes and dislikes.

7.3 Working with Trustees and Committee Members

Most organisations need outsiders to provide fresh energy and new thinking, and to contribute their particular skills to the running of the organisation. The obvious place for such people is on the Management Board of the charity, or on one of its Advisory Committees.

For many organisations, Management Boards are often a self-selecting group of people, which has more to do with the history of the organisation than with its current needs. They can become stale and out of touch with what's happening, and can soon forget that they have a crucial role to play in the organisation's success. A properly structured, well briefed and motivated team of people can play a hugely important role in the life of the organisation.

One of the roles of the Management Board is to ensure that the organisation has sufficient resources to carry out its work and that it is doing all it can to meet the need it is seeking to address. This means having a strategic view of the organisation's fundraising potential, and ensuring that there is sufficient expertise and administration within the organisation to raise the money that is needed. So for the fundraiser, it is imperative to get people on to the Management Board or Fundraising Sub-Committee who will ask the right questions, think long-term, advise on crucial issues, suggest useful contacts, and bring clear thinking to the fundraising.

But what do you do if you have a Management Board that seldom meets, does not understand its role and has lost interest? There are several steps you can take:

- The staff team, including the Executive Director and of course the Fundraiser, should recognise the **potential contribution** that an effective Management Board can make to the running of the organisation.
- The matter might then be **discussed with individual Board Members** who share the concern that the Board is not operating effectively, and who are committed enough to want to do something.
- You could then undertake **an 'audit' of the skills and expertise** that you would like to have amongst your Board Members.
- **Fresh people** might be identified and approached who are willing to become involved as Board Members bringing these skills and expertise.
- **A plan** can then be drawn up for reforming the Board, replacing those who have lost interested with new people, setting an agenda for the Board, and allocating roles and responsibilities to individual Board members.

The Management Board

The role of the Management Board

1. Giving direction to the organisation: Setting and reviewing the mission of the organisation, developing priorities and agreeing plans, monitoring progress, steering the organisation through good and bad times.

2. Managing people: Being responsible for the performance of the Chief Executive, and ensuring that the organisation is getting the best out of all its people – paid staff as well as volunteers.

3. Making the organisation accountable: Ensuring that the organisation accounts to all those who have a stake in it, including the community it is serving and those providing funds for its work.

4. Keeping within the law: Ensuring that the organisation abides by its governing instrument and fulfils its objects and purposes as stated in its constitution, and that it operates within the law at all times.

5. Managing resources: Ensuring that money and property are used properly and for best effect, and that there are sufficient resources to cover all liabilities and for the organisation to keep going and develop its work.

6. Managing itself: Ensuring that the Board operates successfully as a team, that its meetings are effective, and that all individual members are contributing and involved.

Who to put on the Management Board
1. **Professionals**: accountants, lawyers, teachers, welfare workers, architects, etc.
2. **Experts**: in the service you provide.
3. **Clients**: who have benefited from your work.
4. **People drawn from your local community**.

Qualifications required
1. **A genuine interest** in your organisation and what it is doing.
2. **Specialist skills** which your organisation can benefit from.
3. **Contacts and access** to people that will be able to help you.
4. **Time** to devote to your work.

Fundraising Committees

Besides appointing people to serve on the Management Board, there are other ways in which you can bring outsiders into your organisation. One is through the Fundraising Committee. There are a number of different models for such committees:

1. The Fundraising Strategy Committee, which reports to the Executive Committee. Its role is to monitor regularly and improve the fundraising across the whole of the organisation. Its role is purely supervisory. This group will not raise money for you.

2. The Fundraising Advisory Committee, which is a looser grouping which may meet less frequently. It consists of 'ideas people' drawn from different walks of life, chosen because of their occupations or talents. It can be a useful source of ideas for the fundraiser and can sometimes be a means of getting new ideas taken up by the organisation.

3. The Event Committee, which can play a crucial role where any sort of fundraising event is being organised. It is likely to be an ad hoc group specifically created for the purpose of running a ball or film premiere or other activity. It has room for both the great and good (useful for the sale of tickets!) and also the unknown but committed (useful for doing all the work!).

4. The Appeal Committee, which can be most effective where individuals are recruited specifically to help raise large amounts of money for a major appeal. Members of this group are chosen because of their ability to give substantial donations themselves and for their willingness to ask others (the rich, the important philanthropists, the leaders of industry and commerce, and those in charge of government programmes) to give. Meetings are likely to be rare, and the role of the Chairman in leading the group and ensuring that the money is raised is crucial.

5. The Local Committee, which is a group that acts as the local representatives of your organisation. They will consist of the activists in a given area and will usually be prepared to get involved in any activity that is needed, including fundraising, public speaking and media work.

Sometimes the role of the committee has not been clearly thought through. Getting the right brief for the committee is as vital as recruiting the right people. It is much better to start with the right concept of what the committee is going to do, than to try to change the approach or brief once members of the committee are in place.

How to get the most out of your Committee Members

Collecting a group of skilled and experienced people to help you is only the first stage. Getting the most out of this group of people and ensuring their continuing interest and involvement is equally important. Here are a few things to consider doing:

- Give each new person a **proper induction**, showing them the work of the organisation, introducing them to some of the clients and beneficiaries so that they understand the impact the organisation is having on people's lives, introducing them to members of staff so that they understand who is responsible for doing what, and giving them printed literature about the work of the organisation (including a copy of its constitution, the latest annual report, research reports and papers, other publications and fundraising literature).
- Discuss with each person how best they might contribute to the success of the organisation and what **personal objectives** might be set for them. It is better to ask for specific contributions and commitments than just ask people to help as required. And it is better to get people to do something significant for a limited period of time than to continue doing little until they grow old. If you set performance targets, then they will be able to recognise their achievements,
- Agree matters like **regular attendance** at meetings, remuneration of expenses, training, attendance at conferences, etc.
- **Review their contribution** (as a group if everything is going well, or individually if it isn't) on an annual basis.
- Find **ways of keeping them motivated** by continuing to impress them on the importance of the organisation's work, showing them its successes and achievements, involving them in discussing matters of current interest or concern, and continuing to expose them to the organisation's front line work.

7.4 Getting the most from your donors and supporters

Your existing donors and supporters are a really important part of your fundraising future. They have demonstrated their commitment to you through giving, and you should try to retain this commitment and to develop their involvement in your organisation. In this section, we look at two important aspects of developing your relationship with your donors and supporters – saying thank you, and involving them further.

Saying thank you

Saying thank you to your supporters is both an essential courtesy and a piece of enlightened self-interest that fundraisers forget at their peril. And this applies as much to grants from donor bodies (such as government departments or international donor agencies) as it does to donations from individual supporters and participants at fundraising events.

Saying thank you makes donors feel good about their giving; it tells them that their donation has actually been received, and that it is being put to good use; it gives you the opportunity to find out about the depth of their interest, and perhaps some of the reasons why they have decided to support you; it enables you to tell them more about your work and your future plans; and all this will help you to get further support from them in the future. Your best prospects for a donation are those people who have given you a donation. So the thank you process becomes crucial. There are many ways of saying thank you:

By letter

Some charities reply to all donations, while others reply only to certain classes or levels of donation. The cost of replying can make it expensive to reply to smaller donations. But there are important advantages in thanking all donors in some way if you can – as a small donation now may turn into a large donation later, or for the donor, what is a small amount of money to you may be a major commitment of money and concern for them. But if you are worried about cost, you might ask donors to tell you if they do not want a reply (to save administrative costs).

When you do say thank you, make your reply swift – say within three days of receipt of the donation. Make the letter personal to the donor, and recognise their giving history (the length of time they have been supporting you and their level of giving). A word processor can help here, using standard forms of thank you letters as the basis, and adapting these as necessary.

Some organisations wait to get the Chairperson to sign the letter. This is not necessary – your smaller and regular donors are probably much more interested in building up a personal link with your donations administrator, who they will be able to contact if they have a query or want further information.

By telephone

To give a really fast and personal response, little can beat the telephone. This is not recommended for small donations, but is an important medium for thanking larger donors. As soon as you receive an exceptional gift, ring the donor. Thank them personally. Reassure them that their cheque has arrived safely – donors often feel concerned about committing their generosity to the vagaries of the post. Find out what prompted the gift. Find out what they think of your organisation.

Fundraisers will need to use the evenings to do this, as donors will often be out during the day. When making a phone call, try to create a sense of excitement, enthusiasm and urgency – the money will really help, it is being put to good use immediately, and it will bring real and important benefits.

By visit

Personally visiting donors who are likely to be of importance to the organisation may be a very time consuming business. But research shows that it can be an extremely worthwhile way of saying thank you. You need to be able to identify those whom it will be worth your while to visit and those whom it is possible to visit geographically. The visit can be made by the fundraiser, by a Management Committee or Fundraising Committee member, or by a trained volunteer. A preliminary phone call can be made to announce when they are going to be in the area, and an appointment can be set up.

Donors may be wary about the object of such visits until they have actually received one. A simple chat to tell the donor more about your work and to thank them for their gift will often naturally lead on to discussion about committed giving or how they might help as a volunteer – and even about the possibility of leaving a legacy – without your having to introduce the subject yourself or ask directly.

By meeting

Where personal visits are not possible, some charities set up meetings, receptions or open days for much the same purpose. Supporters in a particular area are invited and refreshments laid on. A senior person from the organisation will give a short talk. It is important then to have staff, committee members or other volunteers present to chat to those invited to the event.

One possibility is to hold the event at your office, where all your staff and committees are available. People are always interested in seeing your offices and your facilities. Such events are usually very well received, even when all they are able to see are desks and filing cabinets. Another is to organise a site visit to see the project at work and enable the donors to meet some of the beneficiaries or the local community. It is the people that donors and volunteers most enjoy meeting at such events.

By gift

Some fundraisers offer some inducement or token in return for gifts of a certain size. There are two distinct circumstances: one is heavily promoted by the charity to encourage a particular type or size of response, whilst the other is a token of thanks used to build commitment and help spread the message to others.

Paper items of low cost and high perceived value are more frequently used for this purpose. A special Christmas card from the president; a certificate for a pledged legacy; or a wildlife print in return for a donation of more than a certain amount. Though giving is often a private matter, some supporters welcome opportunities to discuss their favourite cause with their friends. A thank you token or certificate of support which they can display in their home can help them do this.

By public acknowledgement

A further way in which thanks can be given is through a public announcement – such as an advertisement in a newspaper, or a mention in your newsletter, magazine or annual report.

The use of the annual report is sensible. Not only are you able to thank your donors, this sends signals to others too that you are interested in receiving donations and publicly acknowledge the support you receive. If you indicate the level of their gifts, this will create a certain peer group pressure for others to give at similar levels. Perhaps more important is the credibility factor – *"If they have given, then it must be a good organisation"*. As an organisation grows, this becomes no longer feasible, as the number of donors then gets too large to be able to list everyone. Even then the major donors can be listed or mentioned.

Taking paid advertising to thank donors can be expensive but can be worthwhile if there are other messages to communicate (for example that the cause has widespread or prestigious support). Remember always to get the donor's permission before you do this, as most do not expect to see their names publicly in print (and may become frightened that they would then receive an avalanche of appeals from other good causes).

Getting donors involved

Donors and supporters are likely to give more generously the more they understand your cause. If supporters are aware of the issues and policies behind your work, of your difficulties and failures as well as of your success, then they are much more likely to become firmly committed to your work. Fundraising effectiveness can be enhanced by using a number of devices which give the donor a feeling of much greater involvement in the work and the concerns of the charity.

There are a number of ways of giving them a fuller picture of what you are doing that will build their commitment and their support.

Thanking your supporters

We are grateful to...
  Arab British Charitable Trust
  Association of University Teachers
  Austcare
  BandAid
  Britten Pears Foundation
  Comic Relief
  Christian Aid
  DES...

A well used way of recognising the role of major donors to your organisation is to publish a list in your annual report. This is the beginning of a longer list published in the World University Service Annual Report.

Involving your supporters in the campaign

The Anti Apartheid Movement in the UK needed both to raise money from its members and to make a political point about sanctions against South Africa. They invited both their supporters, and also the supporters of the Campaign for Nuclear Disarmament, to send a donation and to send in a card printed in the shape of an orange with their name on. A thousand oranges, each one addressed to the Prime Minister, were then hung on a huge model tree and taken to the Prime Minister's official residence. Using this method they both persuaded more members to give a donation and got more of them active than they would otherwise have done.

	Cash response	Responders sending oranges
AA members	7.5%	20.0%
CND members	3.0%	7.8%

Regular mailings to supporters

Sending mailings to supporters is a necessary and vital form of communication. It keeps them in touch with what's happening. It reports back on your progress, and, by implication, how you have been able to use their money. It highlights successes and achievements, including major grants that have been received. It sets out future plans and further opportunities for giving support.

In communicating with your supporters, you want them to read what you have sent, and you may also want them to respond in some way. Both these are difficult in a world where people are constantly receiving unsolicited information from all manner of sources. So you may want to find ways of improving the communication process. Here are some possible ways:

1. Questionnaires: Where you have a large number of supporters, you have an opportunity to use the strength of their numbers, both to inform yourselves better on what they think (and who they are), and to use their views to make important campaigning points. Sending a questionnaire to supporters in a regular appeal mailing can increase response rates. Some people will be motivated by the appeal and some will be motivated by the request to provide information.

2. Campaigns: Asking supporters to return cards to a government minister or to a planning authority, either directly or through the organisation's offices, can achieve much the same.

3. Contests and competitions: A quite different way of encouraging involvement is through some form of contest or competition. Competitions where the skill is knowledge of what your organisation stands for can often develop greater understanding of what you are trying to do. But use this technique with care. Attractive as it may be to get supporters looking at every line of your copy for the answer to a clue, some tests have indicated that large and regular donors do not respond well with this sort of device, which they might find too childish. But there are other sorts of competitions that you might consider – for the best idea or suggestion, on some matter that concerns the organisation and its work, for example.

Other involvement techniques

There are also other ways in which you can try to involve your supporters much more in the work of the organisation. These seek to provide greater understanding and to expose the donors to the people behind the organisation (staff, volunteers, clients, beneficiaries, the local community where the projects are based).

1. Visits: Most supporters never get to see the work you are doing. You can build their commitment by inviting them to visit you. This can be done in a number of ways. Open days at your office will yield a surprisingly high level of interest, even if your office is remote from the projects you are organising. If possible, site or project visits are even better. Overseas development charities have for years organised project visits for their staff, donors and volunteers. Not because the much visited projects want it, nor because they enjoy the administration involved; but simply because the excitement and understanding that is generated by such a visit can never be replicated through less direct means.

2. Events: Inviting supporters to events such as annual meetings or celebratory receptions can be another way of getting them involved in your work. Try to ensure that you have enough explanatory literature around, and that members of staff make a point of meeting people and discussing the work of the organisation with them.

3. Lectures and talks: This is another form of getting their involvement, where you lay on events specially for your supporters where they can hear experts discuss the problem or issue. This gives them the chance to understand more fully the cause you are addressing, and makes them feel that their contribution is important and useful. You can tactfully introduce the notion that you are looking for support to develop some new initiative whose importance has been highlighted in the talk. But the essential purpose of such a meeting is not to raise money, but to build interest and involvement.

4. Involving donors in your fundraising: On the principle that the best person to ask is someone who has already given, you might try to find ways of inviting donors to accompany you to fundraising meetings, particularly where you know that their support is enthusiastic. If they can convey something of what motivated them to get involved, it can encourage others; but equally importantly, it will cement their relationship with you.

5. Friends' groups: By 'enrolling' donors as members of a friends' group or a supporters' club (either free or for a subscription) and sending them a regular newsletter which focuses as much on the donors and what they are doing for the organisation as on the work of the organisation, you can create a sense of belonging. You can then organise special events for these key supporters. And you can also develop special appeals where you ask your existing supporters to raise a sum of money for a specified purpose. By giving them the responsibility for doing this and a target to achieve, this will encourage them to give generously.

6. Regular giving: This has been covered in *Section 6.5*.

7. Campaigning: Many voluntary organisations have as part of their brief a message to communicate to both public and government alike. The campaigning is usually spearheaded by the paid staff, but can often be reinforced by volunteers. Involving donors in this can also build commitment. Those who become involved in advocating a cause, will develop a much deeper commitment to it. It is exactly these people that are likely to become your best supporters in the long term.

Fundraisers should never allow fundraising to become divorced from the advocacy of the cause. It is important to ensure that there are a number of different ways for people to support an organisation: giving money, volunteering, fundraising, and campaigning. Some people will only be able to do one of these things. However, many want to do more, and by becoming more involved, they will strengthen their concern and commitment to you.

> **Challenges for the fundraiser**
> 1. To get the donor to **give again**.
> 2. To get the donor to **give regularly** and frequently, on some form of committed basis.
> 3. To get the donor to **increase the level of giving**.
> 4. To get the donor to **give in several different ways** at the same time.
> 5. To encourage the donor to **think of giving a legacy**.

Recruiting volunteers from your donors

It is sometimes assumed that volunteers and donors are two separate categories of supporters, which should not be mixed. Many charities feel that they should not ask their donors to volunteer, and that they should not ask their volunteers to give money. This assumes that people compartmentalise their concern and their response – which is plainly not true.

From the fundraiser's point of view, two things need to be borne in mind. The first is that all those who are giving their time should also be given the opportunity to support the organisation by giving money. If you feel that they should be protected from other requests and encouraged in their existing support for the organisation, then you might consider doing some simple market research to find out whether they would like to be asked to give. The second is that donors can be invited to become involved as volunteers in some way. Most will not have the time available or wish to. But some will, and they will continue as donors too. Even if they don't, their support may be reinforced by their being told that other local people are working as volunteers for the organisation.

8. Communication skills

8.1 Writing a fundraising proposal

Writing a proposal is probably one of the most important skills in the fundraiser's repertoire. For many smaller organisations, the difference between a good and a bad proposal will be the difference between success and failure. The fundraising proposal communicates the needs of the organisation to its potential supporters. And it is largely on the basis of the written proposal that many funders will decide whether or not to make a grant.

What follows should not be regarded as a blueprint which will guarantee success. What it aims to do is to identify the key points to enable you to produce a proposal which matches the requirements of a potential funder. The same basic approach applies when approaching any grant-making body, whether central government, a local authority, a trust or a company. Where differences do exist, these are identified in the text.

Planning your approach

In thinking about how to structure a proposal, you will need to consider who you plan to approach, what their priorities and interests are, how you are going to make the approach, what procedure they have for selecting and assessing grant applications, what you need to say about yourself and what you propose to do, and when you will be submitting the application. There are several factors to consider at this stage:

- **Application forms**: You should ascertain whether the donor requires applications to be submitted in any standard format, or has an application form which has to be completed. There is nothing more frustrating than having completed a really good application only to find that it should have been submitted on an application form in a prescribed format.
- **How many donors you plan to approach**: If you are sending the proposal to a large number of donors, you want to try to make it personal to each. The simplest way of doing this is by having a standard proposal accompanied by a covering letter. This can include all the points of previous contact and how the project particularly fits within the donor's guidelines and current interests and (if relevant) whether and how the donor will benefit from the association.
- **The size of the donor**: Large aid and donor bodies, major foundations and government funding programmes will be interested in a great deal of detail. They will be receiving substantial applications from a wide range of applicant organisations. They are looking not just for good ideas, but for evidence of need and professionalism in delivery. Smaller donor bodies, which include smaller foundations and many companies, just do not have the time to read through a mountain of paper. They want everything shortened and simplified

– a page or two at the most. If they need any more information, they can ask for it. But you should try to include all the important points in a short letter.

- **The likelihood of success**: The larger the grant applied for and the greater the likelihood of success, the more it is worth putting time and effort into the application. Conversely, for smaller sums or where the chances are low, then you need to limit the time you put into the application if you are to be cost-effective. It is a general principle of fundraising that it is better to put more effort into fewer things than to scatter your efforts widely. So concentrating on a few applications where you think you stand a greater chance of success, and following these written submissions up with phone calls, meetings and other activity will be a better strategy. You can at the same time send a more-or-less standard appeal to a selection of other donors in the hope that some may respond.

Targeting your proposal

Whom to send your proposal to will depend on a number of factors:

- **Urgency**: If you need the money really urgently, then the best bet may be to approach those who have already supported you. You have already convinced them of the worth of your work, and they may be willing to support you again.
- **Scale of need**: If you require large sums of money, then you have a choice. You can either apply for a few large grants from the larger donors who are known to be interested in your sort of work (or who have already supported you) or from some government source. Or you can mount a wider appeal seeking a range of large and small donations from a larger number of donors. Remember though, if you want a large donation, then you will not get what you need if you approach a small grant-maker.
- **How many donors to approach**: Donors are often interested to know how many other people have been asked and whether others have already agreed to give. The general rule is that only a careful selection should be made, based on an assessment of who is likely to be interested. If this is made clear in the proposal, those receiving it are more likely to take it seriously than a proposal mailed out widely. It also saves a great deal of time for both you and the grant bodies if you can cut down the number of applications you make.
- **Type of project**: New projects and new initiatives are more likely to be of interest to foundations and companies than simply contributing to the running costs of the organisation or providing a basic service. There is a skill here in constructing your proposal to make the work seem new and exciting, addressing matters of current concern in an innovative way. This is often simply a matter of presentation.
- **A personalised approach**: You should try to personalise the approach as much as you can, as the personal approach is likely to be far more successful than what appears to be a standard proposal sent to a lot of people. Refer to previous contacts and any previous support. Match your proposal to their interests as evidenced by their stated interests and policies or other grants they have made. Try to make them feel that you are writing to them personally. This is obviously much easier to do if you are writing individual letters to just a few donors.

Content of the proposal

What to raise money for demands a good deal of thought, and there are many points that you will need to consider. You should decide whether you are seeking support for the organisation itself or for a specific piece of expenditure or project. Once you have done this, you should try to answer a series of questions, which are the questions that the donor will need to have answered before deciding to support you. These are the questions, together with some suggested answers for a village tourism project, where tourists can stay in a local village and experience traditional rural life:

Question: What is the problem or the need that is to be met?
Answer: Local economic development. Tourism is amongst the most important economic development opportunities in the country. But tourism generally has a negative impact on local communities (see the well-publicised report just produced on this subject). This project seeks to harness the potential of tourism for local benefit.

Question: Are there any particular geographic or socio-economic factors which make it important to do something in the area where you plan to work?
Answer: The particular location of the village makes it a sensible place for this initiative. The economic condition and trends in the village and the region, based on research, demonstrate the importance of this initiative.

Question: What are the aims and objectives of this project?
Answer: To use tourism for local economic development, thereby enhancing people's incomes. To provide a demonstration model for the development of 'sustainable tourism'.

Question: What working methods will be used to meet these aims?
Answer: Develop a small tourist complex using traditional village structures, to be owned and managed by the village.

Question: What are the short and long-term operational plans?
Answer: Open the site in 1998, marketing it through the local tourist industry and guidebooks, and through development NGOs.

Question: What are the expected outcomes and achievements of the project?
Answer: Create a self-sustaining project, which will move into profit by the end of Year 2. Generate an income for the village, which will be used for social and economic development projects. Produce a report charting the experience of developing the project. Link with Green Tourism to organise a number of conferences and seminars on models for sustainable tourism.

Question: Do you have a clear budget for the work, and can you justify all the expenditure?
Answer: Yes! See attached budget and business plan.

Question: And what is going to happen when the funding runs out? Will the project continue on a sustainable basis? Or will you be able to identify and develop alternative sources of funding? Or will the project come to a natural end?

Answer: It will continue on a sustainable basis, generating an income for the village which will be used to enhance village facilities, including education and health.

Question: What sources of funds have you already identified? And what has already been committed to the project?
Answer: The villagers have contributed an initial sum, and feasibility plans have been drawn up free of charge using a prominent firm of architects who are leading advocates of the use of traditional technologies. The budget for the project is as stated, and we are looking for support from the following sources.

Question: When do you need the money?
Answer: We plan to start work in September (in nine months' time), and we will need the money in three equal instalments paid over a period of a year.

You need to answer all of the questions as factually and as honestly as possible. This list should provide you with a structure for writing your proposal, and with many of the points you will want to include. You also need to demonstrate the importance of what you are planning to do and achieve, at the same time as describing your work and telling them about your plans.

Fundraising proposals should try to answer the question WHY as well as saying WHAT. The following are some of the WHYs you need to answer:

- **Why is the need important and urgent?** And what are the consequences if nothing is done?
- **Why are you the right organisation** to do something about it?
- **Why is the method you have selected the best** or the most appropriate or the most cost-effective?
- **Why are you likely to be successful?** You can demonstrate this by showing some of the skills and resources you will bring, as well as describing your previous successes. You can show your ability to handle sums of money of the size being requested and to deliver on your promises.

There is also the question of 'leverage'. What will the grant that the donor provides achieve over and above the actual sum of money given. Factors that are important include:

- What **other grants** can be mobilised to add to the sum being requested from that particular donor?
- Will you be able to mobilise the efforts and energies of **volunteers**, and how much value will this add to the work being done? Often this will be considerable and you can show how much you can achieve with a relatively small sum of money.
- Will you be mobilising **the local community**, and how are they involved? Again, their involvement will make your project that much more effective.
- Will you be **collaborating** with other organisations and agencies, bringing in additional skills and resources?
- Will the project become **self-sustaining** in some way? Does the sum requested represent an investment which will continue to bring benefit into the future?
- What are your **plans beyond the project**, to build on and develop from the

work you plan to do during this next phase? This should at least be considered, even if you have no firm plans at this stage.
- If the work is **innovative**, what plans do you have for dissemination, and is it possible that your success will influence how others address the problem?

When dealing with donors that have an application form, what they need to know will be evident from the questions they ask in the application form. Make sure that you answer all the questions as completely and as fully as you can.

When approaching companies, an additional factor to consider is whether and how you can offer something in return to the company. For most companies this will be very important, and for any sponsorship proposal it is crucial. Things to consider are: ways in which you can publicise the company's support (in your annual reports, newsletters, the local press, etc.), and the number of people that will become aware of the company's support; the interest of the company's own employees in your organisation as fundraisers or volunteers; and the proximity of your organisation to any major plant or branch location of the company.

> **Checklist of things to include in your proposal**
>
> 1. Do you really **believe in what you are doing** and the value of the project?
> 2. Have you got a **strategy**?
> 3. Have you **planned ahead**?
> 4. Have you selected a **good project** which will appeal to that particular donor (where you have a choice of things to fundraise for)?
> 5. Have you tailored your application to address the **particular interests and priorities** of the recipient?
> 6. Have you done enough to establish your **credibility**?
> 7. Have you any **personal contact**? And have you plans for using this to progress your application?
> 8. Have you prepared a **realistic budget**?
> 9. Have you been specific (and asked for **what you need**)?
> 10. Have you a **target** for the amount you need to raise to get the project started?
> 11. Is your proposal **concise, factual, to the point**?
> 12. Have you assumed people know what you are talking about? **Check for jargon**, initials and acronyms, and other things that people may not understand.

Deciding how much to ask for

You will have found out the sort of level of grant that the particular donor usually makes through your preliminary researches. Very often this will be less than the total you need to raise. In such cases, you will need to approach a number of funders, asking each to contribute part of the total. There are several approaches to this:

- You can approach, say, three different sources, and ask each to contribute one third of the total (or an appropriate proportion, depending on their size).
- You can break down the project into separate components. For the tourist project described above, this might include: land purchase and basic building work; equipping the complex; marketing the project and the running costs for the first year whilst it gets going; producing the final report and dissemination. Each of these might become the subject of an application to a particular donor, and in each application you will highlight the particular importance to the project of what you are asking that donor to support – as well as the value of the project as a whole.

Then there is the matter of strategy. Do you approach all your prospective donors at the same time? Or do you approach one of them first, hoping to gain their support, before approaching the others? This is something that only you can decide. If you have a funder with whom you have worked closely in the past and who is prepared to make a commitment to support the project, then the fact that you have been able to obtain that support might encourage others. On the other hand, if you have to wait to get a commitment from one funder before approaching others, then that can delay the funding process.

Whatever you decide, it is important to have a funding plan, and to explain to everyone you are approaching how you propose to raise all of the money you need.

Timing

It always takes much longer than you think to prepare a proposal: you should allow up to a month if you have not yet fully formulated your thoughts or if you need to consult others. There will often be a good deal of information to be collected, which will also take time. And after you have prepared a first draft, there will be editing to be done, and finally the perfectly typed copy to produce.

There are the time requirements of the funders themselves. This may mean that some sources cannot respond within the timeframe you require. For example, applications for European Union funding may have to be submitted up to 18 months in advance. Government bodies have their own procedures and an annual budget cycle. Foundations may take up to six months, and smaller foundations may meet only once a year – although companies tend to respond more quickly.

There is the question of the length of time you want the money for, whether you require a single sum or continuing support for a number of years. It is frequently said that you only get what you ask for; from this it follows that if you need three-year or five-year funding, you must remember to make this clear in your proposal, though that is no guarantee that you will get it.

There is the question of what happens afterwards. If your project is to continue, how will it be funded after the initial grant period? If you are applying for money to purchase a piece of equipment or a building, how will the running costs be met? You may not have all the answers now, but you should at least be thinking about the problem.

Writing the proposal

When writing up your proposal there are a range of factors to consider.

1. Length: There is a lot of information you could put in. If you put it all in, your application would be too long for most funders. For a substantial proposal, this may well be appropriate. For less complicated projects, keep the length to a minimum. A page or at most two pages will normally be sufficient; and you can append more detailed information or a photograph or technical information to the proposal, if you feel that it will be of interest to the donor.

2. The key points: At the heart of your proposal, you will describe the needs you are trying to address, the aims of your project, and how you will achieve them. You should include as much detail as is necessary for a person who is not knowledgeable in your area. You should also give an indication as to how you would expect to measure the successful outcome of the project.

3. Your credibility: If the organisation is new or the funder has had no previous contact with you, they may well want to ask who you are and why they should entrust their money to you. You have a credibility problem. This can be overcome in a number of ways: providing CVs of the key organisers and others involved; where you have a well-connected committee or patrons, listing their names; mentioning the support you have previously received from other major donors or a government body, which will help provide reassurance. If you have obtained press coverage, you can include the clippings. If you have had an evaluation done on your work, then that might provide ammunition. If you have received feedback from users, experts or others, then you can mention this or include a direct quote.

4. Recognition of the importance of the problem: If the problem itself is not widely recognised, references to other respected reports or endorsements by prominent people will help.

5. The budget: Your budget will always be carefully scrutinised by potential funders, and needs to be clear, complete and accurate. Most donors will not be interested in the small details of your stationery or postage bill. What they will be interested in are the major areas of expenditure and income. You should identify capital or other one-off costs, salaries, overheads and any other major operational costs. Similarly, income estimates will show the money you expect to generate from the project itself or through fundraising. Beyond this, you may need to show the way in which the money you need in the medium term is going to be raised, say over a period of three years. This may require a summary income and expenditure statement and a capital expenditure statement, both spread over a three-year period. Additionally, you will need to supply your organisation's audited accounts for the latest year for which they are available.

6. Information on the organisation and its status: It is useful to include the formal and legal information about the organisation on the letterhead. This includes the registration details, names of trustees, board members and patrons, which can help create the impression that you are well established, and this will answer points of detail which may

---

Getting the budget right

There is a tendency to under-cost proposals. If you do this, you will not raise the money you need to run your project effectively. So you should ensure that:

- You include **every item** that you expect to have to pay for (travel, training, equipment may all be required, and should be provided for).
- You put in a **realistic price** for each item (based wherever possible on estimates of costs you have obtained from suppliers).
- You take account of **inflation**. Different funders will have different systems for dealing with this. But you don't want to find that the price of something has shot up just when you need to purchase it.
- Include **administrative overheads** associated with the project, where this is possible. The organisation functions to make the projects happen. And the cost of running the organisation has to be paid for.
- Include sums for **dissemination and publicity**, both within the communities where you are operating and to interested parties. Telling people what you are doing can strengthen your organisation and its work.

come up later. Sometimes people include their bank account details – optimistically assuming a grant!

7. Language and jargon: Many applications are frankly extremely boringly written and boring to read. If you have the skill to do so, try to write the application in a lively upbeat way, concentrating on your strengths, the opportunities, the desirable outcomes and your hopes for the future. This is far better than the flat language that most reports are written in. The application is a selling document – selling the idea of supporting your project to a potential donor. Points to avoid are: long sentences, long paragraphs, meaningless words and jargon, which mean something to you but nothing to the reader, and waffle. Far better to have short words, short sentences, short paragraphs, bullet points and bold text to highlight key features, headings and subheads to indicate the different parts of the application, etc. The best advice is to get someone else to read what you have written before you send it off – and the best person is someone who knows little about your work, as that is the position of most of the people you will be sending your application to. They can ask for explanations and challenge assumptions where things seem unclear to them.

8. Facts and figures: It is important to back up your claims – to the extent of the need and to the effectiveness of your methods – with facts and figures, rather than in generalities. Everything may be *'desperate'*, *'urgent'*, *'important'*, *'unique'*; but you need to 'prove' this. Try to include a few selected facts and figures in your proposal, and you can, if you want, also provide a wealth of detail in a background paper attached as an appendix to the application.

9. The human story: If you can include case studies and examples of how people have been helped and what they have gone on to achieve as a result of your help, then this will demonstrate clearly that you are effective in helping people – which is what most donors are interested in supporting.

10. Presentation: How you present your proposal is luckily not the most important aspect, but it can make a difference. Different standards and expectations apply to different donors. A sponsorship proposal directed at the marketing director of a major company will have to have a different feel to that being sent to a national foundation which is receiving dozens of others each day. And government agencies and

---

Fifteen Do's and Don'ts for your proposal

DO
1. Address your appeal to the right person.
2. Tailor your appeal to the recipient.
3. Include a clear statement of your charity's functions/objectives.
4. State clearly the purpose for which the funds are needed and the amount required.
5. Break a large appeal down into manageable, realistic amounts for particular elements and items.
6. Include your latest sets of accounts.
7. Offer to go and see the prospective donor, and follow up the letter within a week.
8. Make full use of VIP contacts.
9. Keep it brief.

DON'T
1. Make your appeal letter look mass-produced.
2. Include irrelevant information or large quantities of printed material.
3. Get angry at a refusal – funders cannot support every request, even those which meet their criteria.
4. Be put off by a refusal – try again next year.
5. Feel obliged to offer expensive hospitality to a prospective donor.
6. Leave too little time – it can often take months for your application to be processed and a decision made.

international donors will have their own standards and preferred styles. Remember to tailor your style of communication to whoever it is you are talking to.

Getting in touch

Skilled fundraisers would not consider sending a proposal out of the blue to anyone but the smallest and the most remote foundation or company. To ensure a greater chance of success, applicants need to know as much as possible about those they are approaching. Equally, if the target already knows something about the applicant's work and reputation, then that will be an important advantage.

For example, you will need to know:

- What constraints are imposed by the donor as a matter of **policy** (there is no point applying for something that they cannot or will not support).
- **What sort of things have been supported** in the past (so that you know their particular interests and can tailor your approach accordingly).
- **Who to write to** (their name and job title), but also who makes the decisions and who they are advised by (so you can plan any lobbying).
- Whether they expect to get any sort of **recognition or benefit** in return for their support (so you can think about this before you write your proposal).
- Their **decision-making cycle** and the best time for applications to be submitted.
- Whether proposals must be written to a **set format.**

To find out about all of this you will:

- **Research** the sources you plan to approach, bringing together information from a variety of sources, and keep this information on record.
- **Telephone** the donor organisation to determine contact person and their application procedure.
- Seek or **suggest a meeting**, if this seems appropriate; or think of other ways in which you can bring your work to the attention of the donor. For large applications this is particularly important. The meeting could be at their offices or on your premises.
- Invite the donor to **visit your project** to see it at work.
- **Find out** as much as you can about the detailed decision-making process by asking the donor and by talking to others who have received support from that donor.

> **Some reasons for refusal**
>
> A large number of applications are rejected because they fall completely outside the funder's guidelines. The Commonwealth Foundation has a series of standard letters it sends out in reply to inappropriate applications, giving these reasons for refusal:
> - The Foundation cannot support students at any level.
> - The Foundation cannot support non-Commonwealth citizens.
> - The activity is being held in a non-Commonwealth country.
> - The Foundation cannot help with general appeals.
> - The Foundation cannot normally support activities limited to one country.
> - The proposed activity is outside our terms of reference or priority areas of interest.
> - The Foundation cannot support research activities.
> - The application has arrived too late – the Foundation normally requires three months' notice.
> - The Foundation cannot support activities of more than three months' duration.
> - The Foundation does not provide capital grants.
>
> Sending a completely inappropriate application is a waste of everyone's time. **Read the guidelines before applying!**

- **Contact** any key advisers or trustees of the donor organisation to tell them about your proposal, if you can get access.
- **Write a draft proposal**, personalised as much as possible to the needs of the donor organisation, seek comments on this and then redraft.
- Produce and send off **the final application**, together with appended information to fill in the detail as necessary.

You might want to ask (tactfully) when you talk to them whether they could suggest other bodies for you apply to. Care needs to be taken here, as this may present an easy way for them to say no.

8.2 Producing effective printed materials

The creation and production of effective fundraising and publicity literature is one of the fundraiser's most important tasks. Good fundraising ideas can be destroyed by poorly prepared or presented material. Good writing skills and an understanding of the design and production processes are vital.

The process of creating any printed material usually follows a similar path. The stages include:

- **Conception or visualisation** (which may include producing a dummy or sample copy), and you need to ensure that you are working to an economic format.
- **Setting aside a budget**, and later on in the process getting estimates of costs (so that you keep within your financial constraints).
- **Copywriting** and gathering together of photographs and other visual material.
- **Design**.
- **Print and production**.
- **Distribution**.

Two simple leaflets printed in one colour (black) only, explaining the work of the organisation. Note the use of photographs.

Many of these stages will be carried out by outsiders and each stage might be produced by someone different. This creates considerable opportunities for getting things wrong – deadlines can be missed as a result – and also for losing or watering down the original concept during the process.

You need to decide who does what. There may be many people, within even a small organisation, who feel they can write effectively. Anyone, after all, can write a letter! You need specific writing skills to present a good, clear logical case and to express your ideas forcefully. This may require an outside professional in advertising or marketing. Then you may be dealing with promotional consultants and designers. They may have the skills you need, but you have to brief them properly and be happy with their approach and that they can produce what you need within your budget.

Principles of effective communication

You must have a clear idea of what you are trying to achieve. It is worth writing down the objectives of any particular piece of communication, and including this in the brief to the writer and designer (if you are not doing it all yourself). Is it to generate awareness? To convey information? And if so, what information? To get a response of some sort? To raise money? This is especially important when it comes to annual reports which may have to serve a number of purposes. If the objective is to raise money, then there must be a clear understanding as to how this is to be done. Is the brochure to be sent through the post and a postal response sought from the addressee? And if so, will that response be a cash donation, a membership subscription, a legacy pledge, or what?

The next stage of the process must be to identify who you expect to read the material. If they are readers of a magazine or a particular mailing list, then you will know something about them and their interests. Have they had any previous contact with you or knowledge about your work? Your past donors might be expected to be fairly knowledgeable, and what you say to them will differ from what you say to those who know little or nothing about the organisation. For your existing donors, you could try to get some picture of who they actually are. Some simple research (through a questionnaire, for example) will tell you something about their age, sex, interests and preferences, and also something about their degree of commitment to the organisation.

You will also need to bear in mind budget factors. You may have limited space (in an advertisement, for example) to get your message across. Or if you are sending out a mailing, the cost of printing all the material and postage weight limits will be a factor. Printing in full colour will be more expensive than in one or two colours. And if you want to include photographs, will these need to be specially taken?

> **Ten suggestions for writers**
>
> 1. Get to know your **audience**.
> 2. Use simple, direct and everyday **language**.
> 3. State your **proposition** boldly and clearly.
> 4. Feature real, identifiable **cases and people**.
> 5. Communicate **the need**.
> 6. State clearly what the reader's support will enable you to **achieve**.
> 7. Remember that cleverness rarely pays.
> 8. Avoid seeming too professional.
> 9. Remove any unnecessary detail.
> 10. Give a clear course of action.
>
> *Ken Burnett, a communications consultant, gives this advice to his staff and clients.*

The next stage is to set a clear deadline for when you need the materials. This is especially important if the material is going to be mailed or presented at an AGM. Give yourself room for slippage, and make sure that everyone involved sticks to their deadlines.

Conception

The concept stage (sometimes referred to as visualisation) of producing any fundraising material is important. This will generate a creative approach, a visual theme, a style and a headline or slogan.

Themes, headlines and ideas can be generated through a brain-storming approach. This involves putting a number of interested people together in a

Illustrations can enliven your publications. This is the front cover of the annual report of the Baroda Citizens Council.

room; identifying the object of the exercise and the rules of the brain-storming process; then asking those present to contribute as many ideas as possible. Some may be zany, others can be done at speed, but all must be written up, so that new ideas build on old. Then there is a process of refinement to select one of the suggestions or develop the approach out of several of the ideas. Out of this will come the general approach. It will generate the actual copy.

At this stage, you will need a designer to produce roughs. This is an important stage, as it is the last major point at which you can turn back. If you don't like the rough design, you should ask for a new approach before too much time has been spent. If you pass this stage and then decide a new approach is needed later on, this will cost money and you may miss your deadlines. The visualisation need be no more than the front cover for a leaflet with a sample page – enough to give you an idea of how it will feel and look.

Writing

Not everybody has the skills to write copy, though almost everybody needs at some time to communicate in writing. A good copywriter can really make your words come alive. However, small organisation do not always have the means to hire copy writers, so fundraisers will usually have to write their own copy.

A good copywriter requires a clear understanding of your cause and a proper briefing of what you are trying to say to whom, and the objectives of the communication. When hiring an outside consultant, always look at their portfolio to see what they have done for similar organisations. Some will have an instinctive understanding of your work, alongside their flair with words, while others will be better at selling condensed milk. Though good copywriters are expensive, you may be able to find one as a volunteer.

If you are writing the copy yourself, there are a number of things you will have to remember. The first is about structure. An acronym is useful here – AIDA. This describes the process of persuasion and communication.

- **Attention**: The reader's attention has to be attracted.
- **Interest**: If you don't identify a reason for the reader to be personally interested, you will lose them.
- **Desire**: To support your cause is the next stage, and finally...
- **Action**: Headlines, pictures or strong ideas can all help attract the reader's attention in the first place.

Their interest can be gained by showing them why you exist and the needs you are serving. Don't imagine that your supporters will continue to support you without a continuing reminder of the importance of what you are doing, or the human cost of ignoring the problem. Desire to support your cause is likely to be generated by an understanding that things can be changed if they give their support. Tigers can be saved, classrooms built and people in need helped and your organisation has the wherewithal to do this. Action demands that you tell them what you want them to do and what sort and size of gift they are expected to make.

Keep everything simple and understandable. One problem is that organisations tend to develop shorthand ways of describing their work. These are useful when talking to colleagues, but can involve language that is quite meaningless to outsiders. Jargon should be avoided at all costs.

Find someone to read your first draft who does not have anything to do with your organisation. Ask them to feed back what they have understood – and what they have not understood! A problem may arise when you have to agree the copy with others. Most people's reaction to checking someone else's text is to check for typographic errors and false statements, and then add their own thoughts. The result can often be an accurate but heavily qualified text that loses all its punch and impact. Accept their comments, but remember that effective text cannot be written by a committee. They may have skills in providing the service or in running the organisation, yours are in fundraising and communication.

> **The KISS principle**
>
> An important principle is that of simplicity. **KISS** is the acronym often used to remind us of this:
>
> |K|eep
> |I|t
> |S|imple
> |S|tupid!
>
> This is a useful reminder. And remember:
> - Pythagoras' Theorem was written in 24 words.
> - Archimedes Principle was written in 67 words.
> - The Ten Commandments were written in 179 words.
> - The US Declaration of Independence was written in 300 words.
> - A recent European Commission Directive on a minor food matter was written in 3,427 words!

Design

The design gives the printed piece its character. Good designers can lift the central idea from a piece of text and make it something infinitely more compelling. The elements of this include the copy, the headlines and sub-heads, the photographs and illustrations used, as well as the design style. There is also the number of colours to be used (and whether it is to be printed on tinted paper), and the use of colour with text reversed out and blocks of the page overlaid with a tint of the colour.

You may already have a house design style, including the use of logos. If you do – and consistency is always important – then ensure that designers are clearly briefed about this. Maintaining a consistent house style will help build up a feeling of continuity and reassurance, and will convey the message of dynamism, safety or whatever is implicit in your house style.

The important elements of the design include the format, colour, layout, type faces, the heading and signposting of the various parts of the text; the use of space and how the various sorts of illustration are used.

Illustrations can take many forms and help bring a design to life. Photographs are the easiest to use; but don't use them if they do not make a point or are not of good quality. Photos should always be captioned, as captions are among the most read parts of any publication. The best are those that involve people doing things – and not pieces of equipment, buildings or groups of committee members posing for the camera. Illustrations, diagrams and plans are a good alternative, and can also be useful for illustrating things that cannot yet be photographed (such as the building you are planning to put up).

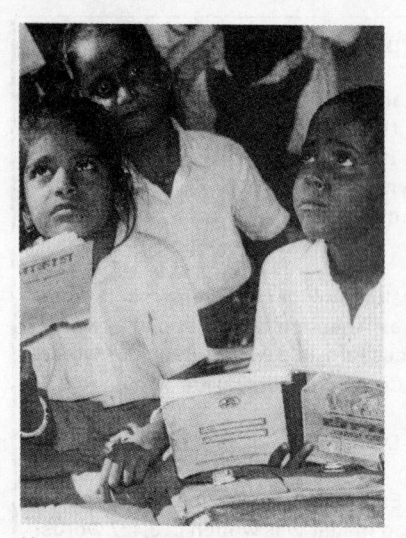

You can use pictures to illustrate your point. This one comes from an annual report of the Aga Khan Foundation, and is captioned "Concern for the quality of education".

A good designer will integrate all these elements for you and, having taken your brief, should be able to satisfy your needs. If you are using an outside designer, do ensure you get a clear quote for the design cost before agreeing to proceed. These days all but the most complicated design can be produced on a Desk Top Publishing system. Newsletters, handbills and leaflets that are produced regularly in a similar format can often be produced in-house to a pre-designed format created for you by a professional designer.

Getting it into print

The final stage in the process is to get the written material into print. This is where you have to spend real money. You will normally want to seek quotes from any outside printers (and from designers if you are using them). With printers, try to obtain three quotes in order to get the best price possible. It is surprising how much the prices vary, even on the most tightly defined jobs. This is a lot to do with how much the printer wants the job and whether what you are producing fits their capacity and their machine size. Do not be embarrassed about asking printers you are dealing with regularly to quote on new jobs. It does not demonstrate mistrust, rather it shows good business practice and a keenness to get the best price. When asking someone to quote, you should have a clear understanding of:

For dealing with designers

- Date of text and instructions to the designer and date of receipt of completed job.
- Visuals needed.
- Format, size and price guidelines for the job.
- Copywriting and who does what and by when.
- Photographs needed: what is required and by when.
- Illustrations needed: what is required and by when.

For dealing with printers

- Date that the completed artwork will be sent to the printer and date required for receipt of completed job.
- Paper size (printers will use standard size sheets of paper; the less the wastage, the more economic the format).
- Print quantity (the unit costs of longer print runs are less than for shorter runs, but it is more expensive producing extra copies you have no need for).
- Paper quality (it usually pays to print on stock paper used by the printer which is bought in bulk) and colour of the paper (tinted paper is more expensive than white paper).
- Number of print colours (one two or four).

- Illustrative photographs and halftones (this can add to the cost, but increase the effectiveness of the communication).
- Folding (complicated folds will usually be more expensive than simple folding).
- Packing and delivery (the price usually includes delivery to one address).

Every decision you make about the design and print quality of a book, leaflet or letter says something about your organisation and its ethos. A most obvious current issue is whether to print on recycled materials. It is hard for an organisation that claims to be concerned with the environment not to be doing this, whatever the economics (and it is usually more expensive). There will be a perception of inconsistency if you don't.

A similar problem surrounds the use of expensive or glossy material paper. Donors expect that when charities communicate with them, they should not waste money unnecessarily. Though they say this, donors will always respond better if what you send them looks nice and appears professional. Remember too, to communicate effectively with new groups of people, you will need to have something much more substantial and well laid out than you would for your existing donors.

8.3 Appeal letters

Appeal letters are also an important type of literature you may need to produce. These are sent to a large number of people, and they will create some sort of impression whether or not the recipient responds. This awareness building is an important factor, particularly when 98% or more of those that the letter is sent to will not be responding.

Perhaps right at the top of the fundraiser's mind will be the fact that direct mail appeals should be raising money at a cost ratio of 10:1, and if the communication is got right, then this fundraising technique can be one of the best sources of continuing income available to any organisation.

There are several parts of the communication to consider. They are the envelope, the salutation, the entry, the appeal, the call to action, the postscript and the supporting literature. Though only a few of these are actually contained in the letter itself, they all play their part in making the appeal effective.

The envelope

Research suggests that 70% never get beyond opening the envelope. Hence you may want to include a slogan or a teaser line on the envelope intriguing the recipient into opening it to find out what is inside. Alternatively, you may feel that since no personal mail ever has advertising copy on the outside, a plain envelope with a stamp may be more compelling to open, rather than immediately thrown away as a piece of 'junk mail'. Only a knowledge of your audience and careful testing will determine the best approach. However, the more personal the letter seems, the more likely it is to get immediate attention.

The salutation

The salutation (Dear...) should be as personal as possible. This is possible when writing personal letters (only possible for small numbers of addressees), by topping and tailing letters personally with the salutation at the start and signature

> **Grabbing attention**
>
> It took us 3,000 years to discover leprosy is curable. How long before we can eradicate it?
> *The Foundation for Medical Research, Bombay*
>
> Do you have a roof over your head? Do you eat at least one square meal every day? Do your children go to school? Do you have easy access to medical help?... For you the answer is 'yes'. For more than half of Bombay the answer is 'no'.
> *Nivara Hakk, Bombay*
>
> Only one person can help this man... This man, because we believe that people have the power to change their own lives.
> *Concern India Foundation*

at the end (only possible for a few hundred addressees or by getting volunteers with good writing to do the topping and tailing for you – this can be very effective), or by using a laser printer fed by computer data to do the job.

If none of these is possible, then fall back on "Dear friend" or "Dear supporter". Both of these are an admission a circular letter is being sent, and that you can't do more than treat the recipient as a statistic. Most word processor systems have mail merge software the enables you to link a list of names and addresses with a given letter.

The entry

You need to grab the reader's attention immediately. If this is not done, there is the danger that the letter will be thrown away before it has been read. The first paragraph you write might be the last paragraph that's read. A letter from a respected celebrity or an amazing statement may make people read on. Or an intensely emotional opening to the letter can do the trick.

The appeal message

Once the reader's attention has been gained, it must be held. The appeal must be simply written; it must be well laid out with short words, short sentences and a variety of paragraph sizes. Key ideas should be underlined, indented or highlighted. In terms of content, you need to:

- State the **problem**.
- Show how you can **help resolve the problem**.
- Demonstrate your **credibility** by showing what you have achieved in the past and others who have helped you.
- Indicate **how much you expect** the donor to give and what this will achieve.
- Make the **call to action** clearly.

The call to action

The call to action is crucial, and where many otherwise well written appeal letters fail. Perhaps this is to do with the reluctance to be direct in asking for precisely what you want. Yet that is exactly what is required. Start flagging up the call to action early on in the letter. Repeat it throughout the letter. And make it absolutely plain near the end. It should consist of:

- **What you want** (money, time, goods, etc.).
- **How much you want** them to give (perhaps indicating a list of amounts, and linking these to what can be done with that amount of money).
- **How you want the amount paid** (in cash, by credit card, by standing order).
- **When** – how soon must it arrive (usually immediately, to create a sense of urgency).

- **Who** – send it to me personally (a personal name to reply to will always be better than an anonymous department).
- **Where** – the return address (which can sometimes be forgotten!).

The call to action

Join a Movement against Blindness by Filling up a Coupon
Lok Kalyan Samiti, New Delhi

Unite to fight against Dowry... How you can help
Sakhya is a non-profit organisation largely dependent on volunteers. If you are convinced and motivated to fight against the dowry system, you could help us in various ways. We are always looking for artists, musicians, writers and others to help us spread our message. You can choose the type of work you wish to do and the number of hours you can devote. Sakhya welcomes donations too. You can contact us at the following addresses...
Sakhya Anti-Dowry Guidance Cell, Bombay

Your help is important
Nivara does not believe in charity. Rather it sees the development of a cleaner, safer environment in the city as a people's movement fuelled by people's participation. You can help us fight for a better city. Setting up medical services, balwadis and running legal aid for the poor is an expensive business. While we try and ensure that the poor themselves finance as much of these activities designed for their benefit, there is always a massive shortfall. To meet the ever-increasing demand for these services, it is crucial we form a large, functioning network of voluntary participants to meet the social challenges thrown up in the city. Do participate. And donate generously. Cheques can be mailed to...
Nivara Hakk Welfare Centre, Bombay

The postscript

Save an important idea for the postscript (or PS). This is one of the most read parts of the letter. So use it for your final argument to clinch their support or reinforce the message. This can be produced in a printed typeface or a reproduction of the same handwriting used for the signature.

Supporting literature

Supporting literature should be used to reinforce the message of the appeal. Don't be drawn into the temptation to squeeze in thousands of words of text that you couldn't find space for in the letter. Use all the same considerations. It is often a good idea to have photographic material with little text. Don't forget to repeat the call to action.

Response mechanism

There will need to be some way of donors getting their reply and hopefully their donations back to you. This could be a simple reply envelope. Or a credit card hot-line. Or an instruction to pay money into your bank account.

8.4 Annual reports

Every organisation has to produce some sort of annual report. This can be an extremely useful publication for your fundraising. The annual report is an opportunity for the organisation to promote its strength, highlight the importance of the need, demonstrate its effectiveness, celebrate its achievements and also raise money both directly and indirectly.

> **Thirteen criteria for the ideal annual report**
>
> 1. A well planned structure.
> 2. A clear statement of objectives.
> 3. A clear understandable financial picture.
> 4. Visible economy, demonstrating sensible use of resources.
> 5. Instant appeal.
> 6. Legibility.
> 7. Good design.
> 8. Well written copy.
> 9. Good use of photos and illustrations.
> 10. Overall appropriateness of style and feel to the organisation.
> 11. Empathy with principal audience.
> 12. Completeness: all components working well together.
> 13. A sense of excitement.
>
> Source: 'Charity Annual Reports' by Ken Burnett

Almost all your major funders will require a copy of your annual report and accounts as a condition of their grant. Legally, too, you will be obliged to produce accounts annually, and as a minimum your report could be no more than a paragraph contained within the accounts. Most people would expect you to take the opportunity to do a lot more than this. And you will probably want to too, seeing it as a useful promotional opportunity rather than a chore.

Since many organisations produce annual reports out of habit or somewhat grudgingly, if you are to make the most of the opportunity, it is really important to identify what you are trying to do and how you can justify the expenditure. Here are a few important points:

- Don't use the annual report to complain. Use it to promote and celebrate.
- Use illustrations and photographs liberally. They can convey more than the printed word.
- Don't start with long lists of supporters and committee members. You are writing the annual report to create interest in your organisation.
- On the other hand, do list major donors. This recognition (and you will be sending them a copy) will encourage them to think about giving a repeat donation, and encourage others (to whom you could send a copy of the report with your appeal letter) to give.
- Think about who you might send a copy to, as good PR for your organisation or to create interest as a prelude to making an appeal.
- Annual reports are good vehicles for sponsorship. It is a reasonably small amount to cover the costs of design, production and dissemination. The sponsorship is visible, and will be seen by key supporters. And with sponsorship you could mount a more effective PR campaign using your annual report.
- If you want to use the report to raise money directly, either print an appeal at the end of the report or enclose an appeal leaflet inside the report (which could be stitched in).

8.5 Using the telephone

The telephone is an extremely important and often under-used tool for the fundraiser. It can be used in a variety of different ways, either on its own or in conjunction with other media. In thinking about the phone, you have to distinguish between outgoing phone calls and incoming ones.

Incoming calls may be requests for information or to discuss making a gift. Outward telephoning requires more skill (and sometimes courage) and can be used for a whole range of promotional and fundraising activities.

Donation lines

With the increasing use of credit cards, it may be sensible to have a phone line for donors to use to send in their donation. Most response lines are answered by telephone answering machines. These need to have good clear messages and long answer tapes to record a number of calls. Donors need to be told exactly what information to leave.

Some donors will want to speak to a real person, to find out more or to offer a large donation. Not many people would leave a donation of £1,000 on a telephone recording device. So, if you are receiving support from individual donors, it is important that there is an effective procedure for taking calls from potential supporters at your switchboard or reception. Although you might want to use a special number for credit card donations in your appeal literature, it is sensible to list your main telephone number too, to ring for advice and further information.

Recruitment

Outgoing telephoning can be used for a range of things, but perhaps most frequently for the recruitment of people. Teams of callers can be used for purposes ranging from the sale of raffle tickets to the recruitment of house-to-house collectors.

> **What can be done over the phone**
>
> | Donors phoned | Response rate | Average pledge |
> |---|---|---|
> | £20 + donors | 61% | £54.42 |
> | £35 + donors | 67% | £65.36 |
> | £50 + donors | 83% | £102.83 |
>
> These results were achieved by Friends of the Earth in a test which targeted groups of existing donors who had given in three different donation ranges. They tested 1,250 donors and raised £64,000 in pledges. Two problems confront telephone fundraisers:
> - How do you convert the pledges into reality; and
> - How do you carry the operation out without offending supporters? Complaints of unsolicited telephoning are a common occurrence.

Membership and subscription renewals

Telephoning existing supporters can be a much more acceptable than unsolicited calls to potential new supporters. And especially if there is a reason for ringing them. Examples of this include the renewal of a membership subscription, where supporters may have forgotten to renew and so may welcome the reminder. Additionally, this is an excellent way for any charity to find out why members are not renewing. Another example is for an emergency. If there is a famine and people are dying, then that is a good reason. Or if the medical costs for operating on a child need to be met immediately if the child is to get treatment, then again that's not likely to cause offence.

Phonathons

One major technique that is used extensively in the United States, but has yet to catch on elsewhere, is the Phonathon, or telephone fundraising campaign. This is different from a Telethon, which is a television fundraising campaign, usually involving a TV programme broadcast over several hours or sometimes a whole day, where donors pledge their support by ringing in. In a Phonathon, the appeal is made directly by telephone, ringing up people and asking them to give.

There are two ways of organising a Phonathon. One is to assemble a team of volunteers and get them busy phoning supporters. Another uses the same technique but employs professionals who may be selling air conditioning in the morning and fundraising for your cause in the afternoon. Telephone fundraising works best if the cause is really urgent, or if it can be made to seem so. If the need is obvious then it also becomes simpler to recruit volunteers to do the telephoning.

The phone is quite an expensive way of contacting people and so the technique needs to be used with care. It is unlikely to be of value in soliciting small donations. The response rates can be over 50% when calling past donors, which is well in excess of normal mailing response rates. However, the pledge rate may not turn into cash in the bank unless donors are giving credit card donations. For the rest you will need to send a letter to pledgers to clinch the donation. You might expect 60% of pledged donations to be converted into actual support at the end of the day (maybe with a telephone reminder).

The essential tools for successful use of the telephone are the script and the list.

The script

Creating a good script is a difficult task. Until you have experienced the huge range of responses possible, it is hard to create a good script. Unlike with a written communication, with the telephone there is the opportunity for the recipient to interrupt or ask questions. But the essential elements will be similar. A script should contain:

- Information about **who you are** and about **the organisation** you represent.
- Whether it is a **good time to talk**. Anyone who has received calls at 6pm in the evening just as the children are sitting down to a meal, will vouch for the potential hostility that can be generated by a caller presuming that now is the most convenient time to talk; so callers should attempt to ascertain whether this is a good moment to talk. Failure to do this can diminish the results of the call.
- Reference to **previous support or past contact**. When calling people, who have supported the organisation before, it is important to refer to their past help and thank them again. This can usefully lead into...
- An introduction to **the work and needs of the organisation** – a short preparatory introduction about the current needs of the organisation or something else about the development of the work, and this should help set the scene for a further request for help.
- A **call to action**. As with any other form of communication, you should not expect that supporters will necessarily know why you want to talk to them unless you state it explicitly. The call to action must be very direct and clear, and should state precisely what you want them to do. Getting a pledge or a verbal agreement is usually the best you can hope to do over the phone, unless

you are seeking credit card donations (in which case you can complete the transaction there and then).
- The **follow up reminder**. The call can be followed up by a letter or form to sign. The follow up should be done immediately to achieve maximum response.

The list

Producing the list of people to telephone is not always easy, since most databases do not include phone numbers. This is something that is changing. If you plan to use the telephone, then perhaps you should include space on the reply coupon in all your promotional literature for the supporter to put a phone number. There is then the implication that if they do so they will not mind being called. Then at least you can keep the telephone numbers of your own supporters on file.

When telephoning individuals and companies out of the blue, the local telephone directory is probably the only available starting point. In many developing countries, having a telephone at least indicates potential wealth. And the business pages, where companies are classified by activity, can be a good hunting ground for soliciting gifts in kind.

8.6 Market research

Market research is a vital tool if a charity is to maximise the funding and support it receives from its donors and from the public. The more you can find out about your donors and potential donors you plan to approach, the more you will be able to communicate effectively with them and to motivate them to give.

There are many different types of market research that you can carry out, and for a wide variety of purposes. In this section we look at researching your own donor base, finding out what the public thinks of you, and using research to seek out new supporters.

All research involves collecting data gleaned from small groups of people and making extrapolations from that to derive views about the attitudes of the public at large. There are three basic types of information that are used:
- Demography refers to the vital statistics of age, sex, and location of individuals in the general population.
- Psychographics denotes people's attitudes and preferences, as shown by newspaper readership, church going, voting patterns, and so on.
- Opinion research usually refers to the attitudes of the public to given questions. This might be put in a question such as "Do you think stray dogs should be shot" – agree, disagree, don't know.

Donor research

There will often be a group of supporters upon whom the organisation's well-being depends. These may be volunteers, donors, sponsors or others. When an organisation is very small, it is quite often just a small group of enthusiasts and well-wishers who are involved. At this stage, it is possible for the organisers to keep in touch with all their supporters personally. But as numbers grow, this becomes no longer possible.

It is at this point that the organisation will need to find out more about its supporters. You will want to know who they are and what they think of you. Knowing who your supporters are will help you identify other sorts of people you might try to recruit as new members – and it could indicate people that have not yet been influenced by your message. What your supporters think is also important, as you are dependent on their time or money to carry out the organisation's work. If they are becoming disenchanted with what you are doing or can no longer meet your expectations, you have a problem which you will need to address.

You can always chat informally to your supporters at events and open days, or indeed whenever you come into contact with them. You should be doing this as a matter of course, to show that you are interested as well as to find out more about what your supporters are thinking. But you may want to do a more formal research survey. A postal survey is the most usual form of supporter survey. If you have a mailing list or can enclose the questionnaire with a newsletter, then this is relatively easy and cheap to do.

There is an important issue behind interpreting results: to what degree are the results of those people who responded representative of the whole (including those that didn't respond)? The responders are likely to be people who are more keenly interested than an average sample. If only a minority has responded, they have one thing in common – that they have responded. Do they also have other things in common? For example, if it was a long questionnaire, then only those people who had the time might have responded, and thus your results could be biased in favour of older people or those not going out to work. Poor survey techniques can lead a misleading results.

Surveying your own supporters is a great deal cheaper than doing the same job for the public at large. It can be relatively easy to carry out yourselves, especially if you pay attention to the question composition and to the methods of getting the responses back to you with a minimum of effort (by making the survey seem important and easy to respond to, by enclosing a reply paid envelope, or by offering some incentive to those responding, such as a free entry into a prize draw, etc.).

Public opinion research

Finding out what the public at large feels is more difficult and expensive. But for some organisations it can be essential – for example, if you are trying

---

Supporter surveys

Examples of questions you might want to ask in addition to those that seek to find out their attitude to your organisation and its work, might include:
- Age.
- Sex.
- Marital status.
- Number of children.
- Income band.
- Working status.
- Job.
- Newspaper readership.
- Voting habits.
- Religious membership.
- Trade union and other membership.
- Giving methods to the organisation.
- Frequency of giving.
- Preferred areas of support.
- Other good cause organisations supported.
- Voluntary support (whether and how much time they give).
- Legacy support (whether they have written a Will and included a charitable bequest).

With this information, you can also begin to build up a profile of a typical supporter, which will help you do two things:
- Communicate more effectively with them. If you have a picture in your mind as to who they are, then this becomes easier to do.
- Think about where else you might look to recruit people with a similar profile to your supporters.

to change the government's environmental policy, it will add weight to your argument if you can show that the public feels extremely concerned about the present state of affairs. There are a number of ways this can be achieved. Postal surveys are not usually effective here, and so are not frequently used. Omnibus research is one useful technique: this is where a research company puts together the questions from several organisations and sends interviewers out to ask all the questions in one survey. If you want to know just a few things, then this can be cost-effective and can be done quickly. If you want to know how the public are likely to react to a given appeal or style, then focus groups will be better (see below). This is what is called qualitative research which ends up with different sorts of answers, and is particularly useful for situations where yes/no answers will not do.

Interviews

Interviews take time, requires professionals and are expensive. However, the findings can be invaluable. Using this type of research, an organisation can learn how it is perceived, how it is compared to others in the same field, who are its prospective supporters, and what their attitudes are to the cause and the work being done. The interviews are invariably conducted by professionals, as is the construction of the questionnaire to which they work. You should get responses which are well-balanced and results that are reliable. One important result that can be derived from this sort of survey is the differences between supporters and non-supporters. If you depend upon high levels of current public awareness of your cause for your success, then this type of research will tell you how well you are doing. Prompted and spontaneous awareness are two useful measures of how well your publicity is working.

Focus groups

Focus groups are useful when you have a new strategy that you want to explore prior to launching it. It works by gathering a number of people in one place for a period of discussion. There should always be an experienced facilitator to help steer the conversation and record the results. A new name of the charity, new advertising strategies, and attitudes to important issues can also be explored in depth this way. The groups themselves are formed in different locations to give balance and compare different types of supporter and public. Reports and transcripts are made available to the client. The results can prove extremely interesting, and you can use this technique to test out the response to proposed fundraising materials.

Sources of data

Regular information is available to the keen observer from a number of places. The National Archive or the public library system is always a good starting point. Reports from Census will contain a wide range of research at a national level. For other information about people's behaviour and buying habits market research companies may produce interesting reports which may be available in business libraries. Your local reference library or university social studies department should be able to tell you about any local research that has been carried out and help you find out about relevant academic research that has been published. This information can be particularly important in highlighting the importance of issues and social problems.

Statistics

Not all research data is reliable. Proper samples are needed to give meaningful results. Samples can suffer from several forms of bias. One is associated with the nature of the sampling process. For example, does it cover all the areas of the country? Does it cover all age and income groups? And is the sample self-selecting, or have you only selected those who answered?

Equally important is sample size. For example, if you were to ask two people about their views and hope that they were representative of a group of four people, then you might be in for a shock. The question may be a simple yes/no attitude questions, such as, "*Do you agree with hanging as a punishment for murder?*" Suppose that two people said yes, and two no. Researchers using a sample of two might get two yeses, or two noes, or one of each. In all cases they would have got the answer completely wrong if the actual split in the population as a whole was 70:30. There are statistical formulae to determine the sample size required to get it right 95% of the time. You might be able to find a university lecturer or graduate to help you as a volunteer to design your sampling procedures.

8.7 Marketing

Marketing is not the exclusive concern of aggressive companies, nor is it just about selling. Fundraising demands marketing skills and a full understanding of the principles of marketing will help the fundraiser a great deal.

Marketing is often described in terms of the five P's. These are:

- **Planning**.
- **Product**.
- **Price**.
- **Place**.
- **Promotion**.

Though the term may not be familiar, the whole of this book is in fact about marketing – about marketing a cause to someone who can contribute money and time to supporting it. This section simply sets out the link between marketing theory and fundraising. Most of the points covered here are dealt with in more detail elsewhere in the book.

Planning and market analysis

A key part of the marketing process is the planning that precedes it. This should start with a clear understanding of the organisation and its work, the market in which it is operating, the other (possibly competitive) organisations (in the non-profit, the public and the private sectors), and the attitudes of potential supporters. Useful tools for this include:

- **SWOT analysis** which gives a picture of the strengths, weaknesses, opportunities and threats to your organisation.
- A **positioning map**, which plots where you are in relation to other organisations, and significant variables such as reliability, urgency, and so on – derived from how you perceive yourselves and from market research based on the public's perception of you.
- **Market share analysis**, which measures what proportion of a given sector

of donated income you are currently receiving – for example, how much support is given by local companies, and how much of this your organisation is receiving.
- **Market research**, which identifies the attitudes of your potential or actual supporters to giving to the cause in general, and to your particular charity in particular.

The outcome of all this analysis should be a picture of those groups in the population which are the best for you to target – in jargon, your target audiences.

Product

The service provided by your organisation is, in marketing terms, the product. It consists of the following ingredients:
- The actual 'tangible' product or need which your charity exists to meet.
- What the donor gets from the association with you – perhaps the satisfaction of knowing that one more child will walk, or of being publicly seen to be generous.
- The frills: the invitation to meet the child you have helped; the attendance at a special function each year; and so on.

All these can be added together, so that the concept as a whole appeals to your target audience. The point is, you are competing for a share of the disposable income of your supporters. You have to tempt them to purchase your product, rather than someone else's. You need to make your product as attractive as you can to your supporters.

Each product you create will have a life cycle. According to marketing theory, from time to time you will need to re-promote your product to keep it attractive and in people's minds. Equally, theory teaches that every product will eventually run out of steam and have to be replaced by another – although, in practice this is not always the case.

Just as each company will produce a range of products, so any charity is likely to have a range of its own fundraising products. These might include a big gift scheme with recognition for major donors, membership subscriptions for the mass support, a friends group for committed supporters, and a schools fundraising scheme for the young. These can all happily co-exist, so long as they are not in competition with one another.

Price

Donors do not automatically know how they are expected to respond, nor how much they are expected to give. Your role as fundraiser is to steer them towards what is likely to be achievable and affordable to them, and at the same time ensure you meet your own needs. This is a vital part of the process.

The most obvious way of doing this is to ask for a precise amount. "We are asking each person to give £10", for example. However this is not always satisfactory as it begs the question of "why £10?". The response to that is to offer a specific example of what the money will do – £10 can buy a new walking frame for a disabled child. The donation may not actually be spent on that, so the wording has to be carefully constructed if you are not to create a binding obligation to spend the money in precisely the way you have indicated or commit a breach of trust. There are three useful approaches:

- **A shopping list** which illustrates a range of things (at different prices) that their money might be spent on.
- **A range of levels** of support from which the donor can choose. Each will be set in such a way as to confer a greater status to those who give more (for example, friend, good friend, best friend).
- **A range of possible frequencies** (annual, quarterly, monthly, or even weekly). You will find that smaller amounts given more frequently yield larger amounts to you. This is because people respond to the headlined figure more than to the actual cost.

Not only does the price you ask determine the type of supporter you get, it also determines the amount of benefit you generate for your organisation. This will be the amount you ask for less any costs of raising the money and administering the donation. A £5 subscription will cost as much to service as a £25 subscription and a £5 donation might be immediately swallowed up by administration costs. There is often a tendency to ask for too little. Generally people are far more generous than you think. Then there is the opportunity cost. For major potential donors, you will do yourself a disservice asking for only £50. Not because it is expensive to administer, but because they might have given £5,000!

Place – the type of gift

The place of giving refers to the channel through which the support is given. It will usually be closely linked to promotion. For example, a personal request to help provides an opportunity to write a cheque and hand it over. A request made in a speech or over the radio, should also include a way of giving support (a return address).

The place – the way the donor makes a commitment and gets their help to you – is always important. Whether it is providing pledge forms on each table, a bucket at the door, a credit card hot line or a well placed advertisement, this needs to be thought about when the promotion is being devised.

The place will determine not just what you can ask for, but will also affect how they see the charity. For example, a charity that decides to raise money from running a series of balls or dinner dances, will only interact with a certain range of people in a particular atmosphere. Equally the same charity could appeal to a wider audience by running a series of village fetes. The two approaches might ultimately achieve the same result in terms of money raised. However, they would have done this by using completely different techniques, from quite different sources, using different resources and helpers, and in the process creating a completely different organisation.

Promotion

Promotion of your cause is about how you project yourself to the public. It is not only the medium, but the message too. The message is conveyed by a whole range of things within your control. Your name – or at least the title of your appeal – sends an important message, particularly if you have made this name well-known. People recognise World Wide Fund for Nature (WWF) or Save the Children, and these names evoke images of what the charity is doing (which may not be quite what it is doing!).

How you present yourself creates an impression of credibility, urgency, dynamism, and so on. Most important is how you express your needs in your written and visual material. Is it a rational or emotional appeal? Is it supported by human content that makes it personal? Good designers and copywriters can create the image and feel you require for your organisation, if they are well briefed.

The medium of your promotion is another important ingredient. Are you going to rely on personal recommendation to get your message across? Or are you going to use other means of communication? Possible media include TV, radio, newspaper advertising. public relations, direct mail posters, house-to-house calling, exhibitions, company promotions, booklets, events, speaking at meetings and many others. The five P's of the marketing mix are in fact all interdependent; if one factor is changed then it will affect all the others.

8.8 Public relations

Good public relations can create a positive climate of opinion and counter negative feelings or images that people may have about your organisation, its work and the cause it's addressing.

Effective PR is an essential ingredient of successful fundraising. For a fundraiser the value of PR lies in two things. First, it can draw the public's attention to a cause or a need, whether this is national or local. Without this attention and understanding, the task of the fundraiser becomes much more difficult. If when you get to see the head of the local company there have recently been articles about the good work that your organisation is doing in the press, you will already be starting from the point where that person accepts your cause as being serious.

PR can also help position the organisation in relation to other organisations in the same field. *"Why do we need so many charities, all apparently researching the same diseases? Shouldn't they all combine?"* will be a natural response of the public. Good PR can help identify the special importance of your work and its particular ethos and contribution as against all the 'competing' organisations, and get this recognised by the public. This can help eliminate an important barrier to public generosity.

How public relations can help your fundraising

- PR can be used to highlight the importance of the need or the urgency of the problem.
- PR can be used to show that it is possible for something to be done.
- PR can be used to tell people of your achievements and successes – to build the credibility of your organisation.
- PR can be used to show that people can help by making a financial contribution, or by volunteering to do something. And not just rich people or large businesses.
- PR can be used to explain what you have been able to achieve with people's money. And how you have been able to change the lives of the poor and the disadvantaged for the better.
- PR can be used to bring a sense of excitement to your fundraising work. And motivate you to do better.

Damage limitation

The media relishes a good story which harms the name of a charitable organisation. So you need to ensure that you are capable of countering the bad press and media coverage you may occasionally receive. There are a number of possible situations all of which need proper handling.

A newspaper might publish an article claiming that you are badly administering your money or that someone has run off with it. The readership and reputation of the newspaper will be enough to do you a great deal of damage. In such cases, action needs to be taken quickly.

The first people to contact are your donors. They need to be reassured that what they have read is not true; and they need to be given the facts. Next you should reply to the offending article as quickly as possible. Though the damage at this point has already been done, it can be mitigated by an article or letter in reply. Then you should issue a statement to other papers and to your own staff and trustees setting out the facts of the matter.

On some occasions you will get advance warning of media interest. On these occasions you should: establish the exact facts; identify a spokesperson to put your case to the media, making sure you keep the message consistent; or consider inviting the senior management of the paper or the television station to withdraw the offending article.

If in fact the bad coverage has some element of truth in it, you are in a less defensible position. In such circumstances, a different approach is required. You should accept responsibility for the situation; identify the immediate action that has been taken to remedy it; and invite the paper to do a follow up in a more positive vein to help rehabilitate the organisation.

In all these situations there are a number of useful guidelines:

- Ensure that the staff of your organisation do **not speak to the media unless they are specifically authorised to**. There is nothing so damaging as the leaked report or the inept interview from a well-meaning staff member.
- Make sure that the **facts are established** at an early stage and are accurate. Then make them well-known.
- Make sure that your **internal communication systems** are working well, that you can get any new twists of the story across to colleagues speedily, and that trustees and supporters are kept informed.
- If you haven't already got one, draft **an emergency plan** in which you anticipate the possible disasters that could happen and allocate responsibilities accordingly.

Campaigning and PR

For organisations that do campaign, PR is clearly a major tool to help them achieve their aims. This also has important implications for fundraising. Sometimes campaigning and fundraising are seen as two separate activities that require different people and skills. The truth is that if the campaign is seen to be an intrinsic part of the organisation's reason for existing, then when the campaign gets good coverage, good fundraising results will follow.

Fundraising and PR

Most not-for-profit organisations do not see campaigning as the primary part of their work, but many need to campaign on particular issues from time to time or have successfully set themselves up as experts in a particular area. This creates an interesting opportunity, since the media will naturally turn to the organisation when there is a story and they need informed comment.

You can also try to get the name of your organisation mentioned in the media, as many times as possible, hopefully in a good context but almost irrespective of whether there is any informed comment on the cause. This can be done by:

- Issuing **press releases**.
- Setting up **stunts and events** which will naturally attract publicity. Better still may be to use these same skills to set up interesting fundraising events that the media will want to cover.
- Holding **press conferences**.
- **Writing letters** to the letters page of newspapers and magazines (*see below*).

Timing is all important in media work. Not only because of the natural deadlines of the different media, but also because of the need to use the coverage to enhance your own fundraising. Thus the media exposure should ideally be timed to happen just before you launch a major fundraising initiative, targeted towards the people you are approaching for support and in whatever form you can obtain it.

Letters

One of the most helpful ways of creating the positive climate of opinion about your cause is to write letters to the newspapers. This can be done by staff, or better still by volunteer supporters.

The best papers for a local organisation or a local branch of a national organisation to target are the local newspapers in the area. In this way you can spread the word about your charity quite widely for little cost. The theme of any letter should be topical. If it is linked to a local event or signed by a well-known local personality, your letter is more likely to be published. But letters just alerting readers to new needs or services you provide may also be published.

Answering letters that others have written to the press is another opportunity. A letter of thanks for local help after a flag day or other event can give you the opportunity to show how successful the event was, how efficiently the money was raised, and how well it is going to be spent.

Exactly similar is the use of local radio phone-in programmes, where you or a volunteer can ring in to make a point, announce a development or even appeal for support.

News releases and press conferences

When you have something new to report, sending a press release to a selected list of newspapers, radio stations and TV channels is one of the most effective ways of publicising it. This can be in response to a recent development in your work, a major donation received, a new publication produced or research completed, a celebrity supporter joining your ranks, or some form of stunt designed specifically to highlight your work or generate publicity.

An effective press release answers the questions who, what, when, where, and why. To be effective at a local level, it should have a clear local angle – a link to a local person or a local event, or a local organisation. Ideally, you should write it in the form of a short article, so that editors can use it verbatim, if they wish. Some might be really interested in the story and want more background information, which you can include separately. Picture editors will appreciate good photos.

If the event is of real interest, then you might consider holding a press conference. You invite the press to come in person to hear your story, and you can expect to be closely questioned on the project and on your organisation.

The timing of the press conference is critical. Its proximity to other important news stories can make or break yours, though you may have relatively little control over this. For example if there is a major political development or financial scandal, there will be little room in the newspaper for other news breaking at the same time. The timing is also important, in that you need to know the schedules and deadlines that the journalists are working to. If you are not sure, then talk informally to a journalist or newspaper editor first before planning your PR initiative.

Location is extremely important. An interesting venue can add to the feel of the story – launching a campaign on climate from the roof of the Meteorological Office would be ideal, for example. The venue should also be easily accessible to journalists. Or you might want to hold a press conference at an event which is guaranteed to get good coverage itself – such as a national conference.

One way of making the press conference go with a swing is to announce that it will be given by some well-known people, renowned either for their entertainment value or for their serious interest. An actress or celebrity will often use pithy words for journalists or be well rehearsed in the photo call for photographers. Similarly, reporters will know that senior figures at press conferences can usually be drawn on the issues.

If you are using a celebrity, having a conference chaired by a senior person from your organisation will help control the questions and steer them away from the celebrity who might not know the answer. To get your message across with no deviation or hesitation, there is nothing quite like a dry run first. If you can't manage this, you will have to give the spokesperson a full briefing.

For those who don't get to the conference, you should compile a briefing pack. It often transpires that some of the fullest coverage from a press conference comes from journalists who have not even attended. But you might never have got this coverage without having organised the conference in the first place!

Photocalls and events

The media are always attracted to the unusual, the famous and the picturesque. Sometimes it is necessary to express your needs in this way, rather than expect that your campaign or fundraising message alone are in any way newsworthy.

If your main way of raising funds locally is to run coffee mornings, how might you use the media to help boost those events? Apart from a one-line mention in the local paper, nobody in the media is going to take much interest. One answer is to use a celebrity. Celebrities do not have to be major national names to be of interest to the local media, though it does help if they are. You could find out which celebrities live in your area and who will be visiting the area at the time you plan to hold the press conference (the theatre, the ballet, or a sporting event often bring well-known people). Just by getting them to pose for an appropriate picture you can raise the chances of getting coverage for your coffee morning. Another possibility is to get photographers to come to a coffee tasting to select the best brand. Another is to hold a coffee morning with supporters drinking from a huge coffee cup. It is the extra dimension that makes the event newsworthy, and the visual aspect will attract the photographers.

A development of this is to organise a stunt of some sort. This need not depend on a well-known person, but can use the stunt's zaniness to attract attention, and its excitement to attract TV or radio coverage. A stunt built around your coffee morning campaign might have a group of air cadets having a coffee morning in the back of a airforce transport plane in flight, or someone leaping off a bridge (with the usual strong elastic attached!) sipping their coffee as they go and as if nothing were happening!

The challenge with these sort of activities is not just having to set them up, but also selecting an activity that is relevant to your work so that any publicity can be linked to it to good effect. Needless to say, dangerous stunts should not be encouraged. There is the additional risk that if anything goes wrong your organisation will receive the blame, whether it was your fault or not.

Managing public relations

Ideally, the control of your public relations should be integrated with the fundraising work. Some organisations see the two roles as being quite separate – with the result that the PR person does not maximise the fundraising potential of the organisation, nor does the fundraiser maximise the PR potential. If there is someone who has a specific PR role, they should be asked to produce plans to show how they can best support the fundraising needs, as well as meet the PR objectives of the organisation.

In small organisations, PR will not be a separate function, and will probably be carried out by a senior member of staff or even a committee member. This is as it should be, but everyone should be encouraged to give PR the importance it deserves, recognising the effectiveness of good PR in generating extra funds for the organisation.

One option is to appoint a public relations agency to handle your public relations. You may find some which work mainly with the non-profit sector, or you may find a commercial agency interested in your cause and willing to take you on as a client at a reduced fee or even for free. Any agency you use needs to be briefed well, if they are to present your work as you would wish them to. You can monitor the results of your PR through the use of a press cutting agency. This will show you whether you are getting your money's worth.

However you handle PR, there should be proper co-ordination. Links with the press should be handled only by designated people, and preferably be channelled through one individual. The risks of any well-wisher discussing confidential issues, getting information wrong or just appearing ill informed are just too great to allow.

Afterword

In this book, I have tried to describe the many sources of money that exist or that can be tapped for charitable support, some of the techniques that will help you in raising money, and some of the practical and personal skills that you will need if you are to be successful.

There is a massive amount of information and advice in this book, which covers an extremely wide range of topics. All of this may seem overwhelming to an organisation just starting out in fundraising or somebody who has never raised any money before. I hope that you will have picked up some good ideas which will be useful to you, and that you will take heed of much of the advice, which is mostly just good common sense. But when it comes to getting started in fundraising or trying to identify some new sources or new techniques or new approaches that you can use, then I have one or two final words of advice.

1. Select just one or two things to concentrate on, which you believe can produce real returns for your organisation and which you have the capacity to make a success of. Spreading yourself over too wide a range of activities will in the end probably mean that you will be able to do nothing well.

2. Take time to think clearly about what you are proposing, whether it is relevant, and how you might best approach the business of raising money. This thinking and planning time is important. But don't make it so long that you never get started!

3. Find out as much as you can from other people. Most people should be happy to share their fundraising experience with others, as you should be too. Other people's practical experience can give you a good idea of what you might expect. You can learn from it so as to do better. You can decide on the basis of what you have heard whether it is worth proceeding at all.

4. Learn from your own experience, and continue to learn. There is no magic answer to the problem of fundraising, no formula which will bring in the money with any certainty. What works best for you is best for you – and you have to discover what this is. It will be a mixture of your skills and personality, the type of organisation and cause you are raising money for, the culture and attitudes prevalent in your country and amongst potential donors, and the personal relations you can build with those you are intending to recruit as supporters. You can write the perfect application, taking a week to do it – and fail. You can dash off a note and make a phone call – and get the support you are asking for.

5. Remember too that there is a lot of luck. This means that you are much more likely to succeed if you keep on trying. Indeed if you give up, it is certain that you will fail. It also means that you should try to make your own luck. The successful fundraiser, as has been said again and again throughout this book, is someone who never gives up and someone who enjoys the business of raising money and of giving other people the opportunity to help create a better world.

My best wishes to you for success in your fundraising, and that it will enable your organisation to thrive, and to continue and develop its important and valuable work.

Michael Norton
London, February 1996

Appendix 1
Testing

In order to improve fundraising performance, you need to be able to test what you are doing against some known control. If you don't test, you will only be able to guess at why your appeal appears to have worked better (or worse) than expected. If you do test, then you can identify which approach really does work better, and then incorporate this into your future appeal material.

There are a very large number of things you can test and many opportunities for testing. First you need to decide what to test. The important thing is to test only one thing at a time, since if this is not done you can never be quite sure about what is causing the different result. In any test programme, there is one control group, which is sent a previously-used appeal message, and then one or several test groups in which for each just one element in the appeal has been changed.

The first things to test are those things that will make the most difference. So, if you are to launch a postal appeal to supporters for cash, then here are some of the important things you could test:

- **Which supporters** to appeal to – testing the results from different lists.
- **The message** you use. The headline; the way the appeal is framed; how much you are asking for; whether to use a celebrity endorsement; the length of the letter; printing the letter in one colour or two colours; all these can be tested – but only one factor at a time.
- Whether you ask for **a single donation or a regular subscription**, and whether the subscription should be paid in one annual sum or at more frequent intervals.

For example, if you are raising money for a hospital, you could test whether asking for money to pay for an eye operation for one patient works better than asking for the same amount of money for an inoculation programme. Or you could test whether it is better to ask for a larger sum for the eye operation, than the sum you have previously been asking for. Or you could test whether to ask for a monthly contributions brings in more support than asking for annual contributions. Your test programme should try to identify those factors which are likely to have a significant impact on the number of people giving and the level of their giving. Unless you are organising a very major fundraising programme you should not seek to test things like the letter heading, the colour of paper or other things less likely to have an impact on the results.

In some areas of fundraising, testing will have a quite limited role. A single campaign to raise a capital sum will not be easy to test (though feasibility studies can be carried out). However a continuous mailing programme to supporters lends itself to testing and improvement. The larger your fundraising programme, the more you can test. The more you test, the more effective you will become, and the more you will understand about the psychology of giving and how to use this to advantage.

Six ways to test your appeals

1. The A/B split: use the facility that many newspapers offer to print different versions of your advertisement in the same position.

2. Split run inserts: best done by printing two-up, where half the leaflets are printed with one form of wording and half with another, and the leaflets are then inserted into a magazine so that half the readers receive Version A, and half Version B.

3. Split run mailing: divide your mailing lists randomly into a number of groups (all of sufficient size) and send different messages to each group.

4. Geographical splits: first run the same appeal in all regions, then in your next mailing, use one region as the control, sending the same appeal again, and for the other regions send a different version to see if there are any geographical factors that might be significant.

5. Questionnaire: use information gleaned from surveys to guide you as to what are likely to be popular themes. This is more guesswork than science.

6. Using the phone: call up people who have received (and not responded) to find out why, using a planned questionnaire.

Adapted from Commonsense Direct Marketing, by Drayton Bird.

The statistics of testing

When you are testing, some of the differences you find will have occurred randomly. But if the results are to be useful, you need to be confident that one test group genuinely did do better. Your job is to structure your tests so that you get statistically reliable results that tell beyond reasonable doubt which approach is performing better.

Statistical theory can tell you whether the different results you get are significant or just due to chance. There are two mathematical formulae that are used. The first tells you the size of the test sample that is required to give a reliable result. You will need to have a certain number of people in the test sample if the result is to be meaningful. The second indicates what the margin of error is once you have the results. Using these two formulae, you can determine which group performed best. For example, if you want to test donor mailings where your response rate is expected to be around 15%, then using these formulae tells you that you can be 95% confident that your results will lie between 14% and 16% if you use a sample size of 4,896. So you would plan on a test sample of 5,000 – which means that you can only do the test if you are using a mailing list of at least 10,000 names.

The mathematics of testing

The formulae you use for determining sample size and reliability are mathematical – and you need to understand the mathematics (or find someone who does, to advise you) in order to plan a test programme.

Sample size determination

To determine the number of any group that should be included to make a test valid you should use the formula:

Sample size = 3.84 x c x (100 – c)/b x b where:

- 3.84 gives a confidence level of 95%
- c is the expected response rate in %
- b is the tolerance in %.

Margin of error

Once you have done a mailing you may need to know how accurate or reliable the results are. To do this you can use a version of the same formula.
This gives b = Root 3.84 x c (100-c)/s where:

- s is the number in the sample
- c is that actual response rate in %

b is the margin of error in percent.

This will give you a result that is reliable 95 times out of 100. For a typical appeal where the response rate is 1%, and you wish to be 95% confident that the true result is within the band 0.75% to 1.25%, then the numbers you should have in your sample are 6,082. This demonstrates how difficult it is to get good test results for cold mailings.

Test against previous results

If the size of your mailings is too small to test a sample, then you can try to measure the effectiveness of the result you achieve from the whole mailing by comparing this with what you achieved last time. If this shows that you can be confident that your new mailing is better than the original version, then you should move to the improved version for all your future mailings. Again, you will need to know whether the difference between this time and last time could have occurred quite by chance. If the result of the test is inconclusive, further testing would be needed before you would be able to change your approach with any confidence that you are doing the right thing. This also will involve the use of complicated mathematical formulae.

The design of a test and the assessment of the significance of the result is a highly technical business – one where you will normally need to take professional advice.

Appendix 2
Tax-effective giving

Many countries offer tax concessions on donations to charitable organisations. Though saving tax is rarely a motive for giving by itself, it can combine powerfully with other types of motivation to encourage giving and to raise the level of gifts. Fundraisers need to have a clear and full understanding of how tax-effective giving works in their own country and how to use tax incentives to encourage giving, and how to convey information on the benefits of tax-effective giving to potential donors.

The tax structure on the treatment of gifts to charities by individuals, companies and foundations will vary from country to country. In some countries the benefits are received by the donor, thereby reducing the cost of the donation. In others, the benefits are received by the recipient, thereby increasing the value of the donation. And in yet other countries, it might be a mixture of both. It is beyond the scope of this book to cover the tax structure to your country. This is something that you will need to find out about. You should try to:

- Have a **clear understanding** of the tax treatment of all donations, gifts and legacies (by individuals and by companies).
- Be able to **explain this clearly** and simply to intending donors.
- Incorporate tax-effective giving into **the requests and response mechanisms** when soliciting support for your organisation.
- Have **systems for reclaiming tax**, where this is the required procedure, and for any other administration of tax relief that is necessary.

Tax-effective company giving

Company giving is an increasingly important area for fundraisers who need to know the main rules. Unlike individuals, companies are invariably well provided with qualified accountants who can advise on the best methods of giving. The senior manager and directors with whom you initially negotiate however, may not be so familiar with the tax position.

Contributions made for advertising or sponsorship can usually be claimed as a legitimate business expense, and so be deductible against taxable profits. This means that depending on the rate of corporation tax, the actual cost to the company will be substantially less than the contribution you receive.

Most support you receive from companies will be in the form of charitable contributions. Here you should consider three different types of company:

- **International and multinational companies** that make charitable donations in all the countries where they operate. These will have considered the tax implications and have made they necessary arrangements to make their charitable contributions as tax-effectively as they can.
- **Major local companies**, which may know the tax implications of giving through having given previously, but will certainly have access to good tax advice.

- **Smaller companies**, where there may be no real knowledge of tax-effective giving requirements, and they will depend on you for advice.

Establishing a foundation

In many countries, individuals can gain important tax advantages by establishing a charitable foundation as a vehicle for their charitable giving. There are three ways of doing this:

- **Endowing the foundation** with property, shares or cash, then investing the money to produce an annual income which can be distributed to charities of the donor's choice.
- **Transferring a sum of income each year** to the foundation, which is then distributed.
- **Establishing the foundation on the donor's death**, where an endowment or corpus is transferred to it by way of legacy.

Whatever method is chosen for producing the income, the direction and control of the foundation will be under the control of a group of trustees (which might include the donor) who are responsible for seeing that the capital is properly invested and for selecting the beneficiaries. There will be all sorts of rules, which will vary from country to country, on what investments can be held, on how much has to be distributed each year and how much can be retained or accumulated, on what sorts of body can benefit (which will often be set out in the foundation's constitution), on who can be trustees and on administration and reporting requirements.

The Charities Aid Foundation

The Charities Aid Foundation (CAF) is a foundation established in the UK with a branch in Russia, an affiliate in the United States and partner organisations in France, Germany and Belgium. CAF is seeking to establish a global network for tax-effective giving. The aim is to enable people and companies to give in any country and direct that the gift be handed to an organisation in the same or another country, and at the same time collect the tax relief available for charitable giving in the country in which the donation is made.

CAF is currently conducting feasibility studies on setting up offices in South Africa and India as a next stage in its international development. If an office is set up in India, for example, this will enable donors in the United States and the UK to make donations to charitable organisations in India and claim a US or UK tax deduction. Since there are many successful Non-Resident Indians in both countries, this could open up new areas for fundraising by Indian charitable organisations.

Appendix 3
Using computers

While many small organisations are able to raise funds very effectively with the minimum of equipment, for larger organisations the computer is rapidly becoming an important and even essential fundraising aid. The most important uses of computers for fundraising purposes are:

- Databases to maintain and use supporter lists for appeals and big gift fundraising.
- Word processing to 'personalise' letters to supporters.
- Spread sheets for financial planning and analysis and for general use.
- Desktop publishing (DTP) to produce simple but well designed explanatory literature.

Computers come in a wide range of sizes and with a dazzling array of names and types. The technology is developing extremely rapidly, but at the same time the price continues to fall, making such hi-tech equipment affordable to more and more organisations.

However enthusiastic you may be on the appropriateness of computers to your organisation, you will have to share that enthusiasm with everybody else in the office too. There will need to be a consensus that it is an appropriate use of the organisation's money and an investment in its future. Your staff and volunteers will need to be properly trained to use the equipment.

Security is the other major issue to take note of. You will need to undertake a series of procedures to ensure that your information remains safe and secure. These will include everything from resisting balancing coffee mugs on the machine, to regularly backing up all your files. Finally you must make sure that the machinery is physically secure. Small modern computers are very attractive to thieves.

Databases

The main purpose of having a database is to be able to organise your appeals more effectively. In its most simple form, the database holds a list of donors or members, with information on their past giving and trading purchases, details of standing orders for regular giving, personal information including their address and telephone number, and so on. This information will be used at different times in different ways. You should consider at the outset what you are likely to do with the information, and therefore what information you should be collecting. You can then produce donation forms which allows the donor to provide this information.

Your database should be able to do the following things:

- Add new donors.
- Amend and update donor information.
- Add new categories of information.

- Delete donors when they appear to have lost interest in your cause or ask to be removed from your mailing list.
- Provide fast access to information on any donor.

All of this is necessary just to keep a list of names up to date. To be truly useful the database needs to do a number of other things as well:
- Select particular combinations of donors (such as a list of people who have given more than a certain sum within the past 12 months).
- Output donor information in various formats, for example as address labels or merged into letters.
- Produce letters of thanks and receipts, reminders, etc.
- Print out donation statistics and an analysis of your fundraising performance in the way you want.
- Print out an analysis of response rates for particular promotions.
- Print out analyses of response by different categories of donor.
- Print out a tracking analysis of donor history.

Only in recent years has it been realistic to consider having a sophisticated database on a Personal Computer. This is now possible, and there are a number of specialist software packages for fundraising work now on the market.

A key issue to consider is whether to use a relational database. This will allow you to choose all those donors who are members, for example, by going to each member record directly without having to look up every donor. Systems which are built in this way offer much greater flexibility and speed when it comes to making complicated selections for an appeal.

For big gift fundraising programmes, a database is essential. While the basic usage is the same, you will also be able to make links between those people who have given you support, those who have expressed interest and those whom you want to attract. Your supporters may be members of an organisation like Rotary or trustees of a charitable trust. If you can discover any such links, this can help you make contact at the right level.

The ability to record an amount of background detail on each supporter can be helpful when you plan your approach to them. Your computer system should be able to print out this background information, including details of previous encounters, relevant personal information, or anecdotes about the people you are about to approach at the touch of a button (provided you have recorded this information).

A wide range of programmes have been developed commercially to service the fundraising market with names such as 'The Raiser's Edge'. These are expensive to buy, but are worth considering for organisations with larger donor bases – say 1,000 names or more – where this technology becomes an essential management tool. Advice from another organisation already using such a system – and even a visit to see it at work – can be invaluable.

Word processing

Word processing packages are a great boon to an efficient fundraising office. They can be used to produce a well presented formal letter, and also to vary and personalise a standard form of wording for different recipients.

To make a word processor work well for you, you need to develop keyboard skills (two finger work is extremely slow for anything more than a few pages) and have a good printer. The software package can come in many forms. Three of the top word processing packages are WordPerfect, WordStar and Microsoft Word. Each is tried and tested. However, there are a wide range of other programmes, some available at a considerably lower cost.

You should do three things before purchasing a software package. Try it out for yourself (on your own computer or someone else's). Check that it has got all the facilities you need. And see that there is someone to give you support when you need it. Facilities you might need are:

- Mail merging for form letters.
- The ability to take and send files to other machines.
- On-screen help when needed.
- Spell checking.
- The ability to move large blocks of text around.
- Windows so as to be able to see several bits of text simultaneously.
- Facilities for searching text.

Types of printers available include: dot matrix; inkjet; and laser (in order of increasing cost). The matrix is fast, but of low quality. The image is produced by a number of little dots making up the letter, the more dots, the better the quality. The more recent inkjet (also known as bubblejet) printers are still slow, but produce crisper characters. Laser printers can be very quick and quiet, and the quality is excellent. But they are more expensive to buy and run. Most come equipped with a standard set of typefaces. If you need special fonts, then the cost will be more.

Spreadsheets

Spreadsheets are an electronic means of manipulating figures. An example serves to illustrate their use in fundraising. Let us say that you are building up some income estimates for a fundraising campaign. This involves estimating the number of names on your mailing list, including new recruits and deletions, what the response rate will be, and how frequently you plan to mail. If, having produced your estimate, you need to know what would happen in a worst case situation, you would normally have to do a great deal of recalculation to come up with the answer. A spreadsheet can do this almost instantly, and with no fear of error. They will be useful for a variety of jobs including:

- Budgets.
- Appeal results.
- 'What if' calculations.
- Inflation adjustments.
- Presentation of information in graphs and charts.

The main functions that you may want to specify when buying spreadsheet software are:

- Graphical functions for drawing charts and graphs.
- Database functions.

- Size of spreadsheet (numbers of columns and rows).
- Whether it can it 'talk' to other computers.

Desktop publishing

Another benefit of the Personal Computer is its ability (with the appropriate programme) to design and print material to a very high quality. To be effective, you will need a proprietary DTP programme and a laser printer. The programme will enable you to combine headlines, text and simple graphic design features to produce attractive artwork for your leaflets, reports, posters, newsletters and other publications. If you have a scanner, you can scan and reproduce illustrations and other graphic material for incorporation into your design. If printed out on a laser printer, the quality of the finished artwork is surprisingly good, either for offset printing or for photocopying.

Appendix 4
Codes of Practice

The following codes of practice have been devised by the *Institute of Charity Fundraising Managers* in the UK. Although drawn up for UK fundraisers, we have included them in this book because they relate to important fundraising techniques and contain much sound advice representing best possible fundraising practice.

1. Code of practice for fundraising in schools

When you are fundraising in schools and with young people, you are dealing with a particularly vulnerable and impressionable group of people. You need to ensure that you deal appropriately and honestly with them, meeting their needs and the requirements of the school at the same time as raising money for your organisation. The following is based on a code of practice used by the *Institute of Charity Fundraising Managers* for charities fundraising with schools in Britain.

1. Fundraising in schools should:

- Offer the child a positive opportunity for involvement in helping others by raising funds.
- Put trust at the heart of all fundraising activity with school children. There should be no harassment of children, but the child should be on his/her honour to pay over all the money raised.
- Ensure that the content of talks given to the children is both educational and non-political and at an appropriate level for the particular age group.
- Take into account and accept the Head Teacher's view of the school's charity commitments and to fit in with this.
- Make contact with children in or near school premises only with the prior knowledge and approval of the Head Teacher or a member of the School's staff designated by the Head Teacher.

2. Safeguards for children

- Children should be told both verbally and on any printed material not to approach strangers for money. Every effort should be made by the charity to ensure that parents are made aware of the need for children to approach only friends and relations for support or sponsorship. Children should be encouraged to discuss fully with their parents the list of people they propose to approach. Examples of 'safe' sponsors should be given in the course of the fundraising talk.
- Participation in any fundraising activity should only be via an authorised adult. For children up to the age of 16, it should be for the parents to decide whether or not a child may take part in a fundraising event.

3. Organisation of an event

- The use of incentives to encourage or reward individual efforts to raise money is a sensitive issue, and the greatest care needs to be exercised in offering them to children. Token gifts, such as badges, may be given provided that they are made available to all participating children, and are given for the purpose of encouraging the children to think about the work of the charity. As a general principle, only incentives of purely token value should ever be given to children. Where gifts of some monetary value have been donated, the distribution of these should be under the tight control of the charity's representative and only after consultation and agreement with the Head Teacher. Particular care should be taken with under-sevens, who should not be encouraged to compete for badges or any other incentives.
- Potential supporters should be given the option of sponsoring a child or giving a donation – at a level of their choice.
- Sponsored events should have maximum number of units (kilometres, lengths, circuits, etc.) clearly stated on the printed material in order that the sponsor can determine a maximum for the amount of money promised at the time of sponsoring.
- Fundraising material should be written in clear, simple language.

4. The fundraiser and the school

Field staff should be instructed:

- To discuss with the Head Teacher the educational content of the talk to be given and the pattern of the event that is proposed, as well as all other additional arrangements.
- To go step by step through what is involved for the school staff, for the children, for the parents. All agreed details, including the financial arrangements, should then be confirmed in writing by the charity's representative.
- To organise the fundraising event within a controlled time limit.
- To make the organisation of the event and collection of money as trouble-free as possible for school staff. If cash is collected, the charity's representative should return on an agreed date, and then call again subsequently (or make adequate arrangements) for any late monies. If the School prefers, monies may be paid directly into the charity's bank account. All monies received should be acknowledged promptly by the charity and the onus should be on the charity to ensure that the amount acknowledged is correct.
- An appropriate message of thanks should be given as soon after the fundraising event has taken place as possible to the Head Teacher or any staff involved, to the children and to their families.

5. General

- Any letters of complaint or criticism received should be dealt with as quickly as possible, and monitored at senior management level in the charity.
- The Head Teacher's comments on how the fundraising project is going and on any events undertaken should be obtained on a regular basis.

- The charity's Field Staff, who will be liaising with the schools, should be trained, supervised and monitored on a continuing basis in every aspect of their work.

2. Code of practice for house-to-house collections

This Code of Practice aims to ensure that a collection is undertaken properly and that all the money collected is remitted to the charity.

1. Proceeds of collections

- Organisations should ensure that all collections follow an agreed procedure for the banking of all receipts from the collectors and the return of all collection materials.
- Organisations should establish and implement an agreed procedure for monitoring the payments of receipts from all collectors.
- Arrangements should be made for the receipt of the collection proceeds and all used and unused materials connected with it at a specified point authorised by the Organiser of the collection.
- Collection materials should be opened and the contents counted in the presence of the Promoter of the collection or another responsible person and duly witnessed.
- A record should be kept of the proceeds collected by each Collector, and details of the collecting materials returned (e.g. in the case of envelope collections, the number of envelopes containing cash returned by each collector).
- Where Collectors are asked to count the proceeds of their collection, they should have written instructions to open the returned envelopes and count the proceeds only in the presence of the promoter or another responsible person who must confirm the proceeds of the collection in writing. This should include, if relevant, the number of envelopes containing cash returned by that Collector.
- All proceeds from all Collectors should be remitted to the organiser of the collection together with the Collector's Badge, Certificate of Authority and any unused collection materials as soon as possible. If the proceeds of the collection are not remitted within one month of the collection, the organisation should identify whether or not the collection actually took place and take appropriate action.
- Organisations should ensure that all official returns are completed in accordance with the requirements of any relevant legislation in force regarding public collections.
- It is the Promoter's responsibility to ensure that the Organiser and Collectors acting for the organisation conduct the collection according to the law. It is the Organiser's and Collectors' responsibility to ensure that they comply with all arrangements regulating collections. Anyone deliberately acting in default of these obligations should not be allowed to participate in future collections.

2. Training

Effective training of all those engaged in house-to-house collections is critical in assuring a collection that is efficient, effective and accountable to donors. Training should be conducted by an informed member of staff on a group or individual basis, and be supported by a comprehensive reference folder. The information given should include:

- Information about the organisation in general, its aims and objectives, and specific work undertaken in the area where the collection is taking place.
- Details of collection legislation that is relevant to the collection.
- A clear definition of their role, and the extent of their responsibility and authority.
- How to plan a collection, on a geographical basis or as an annual or rolling programme.
- The importance and necessity of appropriate contact with other relevant bodies – e.g. other voluntary organisations, the Police, the Local Authority, banks, the local press.
- Who to approach as potential volunteers, and how to approach them, and then the information and instruction to be given to them.
- The recording of Collector details.
- The issue of personalised authorisation certificates and badges to Collectors, and the arrangements for their return.
- The recording of the collection materials issued to each Collector.
- The arrangements for the receipt of income.
- The recording of the receipt of income, which should ultimately provide the information for compiling the accounts and any statutory returns.
- How to deal with queries from the general public.

3. Collection materials

Every Collector should be provided with:

- A Collector's badge, which should be signed by the Collector on receipt.
- A Certificate of Authority, which should specify the name of the Collector, the period during which the collection is to take place, and the specific location or geographical area in which the Collector will collect.
- A sealed Collecting Box or Collection Envelopes.
- Clear instructions as to the proper conduct of the collection, which cover:
  How to conduct the collection
  The precise area in which they will collect
  The specific dates and times in which the collection will take place
  How to use the materials that have been supplied
  What to do with the money collected
  Arrangements for the return of all unused materials and badges after the collection has ended.
- The name of a contact (with address and telephone number) in case of queries or an emergency.

Materials should be dispatched to Collectors in good time. All materials should carry the name and address of the organisation, and any registration number.

Organisations should ensure that prospective donors are not put under undue pressure to give, and that all supporting information about the organisation is clear, concise and truthful.

Collectors should normally be 16 years old or older, and courteous at all times.

3. Guidance notes on the management of static collection boxes

The conduct and control of static box collections is the responsibility of the organisation that is benefiting from the collection. The organisation should appoint a Promoter to be responsible for the collection, who should be an official of the benefiting organisation.

1. Administration

- The organisation should obtain the signed written permission of site holders to collect on their premises.
- Collectors who are to service the collecting boxes should be issued with Certificates of Authority and identity badges.
- Boxes should be of a suitable material, properly labelled, numbered and sealed.
- Records should be kept of where each box is sited, and how much money is collected from it.
- Separate records should be kept of all money raised through static collection boxes and any direct administrative expenditure incurred in the course of the collection.

2. Siting of the boxes

- Agreement must be made in writing between the site holder (owner, manager or occupier of the premises) and the Promoter.
- The agreement may follow an initial visit to the site by a Collector or agent of the organisation, at which a collecting box may have been shown or left with the siteholder.
- The Promoter must write to the siteholder giving details of the arrangements for servicing the boxes. Where possible the name of the Collector who will do this should be given in the communication. The Promoter should provide a specimen example of the Badge of Authority to be carried by the Collector.
- Siteholders must be asked to notify the organisation preferably in writing immediately a box is lost or stolen, or if they wish to end their collection and return the box.
- It is the responsibility of the promoter to be satisfied that siteholders will conduct the collection honestly, and to monitor the performance of all collecting boxes.

3. The Collectors

- Collectors should be aged 16 years or over.
- Collectors must possess a Certificate of Authority signed by the Promoter and

bearing the name of the benefiting organisation, together with their own name, address and signature. The Certificate must be shown to the siteholder.
- Collectors must at all times undertake their work in a manner which will maintain the high standing of the organisation, and which in no way places undue pressure on potential siteholders being asked to participate.
- Collectors must notify the Promoter immediately they have reason to believe that the contents of the boxes are being pilfered or interfered with in any way.
- Collectors must return the Certificate of Authority to the Promoter on ceasing to be a Collector or at any time on demand by the Promoter.
- It is the responsibility of the promoter to ensure that these conditions are adhered to, that Collectors perform their duties honestly and that they conduct the collection in a courteous and ethical manner.

4. Servicing the boxes

- Before opening the box, the Collector should check for evidence of tampering, and after emptying ensure that the box is securely sealed again before re-siting it.
- Boxes should be opened and the contents counted by an authorised Collector, and in the presence of the siteholder or their representative.
- The Collector must give an official receipt signed by them and by the siteholder to the siteholder with a copy kept for the promoter and a further copy for themselves. This receipt should show the address of the site, the box number, the date and the amount taken from the box.
- Collectors should ensure that boxes are in a good state of repair, that they are clean, properly labelled, and function correctly. Collecting boxes may be repaired or cleaned on site by the Collector or may be exchanged for a new box with the promoter being subsequently informed.
- Boxes should be emptied and the contents counted in accordance with a regular pre-determined schedule provided by the Promoter to the Collector and siteholder.
- The Collector must remit to the promoter the full sum collected without deduction of expenses or fees. This should be done within a given time specified by the promoter, which should not be more than one month from the date of collection, and be accompanied by relevant official receipts.
- Any expenses incurred in servicing the boxes must be submitted by the Collector separately, and refunded by the organisation according to terms previously agreed with the Collector.
- The promoter must maintain a full list of numbered boxes, and details of the sites where they have been placed, with a record against each box of the amounts collected. The promoter must ensure that all boxes are emptied regularly, and that each Collector's expenses are checked and paid.

5. The collecting boxes

- All boxes must be properly labelled, numbered and sealed, and must bear the name and address of the benefiting organisation.
- Boxes used in static collections must be made of a durable material, such as metal, wood or plastic. Cardboard or other paper products are not normally adequate for this purpose.

- The seal on the collecting box may be a lock, self-adhesive paper or some other device, provided that any attempt to tamper with or break the seal can be easily detected.

4. Code of practice for reciprocal charity mailings

If you are planning to exchange your list of donors with another charity for a reciprocal mailing, then this will provide a framework for the agreement between the two parties.

1. Basis of exchange

The content and character of the lists to be exchanged should be clearly understood. Precise definition of the lists should include:

- Quantity: the number of addresses to be mailed.
- Quality: statistical information on their giving: how recent; how frequent; type of support given and the average value of their donations; and the frequency of which the list, or parts of it, has been used.
- Details of past list exchanges with other charities or other organisations and the total numbers of supporters on the list.

An outline agreement should be reached at the outset about the availability of the list and the timing of the mailing. Each party should ensure at the very least that it is exchanging 'like with like', lists of equal value.

2. Method of exchange

Will you each be sending mailing materials for the other party to send out, rather than swapping the actual names and addresses? If you do this, then each charity keeps control over its own list, and there is not the possibility of unauthorised use. All label or type formats, sizes and positions should be agreed between the two charities.

3. Unauthorised use

To guard against unauthorised use, you should add one or two names and addresses to the list which will be returned to you and which will not be on any other list. So if you receive mailings to these names, you know that unauthorised use has been made of your list.

4. Material

Each organisation should indicate their approval of the other's material by signing a sample copy of each item prior to the mailing. Each organisation needs to have the right to insist on changes being made, if they consider the other's mailing to be unsuitable in any way for their donors.

5. Mailing date

Dates for the mailing should be agreed beforehand and the actual date of the mailing should be evidenced in some way. Any problems in keeping to the agreed dates should be communicated to the other charity immediately.

6. Informing donors

The two organisations should make it clear at the outset whether their donors are to be informed that there is to be a reciprocal mailing. This can become a condition of the exchange. Methods and times of informing the donors can be the list owner's decision, although the other organisation might insist on having the right to see, in order to approve, any such communication.

7. Legal requirements

All legal requirements on data protection and other similar matters (where these exist) should be adhered to.

8. Written terms of agreement

Before entering into a reciprocal mailing agreement, these terms and conditions should be set out in writing and confirmed by an exchange of letters.

9. Exchange of results

Both organisations should agree to exchange results on the outcome of the mailing, and state any requirements for detailed analysis with adequate resources being allocated to carry this out.

10. Dealing with the response and any complaints

Both organisations should agree procedures and the materials to be used for acknowledging the response to the mailing. There should be an agreed standard complaints policy, with discussion between the two organisations on how to deal with non-standard complaints before these are responded to.

11. File maintenance

All non-delivered letters and changes of address should be returned to the list owner as soon as possible so that the file can be updated.

These guidance notes are based on guidance given by the Institute of Charity Fundraising Managers in Britain.

5. Guidance notes for organisations considering taking on a fundraising consultant

These notes will help you safeguard the interests of your organisation and provide a framework for the contractual agreement between the two parties – your organisation and the fundraising consultant you take on.

Preliminaries

1. Have you considered employing one of your own staff, either full-time or part-time?
2. Are you clear what type of advice or assistance you require?
3. Have you taken advice from other organisations who have recently taken on a fundraising consultant to do something similar? Ask them who they

engaged; if they were satisfied; what if anything went wrong; and whether the would do the same again.

Considering a short list of possible consultants

4. Draw up a short list of possibilities and ask them to indicate the following: their experience and qualifications; whether they would be willing to work for you; how soon they could be available to do the work; what their charges will be and what expenses they will ask for (their estimate of these and how they will be controlled); what their views are of your fundraising targets and whether they feel that these are realistic; other charities they have worked for and people to act as referees in respect of these jobs; what provision will be made for premature termination of the contract by either party and the discharge of any outstanding obligations.
5. Carefully consider their responses. Do not simply look for the most enthusiastic, but instead for those who fully appreciate the difficulties that will need to be overcome. What questions do they ask? How searching are they and how much to the point? Do they appreciate your strengths and your weaknesses? Do they share your values?
6. Look carefully at their estimate of the sums they expect to be able to raise, alongside the cost of their time and their expenses. Is this realistic? Is it cost effective?
7. Ask them what methods they plan to use – what they would actually do and how to raise the money. Do you approve of these methods? Make sure that what they propose to do conforms with all legal requirements.
8. Discuss how they will allocate their time to you, amidst all their other work. Will they be able to give your work the priority and attention that you require?
9. What other staff will they be using on this job? You will want to meet them before you actually commit yourself.
10. Be very careful of anyone who asks to be remunerated by charging a commission on the amount raised. A daily rate for charging is almost always preferable, perhaps with a performance bonus if they achieve their target. However, if you do agree to a commission, ensure that it is only charged on relevant gifts (not a legacy or a government grant, for example).

Negotiation with your chosen candidate

11. Ensure you have control over the fundraising methods to be used, and that nothing will be done to bring your charity into disrepute. Make sure that no-one in the consultancy organisation claims to be your employee or represents themself as such.
12. Ensure that all donors are asked to make their cheques payable to the charity and not the consultancy organisation, and that all cash paid into your bank account as soon as possible. Do not agree to any deduction of the consultant's expenses or remuneration from receipts. These should be paid by the consultant submitting a claim with supporting evidence.
13. Take up bank reference. Also ask if they have ever been bankrupt, or a director of a company or a charity that has gone into liquidation. Ascertain whether the contract will be in the consultant's personal name or in the consultancy company's name? If in a company name, is the consultant willing

personally to guarantee the company's adherence to its obligations (as set out in the contract)?
14. Ensure that the consultant cannot incur any obligation on your behalf without your prior written agreement.
15. Make sure that any information obtained from you or obtained for you by the consultant is your property, and is not available for their other clients except with your consent.
16. When everything has been agreed, insist on a written contract. To prevent any unintended commitment before this, make any earlier letters 'Subject to Contract'. Make sure that the contract is a correct reflection of everything that has been discussed and agreed before, as what is contained in the contract will be binding for both parties.

Adapted from guidance notes produced by the Institute of Charity Fundraising Managers in Britain.

Useful Organisations

The following is a short list of useful organisations which can provide information, contacts and networking. It has been compiled with the help of Murray Culshaw, former Director of Oxfam (India).

To find organisations in your own country which can offer you information, advice or help, you will need to do your own researches. For information on aid programmes and donor organisations from particular countries, it is always worth contacting their Embassy.

1. General information on fundraising matters

Charities Aid Foundation
Kings Hill, West Malling, Kent ME19 4TA, UK.
CAF is an international agency promoting charitable giving. It is exploring ways of getting support from overseas donors donated so that the donor can receive a tax deduction and the money is paid to the intended project in the local currency.

Commonwealth Secretariat
Marlborough House, Pall Mall, London SW1Y 5HX, UK.
The Secretariat will be the best information point for any matter concerning the Commonwealth.

Directory of Social Change
24 Stephenson Way, London NW1 2DP, UK.
DSC is the major English language publisher of information to assist voluntary organisations in the areas of management, financial management, communication and fundraising. A listing of some of its more useful publications (for Southern NGOs) is given in the next section. DSC also runs short training courses, and overseas visitors are welcome to attend these when they are in London.

European Foundation Centre
51 Rue de la Concorde, B-1050 Brussels, Belgium.
The main information point for information on European foundations.

Foundation Center
79 Fifth Avenue, New York, NY 10003-3076, USA.
The Center maintains a library and has detailed information on all US foundations. Its International Foundation Directory focuses on donations for international purposes made by US foundations.

International Fund Raising Group
295 Kennington Road, London SE11 4QE, UK.
The Group organises a major international convention for fundraisers in

Holland each Autumn. It also has regional contacts which act as good networking points for fundraisers. Conferences and short training workshops are organised for fundraisers.

2. International organisations dealing with the environment

Greenpeace
Canonbury Villas, London N1 2PN, UK.
The international environment watchdog and campaigning agency.

Friends of the Earth
26-28 Underwood Street, London N1 7JQ, UK.
FoE campaigns for the environment worldwide, and is represented in more than 50 countries.

Friends of the Earth USA
218 D Street SE, Washington DC 20003, USA.
FoE promotes "socially just and sustainable development... pushing for fundamental change in bilateral and multilateral trade, aid and lending institutions".

Rainforest Action Network
301 Broadway, San Francisco CA 941433, USA.
Aims to help save the world's rainforests by working internationally in cooperation with other environmental and human rights organisations on major campaigns to save rainforests.

Centre for Science and Environment
421 Tughlakabad Institutional Area, New Delhi 110062, India.
Publishes 'Down to Earth' a very readable fortnightly magazine on science and environmental issues from a Southern perspective.

Environmental Law Institute
1616 P Street NW, Suite 200, Washington DC 20036, USA.
Canadian Institute for Environmental Law and Policy, 517 College Street, Suite 400, Toronto Ont M6G 4A2, Canada.
Both Institutes seek to advance environmental protection by improving law, management and policy, researching pressing environmental problems, and entering into dialogue with professionals and citizens.

3. Organisations working for human rights

Amnesty International
99-119 Rosebery Avenue, London EC1R 4RE, UK.
Works impartially and peacefully for the release of men and women imprisoned throughout the world for their political or religious beliefs.

Human Rights Watch
485 Fifth Avenue, New York NY 10017, USA.
Monitors and publicises human rights abuses. There are five Watch committees, including Africa Watch which has its head office at 90 Borough High Street, London SE1 1LL, UK.

Survival International
310 Edgware Road, London W2 1DY, UK.
Supports indigenous peoples throughout the world in their right to decide their own future, and to help them protect their environment, their lands and their way of life.

Anti-Slavery International
The Stableyard, Broomgrove Road, London SW9 9TL, UK.
Aims to eliminate slave owning and slave trading and abolish all forms of forced labour including child bonded labour approximating to slavery.

Minority Rights Group International
379 Brixton Road, London SW9 7DE, UK.
MRG exists to promote human rights and increase awareness of minority issues and abuses. It investigates and reports on situations, including those pertaining to women, refugees, nomadic tribes and threatened minorities.

South and Mesco American Indian Information Centre
PO Box 28703, Oakland CA 94604, USA.
Promotes peace and social justice for the Indian people across the Americas.

4. Organisations promoting appropriate technology

Appropriate Technology International
1331 H Street NW, 12th floor, Washington DC 20005, USA.
Works with small farmers and entrepreneurs in developing countries to find ways of boosting productivity and incomes, foster new enterprise and generate broad-based economic growth.

Intermediate Technology Development Group
Myson House, Railway Terrace, Rugby CV21 3HT, UK.
The original appropriate technology group founded by Schumacher, which publishes an interesting monthly magazine with a worldwide perspective 'Appropriate Technology'.

Tool – Transfer of Technology for Development
Sarphatistraat 650, 1018 AV Amsterdam, Netherlands.
Aims to help improve the living standards of the socially and economically deprived populations of developing countries by adjusting knowledge and technologies to local circumstances.

Water Aid
1 Queen Anne's Gate, London SW1H 9BT, UK.
Supports low-cost low technology people participant water and sanitation improvements in developing countries.

5. Organisations dealing with health and disability

Appropriate Health Resources and Technologies Action Group
Three Castles House, 1 London Bridge Street, London SE1 9SG, UK.
AHRTAG is an information centre which supports primary health care in developing countries through information services and publications.

Action on Disability and Development
23 Lower Keyford, Frome BA11 4AP, UK.
ADD's primary role is to facilitate the active involvement of people with disabilities in the development process of themselves and their country, and now supports work in 18 countries.

6. Miscellaneous organisations

International Council of Voluntary Agencies
13 Rue Gautier, 1201 Geneva, Switzerland.
promotes the development and growth of voluntary agencies throughout the world. Publishes a newsletter 'NGO Management'.

International Center for Not-for-profit Law
1511 K Street NW, Suite 723, Washington DC 20005-1401, USA.
A centre of expertise on charity law, which also organises international conferences.

Civicus
919 18th Street NW, 3rd floor, Washington, DC 20006, USA.
An international network for people involved in the independent sector from across the world.

Ashoka: Innovators for the Public
1200 N Nash Street, Arlington VA 22209, USA.
Funds and supports outstanding individuals with path-breaking ideas for social change worldwide.

Third World Network
228 Macalister Road, 10400 Penang, Malaysia.
TWN is a coalition of organisations and individuals involved in issues relating to development, environment and North-South affairs. It publishes a number of magazines (including 'Third World Resurgence'), and has affiliated organisations in Africa, Asia and South America.

TRANET
PO Box 567, Rangeley ME 04970, USA.
Links organisations and individuals worldwide involved in alternative and transformational movements, including those working in appropriate technologies, environment, energy, self-help, peace and self-reliance activities.

GreenNet
25 Downham Road, London N1 5AA, UK.
Provides a global computer communications network for environment, peace and human rights groups, and services to countries poorly served by commercial communications services.

Useful Publications

This is a selection of books published by the Directory of Social Change which will be of interest to Southern fundraisers. All these can be ordered by post from the Directory of Social Change, 24 Stephenson Way, London NW1 2DP, UK. Write or send a fax (+44(01)71 209 5049) for current prices and information on ordering and payment.

Writing Better Fundraising Applications
A practical handbook with worked examples for the proposal writer.

The Complete Guide to Business and Strategic Planning;
Managing Quality of Service
Two practical handbooks with examples and exercises to help you in your organisation and project planning.

Relationship fundraising
Practical advice on how to build lasting relationships with your donors.

Organising Local Events
An introduction to event organising for the fundraiser.

Tried and Tested Ideas for Raising Money Locally;
Good Ideas for Raising Serious Money
Two books by the author of Organising Local Events with hundreds of good ideas for raising money, some explained in detail with 'recipes' for success.

Image Building and Money Raising for Hard-to-sell Groups
A simple practical guide to PR and fundraising for smaller organisations, with handy tips and case studies.

The DIY Guide to Public Relations;
The DIY Guide to Marketing for Charities
Everything you need to know about PR and marketing for charities

The Effective Trustee
A three-part guide to effective supervision of voluntary organisations for Management Board members. There is an associated training programme developed from this which is also available.

The Third World Directory;
Peace and International Relations
List donor agencies which may support southern projects or NGOs.

Index of organisations

A
ACCORD, India 37, 104
Action on Disability and Development 66, 262
ActionAid 66, 104
ActionAid Kenya 133
Aga Khan Foundation 74, 80, 218
Aga Khan Foundation UK 78
Aide et Action 66
American Express 86
Anti Apartheid Movement UK 180
Appropriate Health Resources and Technologies Group 262
Arid Lands Initiative 66
Ashoka: Innovators for the Public 262
Association for the Physically Handicapped, Bangalore 153
Association for the Welfare of the Handicapped, India 146

B
BESO 66
Bolshoi Theatre 44
Bombay Community Public Trust 74
Botswana Red Cross 91
British Petroleum (BP) 87
British High Commission, India 64
British Telecommunications (BT) 96
Brot fur die Welt Stommestiftelsen 66
Business in the Community, UK 93

C
CAF America 78
Campaign for Nuclear Disarmament (CND), UK 201
CAMPFIRE Association, Zimbabwe 104
Canadian Centre for Philanthropy 79
Charities Aid Foundation 243, 259
Charity Projects 78
Charity Projects 78
Churches Mission Association of Zambia, The 111
Civicus 262
Civil Society Development Programme, Hungary 77

Commonwealth Foundation, The 79
Commonwealth Relations Trust, The 79
Commonwealth Secretariat 258
Commonwealth Youth Exchange Council, The 79
Community Aid Abroad/ Freedom from Hunger 158
Community Chest 138
Concern India Foundation 53, 220, 221
Contacts-I Russia 22
CORR - The Jute Works 109
CRY - Child Relief and You, Bombay 9, 176, 185
CUSO (Canada) 192

D
Directory of Social Change (DSC) 79, 259

E
European Foundation Centre 259

F
Farm Africa 66
FEBA 131
Fiji Red Cross 180
Food and Agriculture Organisation (FA0) 63
Ford Foundation 74, 80
Foundation Center 78, 259
Foundation for Medical Research, India 220
Foundation Library Centre, Japan 80
Friends of the Earth 223

G
Gatsby Charitable Foundation 78
Green Deserts 66
GreenNet 262
Greenpeace UK 157

H
Herbert Chitepo Library Trust 169

I
IBM 86
Institute for International Education, USA 79

Institute of Charity Fundraising Managers (ICFM), UK 248
Intermediate Technology Development Group 261
International Association of Lion Clubs 103
International Center for Not-for-profit Law 262
International Council of Voluntary Agencies 262
International Fund Raising Group (IFRG) 29, 259
International Labour Organisation (ILO) 63
IRED 122

J
John D and Catherine T MacArthur Foundation 80
Joseph Rowntree Charitable Trust 78

K
Karuna Trust 67

L
Lok Kalyan Samiti India 9

M
Marlborough Brandt Group 105
Medecins Sans Frontieres, France 66
Mother Theresa 67

O
OECD 67
Overseas Development Administration (ODA), UK 64
Oxfam 66, 70, 183, 185

P
PACT 113
PACT Bangladesh 122
Paraguayan Red Cross Society 145
Paul Hamlyn Foundation 78
Peace Corps USA 66, 192
Philippines Foundation for the Environment, The 116
Plan International 68, 72
Prince of Wales Business Leaders' Forum 122
Prince's Trust, The 79
PROSALUD 112
Proshika 114
Pune Blind Men's Association 176
Radda Barnen 66

R

RAFAD 122
Rajiv Gandhi Foundation 74
Rockefeller Foundation 80
Rotary International 103

S
Sakhya, India 221
Save the Children 66
Send A Cow 66
Shalom India-Israel Centre, India 23
South Asia Fundraising Group 68
Swaziland Red Cross Society (Baphalali) 187

T
Third World Network 262
Tool - Transfer of Technology for Development 261
Tools for Self-Reliance 66
Tranet 262

U
United Nations (UN) 62
Unuted Nations Volunteer Programme 192
United Nations Agencies 63
United Nations Children's Fund (UNICEF) 63
United Nations Development Programme (UNDP) 63
United Nations Educational and Scientific Cooperation Organisation (UNESCO) 63
United Nations Fund for Population Activities (UNFPA) 63
United Nations High Commissioner for Refugees (UNHCR) 63
USAID 116, 122, 212

V
Voluntary Health Association of India, 68
Voluntary Service Overseas (UK) 192

W
WaterAid 261
Willi Musarurwa Memorial Trust 169
Woodland Trust, UK 182
World Bank 63, 111
World Food Programme (WFP) 63
World Health Organisation (WHO) 63
World Vision 146
World Wide Fund for Nature 99, 162
World Wildlife Fund USA 116

Y
Yayasan Bina Swadaya, Indonesia 108

Index of topics

Advertising
Acquisition advertising 192
Awareness advertising 182
Disaster advertising 182
Door drops 184
Handbills 184
Issues 185
Legacy advertising 183
Loose inserts 183
Posters 184
Press advertising 181

Capital Appeals and Big Gift Campaigns
Leadership 172
Planning an appeal 170
Private phase 173
Public phase 174
Stages, the 171

Collections
Checklist for organising a collection 142
Collecting boxes in public places 145
Collecting boxes in supporters' homes 146
House-to-house 141
Street collections 143

Committed Giving and Membership
Administration 162
Frequent giving 161
Keeping in touch 159
Membership 160
Promotion 157
Standing orders 157

Computers
Databases 244
Desktop publishing 247
Spreadsheets 247
Word-processing 245

Codes of Practice
Code of practice for fundraising in schools 248
Codes of practice for house-to-house collections 250
Codes of practice for reciprocal charity mailings 254
Guidance notes for taking on a fundraising consultant 255
Guidance notes on the management of static collection boxes 252

Direct Mail
Advice and consultancy 155
Cold mailings 150
Components of a mailing 148
Definition 146
Finding the right lists 151
Getting started 153
Getting the message right 149
List management 155
Management 153
Ten ways to personalise your mailing 148
Types 147
Warm mailings 150

Donors
Donors don't know how much to give 18
Five good ideas when fundraising from individuals 55
Getting donors involved 201
Individual donors 50
Other involvement techniques 202
Recruiting volunteers from your donors 205
Regular mailings to supporters 201
Understanding the donor's viewpoint 17
Why people give 51

Events
Checklist for sponsored participation events 136
Deciding what to organise 129
Developing extra income 135
Five ingredients 128
Getting sponsorship 134
Ideas for sponsored events 140
Management 130
Organising the event: three stages 139

Promotion 133
Reducing the risk 132
Spin-off for future fundraising 135
Sponsored participation events 135

Fundraiser, The
Commitment 20
Contacts 23
Engaging a fundraising consultant 32
Management of fundraisers 27
Opportunism 23
Persistence 21
Persuasiveness 20
Recruiting a fundraiser 26
Social skills 22
Truthfulness 22
When you need to employ a fundraiser 25

Fundraising
Accountability 19
Challenges for fundraisers, the 15
Commitment 19
Credibility and PR 18
Donors don't know how much to give 18
Fundraising is a people business 17
Fundraising is selling 17
Personal approach, the 16
Saying thank you 18
Understanding the donor's viewpoint 17

Fundraising Office, The
Equipment 30
Publications about your organisation 31
Resources 31
Stationery 31

Fundraising Proposals
Content of the proposal 207
Deciding how much to ask for 209
Getting in touch 213
Planning your approach 205
Targeting your proposal 206
Timing 210
Writing the proposal 210

Fundraising from Schools and Young people
Making the approach 176
National competitions 177
Publications for schools 176

Fundraising Strategy
Constraints, the 39
Developing a fundraising strategy 34
Identifying the sources 37
Other strategic principles 45
Resources available 41
Testing, evaluation and control 46

Fundraising Techniques
Advertising for support 180
Capital appeals and big gift campaigns 170
Collections 141
Committed giving and membership 156
Constituting the local group 125
Direct mail 146
Gambling activities that generate money 177
Legacies and regionals 167
Local fundraising activities 126
Managing a local group 127
Organising a fundraising event 128
Personal solicitation 166
Raising money from young people and schools 175
Setting up a local fundraising group 123
Trading 185

Gambling
Draw, the 180
Issues 177
Prizes 178
Promotions 179
Running a 500 club 180
Types of gambling activities to raise money 177

Giving by Companies
Eight ideas for getting support from companies 94
Getting companies to advertise in your publication 90
Getting support in kind 90
Kinds of companies that give 86
Projects that companies support 84
Questions companies are likely to ask 88
Sponsorship 94
What companies give 85
Where multi-nationals give 86
Where to find out about companies 89
Who decides and who to write to 88
Why companies give 84

Giving by Donor Agencies
Categories 66
Dealing with a donor agency - twelve steps to success 69
How donor agencies raise their money 67

Giving by Foundations
Background 74
Five don'ts in dealing with overseas foundations 77
Fundraising from overseas foundations 77
How a foundation works 75
How to be more successful in fundraising from foundations 83
Information on international foundations 78
International foundations 76
National and local foundations 75

Giving by Governments
Four good ideas for raising money from statutory sources 59
Lobbying 59
Local government 57
National government 57

Giving by Individuals
Different ways of giving 51
Five good ideas when fundraising from individuals 55
Why people give 51

Income generation
Alternative tourism 113
Blocked funds and debt swaps
Charging fees for services 110
Community economic development 108
Financial autonomy 119
Getting started 120
Joint ventures with business 114
Kinds of people and skills needed 121
Money making enterprises 114
Problems and issues 116

Legacies and Memorials
Getting started 169
Memorial giving 169
Target audience 168
Why people leave money to charity 168

Marketing
Place - the type of gift 230
Planning and market analysis 228
Price 229
Product 229
Promotion 230

Market Research
Donor research 225
Focus groups 227
Public opinion research 226
Sources of data 227
Statistics 228

Patrons and Celebrities
Fundraising committees 197
Using celebrities effectively 194
Working with patrons and celebrities 193

Personal Solicitation
Meeting potential new supporters 164
Presentation at events 165
Warm visiting 164
Your own events 165

Producing Effective Printed Materials
Annual reports 222
Appeal letters 219
Conception 216
Design 218
Getting into print 218
Principles of effective communication 215
Writing 217

Public Relations
Campaigning and PR 232
Damage limitation 231
Fundraising and PR 232
Letters 233
Managing public relations 235
News releases and press conferences 233
Photocalls 234

Saying Thanks
By gift 200
By letter 199
By meeting 200
By public acknowledgement 200
By telephone 199
By visit 200

Sources of Funding, The
Companies 84
Embassies 102
European Union Funding 65
Foundations 74

Government grants 56
Individual donors 50
International grant-aid 60
Membership bodies 102
Multi-lateral aid 62
Non-resident communities 105
Overseas government aid programmes 64
Overseas NGOs and donor agencies 66
Religious bodies 102
Returned volunteers 104
Schools 103
Tourists 103
Trade Unions 102
United Nations 63

Sponsorship
Competitions 100
Contractual issues 98
Getting started with promotions 101
Identifying possible sponsors 96
Issues surrounding promotions 101
Joint promotions 99
Licensing 100
Making the approach 98
Self-liquidating offers 100
Sponsorship package, the 97
What can be sponsored 95
Who sponsors? 94

Tax-effective Giving
Charities Aid Foundation 243
Establishing a foundation 243
Tax-effective company giving 242

Telephone solicitation
What it can be used for 166
What you need to succeed 166

Testing and Evaluation
Six ways to test your appeals 240
Statistics of testing 240
Test against previous results 241

Trading
Catalogues 186
Charity shops 186
Other trading activities 187

Using the telephone
Donation lines 223
List, the 225
Membership and subscription renewals 223
Phonathons 224

Recruitment 223
Script, the 224

Volunteers
Management of volunteers 191
Overseas volunteers 192
Voluntary organisations as part of civil society 56
Volunteer recruitment and selection 190
Volunteers from specialist agencies 192
Working with volunteers 188